Escape To Paradise
Living & Retiring In Panama

Richard Detrich

"Moving to another country is a big decision but Richard's book helps you think through all the benefits of moving to Panama. Get ESCAPE TO PARADISE! It is a GREAT book and the best information I have found anywhere about relocating to Panama." - **Jackie Lang**

"My husband and I both enjoyed this book immensely! We made the move ourselves to Boquete, Panama six years ago. If ONLY we had had this book to help prepare ourselves when we were first considering making the move!! If you have any thoughts about finding your own paradise, and particularly finding your paradise, as we and the author did, here in Boquete, Panama, you MUST buy this book!! " - **Sharron "Squirt" James**

"Richard really hit the nail . . . of all places...on the head!! Of all the articles and books I RESEARCHED...this one tells it like it really is, with no personal axes to grind. Even though Richard has obviously been in Panama for quite some time his approach is current. His answers are to questions that the other literature I read failed to ask . . . much less answer! Not only that, his approach is far from lofty or detached . . . it's like you're both sittin' at the breakfast table sharing conversation . . . with a little wit here and an off hand comment there. None of it a waste, but a nice easy way to give you the info YOU'RE interested in!!" - **Bob Little**

"Your book . . . is entertaining, informative, and a quick read. Once I started reading it, I found it difficult to put down." **Harry Kooiman**

"We have gathered several publications, attended a conference and been to Boquete twice , but ESCAPE TO PARADISE is by far the most useful book we have read so far. Thank you for your most comprehensive book." **Bob Milligan**

6

Contents

Introduction

Have you ever thought of "escaping"?

Ever thought of moving somewhere less expensive, with less hassle . . . more romantic . . . maybe even living in Panama?

ESCAPE TO PARADISE is jam-packed with what we've learned and helpful hints of what to consider if you've ever even thought of escaping to Panama or anywhere else. Of course our experience obviously is based on our experience in Panama, and specifically in Boquete.

In the chapters, "Our Experience A to Z" and "Questions People Ask", I've tried to anticipate some of the things about which you may have questions.

We lived in Ventura County, California for twenty years. For most of that time we rarely knew our neighbors. Yes, we waved, and said "Good morning!" and knew their names, but we didn't really know them. Most Southern Californians set themselves off from their neighbors with high stucco walls designed for backyard privacy. When we moved to the Hillside in Ventura we finally had neighbors who were neighbors, people we knew. We could commiserate over garden problems, borrow an egg, a tile saw or go for assistance in an emergency.

My next door neighbor, Shaun, was a techie and do-it-yourselfer who, fortunately for me, had every power tool ever invented. Shaun was also a wine aficionado and along the way discovered, and introduced me to Trader Joe's "Two Buck Chuck" Syrah. Then, at only $2 a bottle for a surprisingly good wine, we could afford a lot of neighborly conviviality.

When we were in the depths of trying to buy our property in Panama, sell our house in Ventura, and make it work and pull this all together, we were sipping "Two Buck Chuck", sitting on Shaun's patio and watching the sun set into the Pacific. In all seriousness, Shaun said, "Richard, you know you've got to make this work, because if you can do it, then we'll know that anyone can escape."

If we could do it, so can you!

* * * *

- By way of disclosure: this book is based on my experiences: ask three different expats their opinions of anything and you will get three different responses. This book is about Panama and Chiriqui in particular and it is not my purpose to cover every country in the world, or every place in Panama that expats call home.

- Yes, I sometimes do repeat myself: I'm retired; I've earned the right to repeat! Aside from that, some things need repeated and some observations fit in well in several parts of the book. OK? If it's not OK, here's some Spanish . . . *Que lastima!*

- If you bought the book on Amazon and liked it, please write a review. If you bought the book and didn't like it please tell your dog.

- I don't know it all so I welcome your feedback, your corrections and I'd love to hear about your experiences.

- I invite you to follow my adventures on my blog at RichardDetrich.com

Regards, Richard
Boquete, Panama
Augusut 2012

1. Work Until You Drop

Well, that's what I thought.

To understand why I intended to work until I dropped, you have to understand a little about me.

I graduated from college in 1964 and then from theological seminary in 1968. I entered the work place with certain basic assumptions:

I would change the world – for good;

I would work one job, in my case the church, all my life;

People would appreciate my work and reward me;

I would be loyal to the "company" and the company would be loyal to me;

Social Security would be bankrupt by the time I retired;

I would need, and want, to keep working until I died.

I guess I grew up in what seems today to be a pretty enchanted, and unreal, world. We lived in a little town in Somerset County, New Jersey, really just a crossroads then, called Neshanic. My father was pastor of a church founded before the Revolution. We even had the charter from King George hanging on the back wall. Every day I rode the school bus an hour to a regional high school in Somerville. But life centered on the church and our gang of high school kids who were active in Christian Endeavor and a Christian boy's club called Brigade. The big events in our lives were "camporees", where we competed with other clubs to see who could be first to start a fire from scratch and burn through a string, and the opening day of trout season.

In later life I would "adopt" or be "adopted" by so-called "at risk" teens. One of these guys, Mario, became a good friend and would lament my deprived adolescence: "No sex. No alcohol. No drugs. What kind of life was that?" Hmmm. Mario sometimes had a point.

I was lucky enough to get a rare four-year, full-ride college scholarship from the state of New Jersey which could be used at any school. I went off to my dad's alma mater, Gordon College in Massachusetts. In the meantime my folks moved to Grand Rapids, Michigan where my dad worked for the Brigade boy's club that had so much influence my friends and me. It was then that I discovered, as the bumper sticker says, "Shit Happens", or as I prefer to think, "Things Change."

"Things Change"

New Jersey didn't look with favor on the idea of paying for my college education when my folks were no longer taxpayers, so they yanked my scholarship. And I ended up in Grand Rapids, which was the last place I wanted to live in the entire world.

What was wrong with Grand Rapids? Really nothing. It's actually a very nice place. My dad was a pastor in the Reformed (sometimes called "Dutch Reformed") Church or Reformed Church in America (RCA). He was called to the ministry late in life, so by the time he had his first church and I assumed the unenviable title of "Preacher's Kid", I was in junior high. I went to Eastern Christian school where almost all of the kids were Christian Reformed. Christian Reformed vs. Reformed is one of those theological and cultural hair-splitting things that only a Dutchman would understand. I was a wise-guy junior high kid, a preacher's kid, and a Reformed (as opposed to Christian Reformed) kid at that, so I had to try to prove myself the most bad-ass kid in the school. Grand Rapids, Michigan for Christian Reformed folk is the equivalent of Mecca. All my teachers had gone to school in Grand Rapids and thought it was the New Jerusalem.

So I ended up in Grand Rapids, living at home, and going to college at the Christian Reformed Calvin College, living in the epicenter of the Christian Reformed, Grand Rapids, Jerusalem-Mecca. It turned out to be a really quality education that provided me with, in Calvin College terms, a "world and life view." We actually read John Calvin's INSTITUTES OF THE CHRISTIAN RELIGION – the whole frickin' thing – and had required courses in Calvinism. It turned out that many of my junior high school friends from Eastern Christian also ended up at Calvin. In those days there were two cliques at Calvin: Grand Rapids Christian and Eastern Christian. But in order to stay in school and pay my own way I had to work full time as a night watchman. Between working all night and going to school all day I had very little time left to enjoy college. Mario looks at me compassionately and shakes his head lamenting more lost opportunities.

I guess I went to seminary because I wanted to help change the world. It was a very Reformed, Calvinistic, more importantly Christian view, i.e. that Christ could transform culture. And I had another assumption and that was that the church and Christians in general were committed to transforming the culture. Please note that "transforming" the culture is something entirely different than imposing your own interpretation and lifestyle on everyone else.

I didn't particularly want to be a minister. Apart from my Dad, many of the ministers I met I thought were pompous asses. I didn't have many illusions about the church or Christian ministries either. In seminary I worked for Youth for Christ. I remember rallies at the local civic auditorium where the faithful were all waiting to be inspired, while the guest Christian speaker, singer, hustler, whatever, was in the wings shouting and swearing and arguing for an increased percentage of the evening's "love offering" take. Of course on stage everything was peace, and harmony, and God's love.

One of the things I learned in seminary, that would later help me keep everything in perspective, was that God's people can be a pain in the butt. Look at the Biblical history: God calls and delivers his people and blesses them and what do they do? They turn on God. They wreck havoc and destruction and fight with each other and even with God.

Eventually I would discover that if God's people can be a pain at times to God – well, who am I?

But it was time to graduate from seminary and change the world. Both Kennedys had been shot when I was in college and seminary. The US was bogged down in the first of what was to become an ongoing series of devastating modern wars, including the so-called War on Drugs.

I was talking with anyone who knew anything about getting a job, including the Reformed Church Field Secretary from New York (a kind of bishop in a church that doesn't have bishops). Somehow he got the impression I was interested in a city church, and I guess if it were Marble Collegiate Church on Fifth Avenue, he would have been right. Instead I was invited to candidate (a dog and pony show to see if a church likes you) at The Protestant Dutch Reformed Church of Mott Haven. The name shouldn't throw you. Mott Haven was a tiny all-black church in a Puerto Rican neighborhood in the South Bronx. My church kids used to explain the fact that the "Protestant Dutch Reformed Church of Mott Haven" was mostly black by saying it was just "Dutch Chocolate."

I knew I wasn't interested, but was told by the Seminary Dean that I would go and act interested. We only had a few black churches in the RCA and in the interest of race relations I would go and candidate. Really! "Race relations"? If you had given me an hour I could probably have thought of one black person I knew vaguely.

I went to the Bronx, preached at Mott Haven, and had a great weekend in New York. The people at the church were gracious and welcoming, but I knew I wasn't interested. Then a few weeks later Martin Luther King, Jr. was assassinated. And I few weeks after that I was invited to become the pastor at Mott Haven, and I accepted. I became the white pastor of an all-black church in a predominantly Puerto Rican neighborhood in the South Bronx.

I suppose if you want to change the world the South Bronx is as good of a place as any to begin.

"Black" – forgive me if Afro American, "people of color", or some version thereof is your preference. Six years in the South Bronx in the late '60s with Black Panthers and "Black is Beautiful" slogans, have forever indoctrinated me.

The people at the church were patient, accepting, loving and amazingly tolerant of this white kid who knew nothing about being black, Puerto Rican, or living in the South Bronx. Together we turned the church inside out to serve the community. We started a day care, community center, drug rehabilitation program, and worked with other churches to build new housing. We worked with anyone and everyone who had an agenda to serve the people.

We tore down the old church sanctuary and built a multi-purpose community center. And when the cops and building inspectors came looking for pay offs, I sent them away a fistful of contribution envelopes instead of cash, "knowing", as I would put it, "that they would want to contribute to the building fund." They'd see me coming to the 42nd Precinct to collect and they'd hide in the locker room. And the building inspector who'd tried to shake me down ended up being busted attempting to pay a bribe while standing at the urinal in the County Court House.

* * * *

While in New York I came to know Norman Vincent Peale. Peale was an amazing man who took a grandfatherly interest in me and my ministry. Later I would write a book about Peale called, NORMAN VINCENT PEALE: THE MAN AND HIS MINISTRY. Peale was pastor of the famed Marble Collegiate Church. The Collegiate Church is actually a collection of churches that go all the way back to the settling of Nieuw Amsterdam and the arrival of the Reformed Church on Manhattan in 1624. What makes this interesting is that much of Manhattan, including the incredibly valuable land in places like Jay Street, Wall Street, and even parts of Rockefeller Center, belong to the Collegiate Corporation, parent of the Collegiate Church. Even more interesting – and this is the part that relates to "Work until You Drop" – the Collegiate ministers, like the Pope and the Supreme Court justices, are hired for life.

So, my long-term goal was to become a Collegiate Minister. I fancied myself someday occupying the prestigious Fifth Avenue pulpit at Marble Collegiate. Aside from the prestige, the real reward was never having to retire. You could work as long as you wanted, and even if you chose to semi-retire retain the Collegiate Minister position until death do you part.

Raising money for the ministry in Mott Haven across the Reformed Church had given me exposure in the RCA and I was developing a reputation of someone who, although brash and opinionated enough to call then President Richard Nixon a "crook" in a lily-white, all Republican Church in Grand Rapids (complete with people walking out of the service in protest!), could get things done and handle tough situations. I married, we lived in New York a while and then we accepted a call to a dying First Reformed Church in Milwaukee, Wisconsin. We renamed the church New Life Community Church and it grew, bought land on the edge of town, and started a new building. Now adding "church growth minister" to my vitae I went on to another difficult situation in Littleton, Colorado. The church was meeting in a shopping center and had a brief but tumultuous history. This church started growing. We added a counseling center, a day care, built a new multipurpose church center. I became known as the Western Field Secretary's (remember, like a bishop only supposedly not) "fair-haired boy" and I became known as a pastor who could help churches turn themselves around.

After enduring winters in Michigan, New York, Wisconsin and Colorado (although Colorado winters were never that bad), I guess it was natural that I'd always wanted to live in Southern California. After all, I grew up with "California Dreamin'" and the sounds of the Beach Boys. The Reformed Church in Thousand Oaks, California had been started in a drive-in theater following the model of RCA television pastor Dr. Robert Schuller. In fact Schuller himself had preached at the first service. But the church languished and never grew so they called me in.

I loved Ventura County and Thousand Oaks. We were fourteen miles from Ventura, nestled in the Santa Monica Mountains and it was the ideal community in which to raise our children. It was warm, the beach was nearby, and the schools were good. My wife Nikki had been a marriage and family therapist in Colorado. But in California the board that licensed palm readers and therapists (interesting juxtaposition) insisted that therapists coming in from out-of-state basically start over. Unwilling to reinvest all that time and money basically to protect California therapists from being overwhelmed with incoming competition, we began to look at other opportunities for Nikki.

When I graduated from seminary and moved to New York I started spending my vacations serving as a volunteer chaplain on board the ships of Holland America Line. Later we started taking groups from our churches on cruises. Nikki and I both loved cruising and for years had talked about opening a travel agency. The timing seemed right and so we opened what at the time was a new concept, a cruise only travel agency called "Just Cruising."

Within a year I knew the Thousand Oaks church had a fatal flaw and would never grow. It had been started for all the wrong reasons and was being smothered by a few families who lovingly sought to control everything. People from Thousand Oaks and Newbury Park were welcome, but people from nearby very affluent Westlake Village were shunned. And our travel agency was in Westlake Village. Ooops.

The church board and I recommended to the Field Secretary (the bishop wantabe) that the church be closed and after a short time reopened in a new location with a new name and vision. Calvary Community in Westlake Village had faced a similar challenge years earlier, had closed their church, reopened in a warehouse down the street, redirected its efforts to reaching the unchurched in a casual, non threatening atmosphere and was wildly successful. Ventura County was rapidly growing and there were fertile areas for church growth. We envisioned an approach similar to that used by Calvary Community and of course I would lead the charge.

Much to my surprise it was decided to accept the recommendation to close the church but the decision was made not to undertake any further efforts in Thousand Oaks. Suddenly I was out of a job!

The Field Secretary felt that I had failed to rescue his project and I went from being his "fair-haired boy" to the head of his shit list. Worse yet, I had dared to criticize his policy of opening loads of new churches without giving them proper supervision and support.[1]

It was two months before Christmas. I had no job. We had to be out of the parsonage the church had rented for us by New Year's. And we had sunk every penny we had into a travel agency that had yet to earn anything.

One of my most memorable moments in the ministry happened then. As we were facing an uncertain and tragic Christmas, I received a call from the Ventura County Sheriff's Department. They explained that they had a program to provide help for needy families at Christmas. I explained that the church had closed and so I didn't know of anyone to suggest. The gal from the Sheriff's Department said, "No, we were thinking of you. Is it all right if we send something over?"

I'll never forget the paddy wagon driving up and Santa jumping out of the back with toys for the girls and food. And some of the former church members would drop by anonymously and leave bags of food on our front porch.

Things change!

---

[1] Unfortunately, as it would turn out my assessment would be spot on. Ignoring the great potential in Thousand Oaks the RCA continued to lap up Orange County properties, starting churches, then a few years later abandoning them and selling off the properties. The Field Secretary was good buddies with Robert Schuller and the Crystal Cathedral folks and allowed them, and them alone to be exempt from Classical supervision. Largely because of that the Crystal Cathedral and Schuller ministry would eventually crash and burn. A sad and tragic story overall and a case where I wish I had been wrong.

Both my wife and I where children of Reformed Church pastors and had grown up in the church with the idea that the church was a community where people cared for and took care of each other; it was fundamental to our understanding of the church. With the exception of the Sheriff's Department and a handful of former members, the "church" or RCA denomination could have cared less.

I remember driving down to Orange County for an appointment with the bishop wantabe Field Secretary. It was a bleak, rainy, depressing winter day in Southern California. I had no job and it seemed none were in the cards. I knew it was going to be a bleak Christmas and I had no idea where or how we would live. As I drove down PCH where the road curves along the ocean at Point Mugu I thought how easy it would be to step on the gas and go flying off into the ocean.

In that fragile state I arrived at the Field Secretary's office, hat-in-hand to see what help the denomination could offer. He pulled down a loose leaf binder and went down a list of names of former RCA pastors, mostly ones who'd gotten into trouble by not keeping their pants zipped. It was an actually a pretty long list! These guys (it was all guys then) were selling cars or insurance and a few were teaching high school . . . he told me that I should go and do likewise and forget about any help from the RCA. It seems that the church, even more than the corporate world, can be ruthless in cutting its losses.

Over the years I would apply for different pulpits, only to be passed over. It took a while before one of the elders in one of the churches clarified the situation for me: the Field Secretary was black-balling me, subtly questioning my competency and not so subtly suggesting churches look elsewhere. It didn't take much to cast doubt. I thought I'd outlive him, but he was a stubborn cuss who just refused to die. It's ironic that some of the guys, who'd been screwing half the women in their churches, miraculously repented, were "rehabilitated" and went on to some very large churches, only repeat the same behavior. Go figure!

Falling assumptions

My initial assumptions were falling like flies!

Turned out I wouldn't change the world.

Although I'd remain an ordained RCA minister, I wouldn't work just one job for life.

Although I wanted the Reformed Church, it didn't want me.

Forget appreciation and reward.

The jury's still out on God's final opinion.

It helped to understand that if God's people were often a pain to God, there was no reason they shouldn't be a pain to me as well. What also helped me was an epiphany I had one afternoon while watching my kids play girls softball. I'm not a sports fan. The only reason I was sitting through an afternoon at a softball game was because my kids were playing. I just wanted my kids to play and have fun. But I'd noticed that girls' softball was a very political thing for some parents. They could have cared less about the kids; it was all about the organization and control. Suddenly I understood the church! It wasn't really about winning the world for Christ, or transforming culture. For many people it was the chance to be a big fish in a little pond. Another assumption bites the dust!

So we had this fledgling "Just Cruising" travel agency with posters of beaches and palm trees. My wife sat at one desk and I sat at the other. A few people wandered in. Occasionally someone bought something. For us at least working in the same tiny office, and struggling for survival was not an endearing couple experience. We decided we'd both put out resumes and whoever got a job offer first would take it and the other would run the travel agency. My wife was obviously more salable. I remember when she was offered a six-month job running a program for pregnant teenagers for Ventura County Public Health. Six months were all we needed! We splurged and bought a split of champagne and celebrated. Nikki went off to public health (a job she would continue for 18 years) and I stayed at the travel agency.

Eventually "Just Cruising" became very successful. We had two offices, sold a ton of cruises, and became top producers for Carnival, Princess and Holland America. We never made a fortune, but there were wonderful fringe benefits!

So I became a small businessman. I watched Carnival grow from a bottom-of-the-barrel cruise line that all the other lines looked down on, to the foremost cruise line in the world. I also watched the airlines start eating away at travel agent commissions and saw the handwriting on the wall and fortunately sold out just before the airlines cut commissions and the Internet took over. Watching the success of Carnival fascinated me and, at 53 years-of age, I decided to get an MBA with the thought of going to work for one of the cruise lines. The hardest part was the math. The last math class I'd had was in eleventh grade. I don't know why it never dawned on me that they called MBAs "bean counters" because it involved a lot of math! Math had changed. At one point my daughter Rebecca was trying to help me understand negative numbers and finally exasperated said, "Dad, just accept it and get on with it!"

I finished my MBA about the time the Internet was just coming into its own. I had been serving part-time as an associate minister at a United Methodist Church in Westlake Village. One of the key laymen was CIO for a company called 24 Hour Fitness, a privately held chain of over 400 fitness centers that was rapidly expanding from the West coast into other areas of the US as well as Asia and Europe. 24 Hour Fitness' Internet presence consisted of a single page which gave an 800 number to call for information. I became Director of Ecommerce for 24 Hour Fitness and jumped into the corporate world.

I worked mostly from my home in Ventura, flew to the corporate offices in the Bay Area for meetings, and spent about two days a week with the IT staff and developers in Carlsbad. Like everyone at 24 Hour Fitness I worked long hours, but I loved it.

I'd go to Internet conferences in San Francisco, which became the Internet Mecca, and I'd hear my peers telling of the lengths they would go to even get their CEOs to try the Internet. I had just the opposite problem: my CEO got the Internet big time. We'd be in a meeting and Mark Mastrov, our CEO, would drop the latest Internet buzzword, and at the break my boss would ask me, "Do you know what that means?" I'd say no, and he'd say, "Well, find out!"

24HourFitness.com became one of the Internet's premier fitness resources. Along the way we gave away millions of free passes that got prospective customers into 24 Hour Fitness centers. And we were the first fitness company to begin selling memberships online. We spent five years writing and rewriting business plans for the ultimate online fitness application and during that time the dot com era came . . . and went bust. I suppose we saved the company millions by never actually perfecting our business plan.

Since 9/11 changed the whole world, it should come as no surprise that it changed things for me as well. Like most companies 24 Hour Fitness was rocked by 9/11. We had been in a program of rapid expansion up to that point, and like everything else it came to a halt and we battened down the hatches to survive. Positions were cut, including mine. And although I would continue to work as a consultant for 24 Hour Fitness and its Apex Fitness subsidiary, I knew that if I wanted to "work until I dropped" I would have to find yet another line of work.

Real estate appealed to me. I'd always enjoyed buying and selling our homes. I'd remodeled several homes and built three churches so I knew something about construction. I enjoyed watching the real estate market and watching our ocean-view home on the Hillside in Ventura go up in value . Real estate seemed to be the kind of thing you could keep on doing at whatever level you desired for as long as you wished. The real estate market was good and I did very well. I was a top producer my first full year in the business. We loved Ventura. Life was good . . . and I finally found something I could do for as long as I wanted. But make no mistake; real estate is demanding and a lot harder than it looks!

What do you want to do when you grow up?

Minister, travel agency owner, director of ecommerce, REALTOR®:
I began to wonder what I wanted to do when I grew up. I discovered
a little earlier than many of my contemporaries that people would no
longer do one job their entire lives. People would migrate from job
to job and have several careers in the course of their working lives.
And this is even truer for my children.

If there was a common thread that ran through these seemingly
diverse careers it was selling, or as I prefer to think of it,
communicating. Faith, a wonderful cruise vacation, health and
fitness, a beautiful home – all were dreams to be communicated and
sold.

Social Security: still ailing, but still kicking. Scratch yet another
assumption! Social Security hadn't gone broke and would in all
likelihood survive me, although I'm not sure it will be around for my
children. But because it was still there, it allowed me to consider . . .

I've worked hard, all my life. I enjoy working hard, whether it's
mental work, or renovating a house or gardening. And I still work
hard, and enjoy working hard. It fits my Protestant Calvinist work
ethic. Maybe it was turning 60. Maybe I was slowing down or
running out of steam. Maybe it was a post 9/11 reaction. Maybe it
was watching what the stress of schizoid California government was
doing to my wife's health.

A successful drop out

I didn't drop out in the '60s but I thought that maybe I should
reconsider the idea now that I was in my 60s.

Whatever it was, for the first time I began to question if I really
wanted to work until I dropped. The world wasn't going to change,
or at least I wasn't going to change it. Maybe I should chill out and
enjoy life.

Your experience and assumptions obviously have been different, but it's important that you identify them and how they have changed. Things change, assumptions change and people change.

Interacting – What's this?

OK, a book shouldn't just be a one way street. If we were talking face-to-face we'd be interacting and you'd be peppering me with questions. Since we can't do that, I'll ask some questions at the end of each chapter in a section called "Interacting". Hopefully this will push you to consider some questions you should be thinking about if you're considering coming to Panama or going anywhere else. And don't just scroll on to the next chapter. STOP. Get a sheet of paper and do your homework! Write it down, if not now, then later.

1. So, what careers have you had? What we there common threads?

2. What were your assumptions when you began and how have they changed?

3. "Things change!" in life. What things have changed in your life?

4. What were/are your retirement plans?

2. Dare To Dream

I was turning 60. As usually happens, life hadn't turned out exactly the way I had planned when I was in my 20s. I was becoming less and less sure I wanted to work until I dropped and retirement, forced or voluntary was looming. I began to seriously look at how we were going to survive retirement.

It was actually the fault of my daughter, Noelle, and her husband, George. George worked for Princess Cruises at the time and Noelle was finishing up her Masters in Education. They had taken a cruise vacation and fallen in love with the little, and relatively unknown, Caribbean island of Dominica. Where others may have seen a dirty and impoverished island, these sun-starved kids from the Pacific Northwest saw paradise. George was growing restless at Princess and Noelle was looking for her first teaching job. They stumbled on a Web site called EscapeArtist.com and a fledgling marina/bar operation for sale in Dominica and they started to dream. Naturally they wanted us to go online and check it out. And so I discovered EscapeArtist.com.

It really is a genius concept! Who of us has not at sometime in their lives just wanted to run away from it all and . . . escape? The name, the artwork, the content – confused and disorganized as it was for a Web pro – captured the concept. It was "Casablanca" revisited. It got you dreaming of escaping to the supposedly notorious and illicit fleshpots of Europe or mysterious orient. Enter visions of The Orient Express, sybaritic Greek islands and exotic Caribbean beaches. Beaches with lush palm trees. Forget about "no-see-ums", those horrible invisible little bugs that plague exotic beaches and nobody likes to talk about. Although cumbersome to navigate, EscapeArtist.com was a virtual paradise of escape dreams.

Now we were dreaming as well as our kids. Our kids eventually settled down to reality; we, however, kept dreaming.

Over the years we had spent a lot of time in the US Virgin Islands. We had friends who lived in St. Thomas and we were the ones who encouraged them to move to the USVI. Over 11 years we visited St. Thomas almost yearly. As chaplain on cruise ships and later as owner of travel agencies we frequently visited the USVI and the rest of the Caribbean. In the back of my mind I had always dreamed of someday living on St. John overlooking Pillsbury Sound.

If money were no object . . .

If money were no object, what was it really that we wanted?

So we began to dream. If money were no object – a big IF by the way – and if we could live anywhere we wanted . . . what was it really that we wanted?

My wife and I each began making list of the things our ideal nirvana would need to have. So we went off to our separate corners and began to come up with our dream lists. Independently. No consultation.

This is what we came up with.

Nikki's Top 15 List:

1. Breezes to mitigate heat and humidity
2. Warm (not over 85 degrees)
3. Good medical care
4. Ocean View
5. Clean
6. Smaller town
7. Basic dependable utilities including Internet
8. Availability of supplies
9. Lower cost of living
10. Clear title and ownership
11. Near nice beach
12. English widely accepted as second language
13. Diverse, accepting, open, tolerant
14. Ample water supply
15. Stable currency and low inflation

Richard's Top 15 List:

1. Warm
2. Lower cost of living
3. Breezes to mitigate heat and humidity
4. Basic dependable utilities including Internet
5. Ample water supply
6. Clean
7. Near nice beach
8. Clear title and ownership
9. Good medical care
10. Availability of supplies
11. Stable government
12. English widely accepted as second language
13. Ocean view
14. Stable currency and low inflation
15. Opportunity for business, investment, owner working

Amazingly, and perhaps not so amazingly after twenty eight years of marriage, our lists were remarkably similar. So now we knew what we wanted, if it were available somewhere, and if money was no object.

It doesn't hurt to dream!

The MBA in me forced yet another exercise to further refine our dream. If we had 100 points, and only 100 points, with which to assign value, how would we assign those points? We needed to further refine our wish list. After much discussion, here's what we ended up with:

- Lower cost of living 30 points -We knew we couldn't make it without lowering our cost of living.

- Good medical care 20 points – Like it or not, someday we were going to be "seniors".

- Warm 15 points – We remembered those cold Michigan and Wisconsin winters.

- Opportunity for investment, business or working 15 points – No matter what, we wanted an additional income stream.

- Basic dependable utilities, including Internet 10 points – How great could life be without drinking water or the Web?

- Availability of supplies 5 points – It was too late in life to start a subsistence lifestyle.

- Clean 5 points – We had seen a lot of beautiful beaches on islands that were trashed.

There you had it – the weighted list. The other wants were still important; niceties, but not absolutely essential. If we could have it all, great, but these were "must haves."

Knowing what we wanted, unfettered by restrictions of budget or reality, we began to dream and to think of places we'd been, or heard of, or read about that might prove our nirvana. We scoured the Web, and kept returning to EscapeArtist.com and dreaming of running away from it all. It's not that we were actually planning to retire, dreaming was just good therapy!

What is it that you would like to do today?

It's not just where you dream about living, but what you dream about doing. What is it that you would like to do today?

If you are at the point where you wake up and can't wait to get to work – as I was when I was with 24 Hour Fitness – you're not ready for this book. Enjoy your work! Save the book, and come back later when "Things Change!" But if you dream about walking an endless beach, sailing the Caribbean, exploring jungles, or teaching kids to read in the South Bronx, now is the time to explore your dreams and give them definition.

We ended up in Panama. I'll tell you more about how and why later, but part of the story involves a group of Embera Indians I met while on a cruise through the Panama Canal.

The Embera and Wounaan Indians together are only estimated to have a population in Panama of around 30,000-80,000, but nobody knows for sure since the Embera live deep in the jungle in tiny villages and survive on subsistence farming, hunting and fishing. The men have generally replaced their loincloths with shorts, but most women still wear only skirts. All have rich tattoo-like body decoration made from the juice of the *jagua* fruit. Aside from being decorative it protects them from mosquitoes and ultra-violet rays.

I had met one Embera Indian, Erito Barrigon, while on a cruise. Lubricated by lots of Atlas beer, Erito, his brothers and I became fast friends and *"hermanos."* They invited me to visit their village an hour's drive from Panama City and then an hour-and-a-half by dugout canoe across a lake and up a jungle river. It was in researching the Embera, so I could fulfill my promise to visit, that I accidentally discovered the retirement benefits of Panama. So, in reality, I'm here in Panama because of Erito!

When we came to "check out" Panama I was intent on visiting Erito's Embera village and spending the night.

"This is not the 101 Freeway! This is adventure! I can die now knowing that I have lived!"

I distinctly remember Erito and his brothers picking me up at a tiny hamlet on the edge of Madden Lake. We loaded up their dug out canoe, or *piragua*, with supplies including three cases of Atlas beer. I thought this strange since I knew at the time alcohol was not permitted in the village. I quickly learned the plan: Erito, his brothers and I would drink all the beer before getting to the village, thus, although arriving very relaxed, not offending anyone.
We crossed the lake, and were making our way up the Río de Pequini to their tiny village of San Juan. We were deep in the jungle and well-brewed, and I remember leaning back in the boat, looking up at the jungle canopy covering the river and thinking to myself, "This is not the 101 Freeway! This is adventure! I can die now and know I've lived!" That was the moment I knew for certain that it was time for a change.

Interacting

We've sometimes seen couples who visit Panama thinking of living here. One member of the couple loves Panama, and the other dislikes it. I can only wonder if they've really done their homework. Have they really sat down and discussed what each considers important and what each wants? We've seen couples sell everything in the US and move here, often on what appears to us to be a whim, only to quickly become disillusioned or realize that they don't want to give up all the comforts of life in Miami, Los Angeles or wherever, and we wonder if they really did their homework.

This book is designed to help you think through what it is that you want before you make a major change in your life. If you come to Panama or go anywhere else that's new, we want you to love it, so do your homework!

1. So, assuming money was no object and you could live anywhere you wanted . . . what is it exactly that you want? Come up with your own "Top 15" lists.

2. OK, Now discuss your lists and come up with a joint Top 15 List. Have fun!

3. What do you dream of doing? Get a pad and pencil and spell it out! Go ahead – money is no object here, dreams are free!

3. Finding Nirvana

Now that you know what you're dreaming of, how do you find it? Where in the world would you like to live?

Maybe, just maybe, you already have found it! Maybe you're *already* living in the perfect place.

Our home was in Ventura, California, right on the Pacific coast, about halfway between Los Angeles and Santa Barbara. We lived on a hillside overlooking the Pacific Ocean. I woke up to the sun rising over the Santa Monica Mountains sparkling off waves rolling in on Ventura beach. I could look out the window and know if the surf was up, if it was a good day for ocean kayaking, or if a storm was brewing. I could sit in my spa at night, sipping wine, and see the famed stone arch at the end of Anacapa Island. At night I looked out over the twinkling lights of Ventura. My neighbors were the best: Ventura was the only place we ever lived in Southern California where we actually knew our neighbors. Property values were soaring. I was a REALTOR® so I didn't have to commute anywhere. Compared to most of Southern California the crime rate was relatively low. And Ventura's weather, except for the summer fog, is probably the finest in the continental US. What was there not to like? Ventura was damn near perfect.

So when you're looking for Nirvana, be sure to include the place you already live. It's a good reality check. A good comparison. And maybe, just maybe, you've already found the perfect place.

So, how do you go about finding your Nirvana?

1. Make a list.

I'd start by sitting down with my partner some evening, preferably by a fire, with a bottle of good chardonnay, a world map, and a pad of paper.

We started by making a list of places that even sounded remotely interesting. Places we'd been to on trips. Places we'd heard of. Places we'd seen in movies.

In our case that gave us:

Greek Isles
Thailand
Polynesia
Hawaii
Key West
Virgin Islands – US & British
Dominica
Costa Rica
Belize
St. Martin
St. Lucia

And on our list, we included the place we already lived: Ventura Interestingly Panama, the place we ended up, never appeared on any of our early lists.

Make a file folder for each of the destinations on your list. As you start accumulating notes and information just stick it in the relative folders.

2. Visit Barnes & Noble.

Start spending a few evenings at Barnes & Noble or Borders. Get a latte and start browsing the travel section, scanning guidebooks from destinations that have sparked an interest. At this point I'd just browse, not buy. Just keep buying coffee and you won't feel guilty for making the bookstore your public library! And of course there is the public library, but in most cases you'll find more of what you want at the bookstore and the library generally doesn't offer cafe mochas!

Don't forget the magazine section. You'll find some great travel magazines, some with features on your areas of interest. Calendars too! If something strikes your fancy here, buy it!

Bulletin boards by my desk had pictures of dozens of beaches and islands while we were in the research stage. There's nothing like looking at a picture to help you escape work and start dreaming. A picture helps you vicariously try a place on for size to see if it fits.

3. Go online.

The Internet is the most fabulous resource in the world! But be forewarned: anyone can put anything on the Internet. Just because you found something online doesn't mean it's true! And the biggest plague of the Internet is that most information isn't dated. People are notorious about not removing outdated information from the Web. Particularly when you get to specifics like prices and cost of living: unless it is actually dated, and not with the applet that automatically gives today's date, it's probably out-of-date.

And don't forget to search for pictures as well. An interesting side note: we ended up retiring in Boquete, Panama. Do a picture search on Goggle for Boquete with your "safe" filter turned "off" and you will be shocked. You'll find pictures of our tiny little town, pictures of rainbows, flowers, mountains and coffee, but you'll also find . . . let's just say that Boquete, like my nickname, has multiple meanings and in Brazilian Portuguese it means something all together different. When I work with crew members on the ship from Brazil and tell them where I live they almost choke!

I collected images online and downloaded them into my own PowerPoint presentation so I could develop a digital file of my research. I had maps, scenic views, stories, and a regular presentation on potential areas . . . it was a great tool for dreaming!

Don't forget the news groups, bulletin boards, and discussion forums. You'll find all kinds of postings from expats online.

Use email. You'll find a lot of expats are more than happy to respond to emails and answer knowledgeable questions. What's a knowledgeable question? I got an email from a man in Minnesota who wrote – I kid you not! – "I'm interesting in retiring to Panama. What should I do?" Not knowledgeable. A lady wrote, "We're falling in love with Boquete. What is the school situation? Is there an American or international school in Boquete or David? I can't find anything online." That was a knowledgeable question which I could answer.

If you are lucky enough to know several languages, include in your search criteria sites in languages other than English. If you're interested in Latin or Central America you'll find a wealth of additional information on the Spanish Web sites.

4. Keep your eyes and ears open.

It's amazing how sometimes you never see something, until you're looking for it. You've driven down road scores of times and you've never noticed a particular shop, until one day you're looking for it. Or you've shopped in the same grocery store and never noticed a particular item, until the day you're looking for it, and there it is!

Once you're thinking it terms of particular destinations, you'll be surprised when they will pop up. A co-worker's parents are retiring there, or your neighbor's kids just got back from backpacking in a country you've found interesting, or the station attendant was born there. Check out newspaper articles, books, magazines, even movies.

A quick word about movies: movies are movies! You know better than to think that every North American lives the way they are portrayed in movies. You know that just because a movie is set in a particular location, doesn't mean that the location is portrayed accurately. Los Angeles isn't really like it's portrayed in the movies, and it may not even be Los Angeles that you're seeing in the movie.

John Travolta's movie "Swordfish" was actually filmed in downtown Ventura. The old section of downtown was closed off for two months and became downtown Los Angeles. Our old two-story Bank of Italy building became a Los Angeles skyscraper. And when the bomb supposedly went off, our little downtown corner of Ventura looked like a war zone. Movies are fun, but basically make believe.

I mention all this because the movie "Tailor of Panama" helped create a negative impression of Panama that almost kept Panama off our short list. Yes, the movie was actually filmed in Panama. It was the first major motion picture to be filmed in Panama and the government went all out, even giving movie makers access to the Presidential Palace of The Herons. Because movie making isn't a Panamanian business there weren't companies to provide hundreds of extras, so the extras were actually recruited right off the streets, no SAG card required. But when the movie came out, people were shocked! The movie, although fun and interesting, bore absolutely no resemblance to the reality of Panama.

5. Use your vacation time.

Depending on your timeline, use your vacation time. Visit some of the places on your list that you find interesting. Aside from having a great time, you can start to get the feel of a place and know if you want to consider it as a place to live. Granted, being on vacation in a place is different than living there, but it's a start.

Go beyond the tourist hot spots. Invest in a good map! This will come in handy not only on your vacation, but also later. Rent a car and drive around. Get off the beaten path and see if it feels comfortable. Chat with the locals, especially the ones not connected with the tourist trade, and see if they feel comfortable. Search out some of the expats already living there, buy them a drink or two or three, listen and ask questions. Usually if I'm having coffee or in a store and a visitor wants to ask me questions about life in Panama, I'm more than happy to share. Tune into some of the local gossip. Pick up the local papers, even if you don't really know the language.

Visit the local supermarkets. Identify products similar to those you buy at home and jot down the prices. Imagine shopping here: what are the items you think you couldn't do without? Are they available? If they have "big box stores" visit them? Price Smart in David, Panama wasn't exactly like Price Club/Costco in Oxnard, California, but it was comforting for us to know it was there and at least some of the familiar products were available.

Talk to some real estate agents. Understand that in most countries real estate practice is very different than in the US, so go in with eyes wide open. Be upfront, and don't forget that you're not here to buy, just to learn. A good real estate agent will be happy for the contact that may eventually turn into a sale, but don't expect a free tour or hours of time. Get away from the timeshare folks and get a feel for the prices of homes that are the type of home in which you could imagine yourself living.

As you visit places you want to ask yourself this basic question, "Can I see myself living here?" There are many places in the world that I love – Amsterdam, the Greek Isles, Menorca, Tuscany, even Alaska – but I don't see myself living there on a permanent basis. Nice to visit for vacation, maybe even an extended vacation or a couple month home exchange, but not permanently.

And just doing the vacation research, even if you don't book the trip, is valuable. You'll pick up a lot of information and travel brochures are a great source for the pictures to decorate your cubicle or office!

Of course all the information you pick up on your trip, or researching a trip, ends up in the relative destination folder.

[Maybe I shouldn't tell you this, but since by now we're friends . . . Since I spend about half the year lecturing on cruise ships, and my wife sometimes would like to join me, occasionally we are looking for house sitters to watch over our beautiful home and feed our three dogs. It's an opportunity to experience Panama for a month or two. Watch my Web site RichardDetrich.com for our needs and openings.]

6. Develop a short list.

As you go through the research process you're going to find yourself eliminating some destinations. "Forget that!" As you do, cross them off your list and trash the folder. Eventually you want to weed the list down to four to eight destinations in which you are really interested, including, of course, where you already live.

In our case we ended up with six destinations, including Ventura. We already knew what we wanted. Remember Chapter 2? Lower cost of living, good medical care, warm, opportunity, dependable basic utilities, supplies and clean.

Our short list ended up with:

- Ventura – Pretty close to paradise in the US and the stuff of movies and dreams.

- Costa Rica – We had heard it was a great US retirement destination and had visited San Jose and along both coasts on a couple of cruises.

- Boquete, Panama – Panama was a long shot that wasn't even on our initial list. We had stopped in Panama on a cruise, found a lot of interesting information online, went back for two weeks to either rule it out or keep it in, and fell in love with the little mountain town of Boquete.

- St. Thomas, USVI – Over the years we'd spent a lot of time in St. Thomas. We'd seen cruise ships change Charlotte Amalie from being a sleepy little Caribbean town to a gridlock of ships, taxicabs, tourists, and shops, but we also knew there were areas of the island that were still remote and beautiful. Because we knew the USVI, and we knew the islands were different, we included each island separately.

- St. John, USVI – I will always love St. John. Much of the island is National Park and Cruz Bay still retains some of the charm that we found in St. Thomas before the cruise ship invasion.

- St. Croix, USVI – The biggest of the three Virgin Islands, and although we'd visited it several times on cruises, it was the one we knew the least.

7. Now's the time to buy some books.

You want to go back to the bookstore and buy some of the guidebooks that seemed most helpful and start to really research and study. Be sure to check out Amazon.com: often some books are out-of-print and you can often find these books being resold on Amazon.

Get some maps. When we were researching we found it almost impossible to get a good map of Panama. Now the NATIONAL GEOGRAPHIC publishes a wonderful map of Panama. If you were wise, and if you've already had opportunity to visit the places on your short list, hopefully you picked up maps while you were there.

8. Analyze the short list.

OK, maybe the MBA in me got carried away. But the best way I knew to analyze and compare was to make a list of all the things that were important to us, rank them, assign values, and see were we ended up. One of Bill Gates' great gifts to mankind is Excel. If you know Excel it is relatively easy to create a spread sheet that will let you make the comparisons.

You've already identified what's important to you: now expand that list. Understanding that no one place can provide everything you want, you still need to expand that list. Say you find a place that looks like paradise, but there is a coup every two years, or inflation is 40% a year – how great is paradise going to be? What if every five years a hurricane wipes half your island paradise off the map? Your kid is gay and the place is homophobic? You have dietary restrictions or preferences requiring foods these folks have never seen? You've already got two cops with shotguns on every corner: is that what you want in your new home? Your dream island is paradise, except for the dumpster on the corner overflowing with foul-smelling garbage. Here's what we came up with. It's obviously not the definitive list, or the list for everyone, but it worked for us.

Climate
Warm
Breeze to mitigate heat & humidity
Outside hurricane belt

Area, Amenities & Economics
Ocean view
Basic dependable utilities including Internet
Ample water supply
Clean
Near nice beach
Good medical care
Availability of supplies
Access for a boat
Opportunity for business, investment
Ability to work
Smaller town
Minimal traffic
Relatively low crime rate
Stable and growing economy
Lower cost of living
Easy to import car tax free (which would turn out not to be that important)
Retiree benefits & incentives
Tax advantages
Clear title and ownership
Stable currency and low inflation
Accessible from the US at moderate cost (we wanted our kids to be able to afford to visit)
Some tourism
Some infrastructure
Home that looks interesting (and affordable) on line

Government
Stable government
English widely accepted second language
Legal system familiar
Minimal corruption
Respect for law but not "cop heavy"

Residency options
Dual citizenship option
Family/friends visa options and ability to work

Culture
Diverse, accepting, open, tolerant
Friendly
Stimulating environment – something to do other than "play golf"
Opportunities to contribute
No official religion or state church
Optimistic and forward-looking attitude

OK, we didn't want much. But, hey, we were dreaming, and isn't that what dreams are about?

I created an Excel spread sheet, with columns for each location on my short list. Arbitrarily I created a ranking system using the information I had at the time based on my research and whether the location had the particular attributes we were seeking. I assigned points based on the ranking as follows:

Definitely = 5 points
Yes = 4 points
Sorta, Kinda, Yeah BUT = 3 points
Depends = 2 points
Unknown = 1 points
No = Minus 2 points

One important item had to do with the cost of housing. The criteria here was the cost of a house that I found listed for sale on line that at least looked interesting to us.

Under $100K = 5 points
$101-200K = 4 points
$201-300K = 3 points
$301-400K = 2 points
$401-500K = 1 point
Over $500K = Minus 2 points

Not perfect and were I doing it again I would definitely refine my rating system, but you get the idea.

This gave us an overall ranking by which to compare our five destinations. Using this system we ended up with:

Panama – 171
Ventura – 145
Costa Rica - 112
St John, USVI – 135
St Croix, USVI – 124
St Thomas, USVI – 122

Interestingly, for us Ventura, where we were living, ranked higher than any of the Virgin Islands or Costa Rica!! So why would we change? But remember, not every item on the list was of equal importance to us.

So we said, "If we had 100 points to 'spend', and only 100 points, how would we allocate that? What is really important to us?"

And here's what we ended up with . . .

Lower cost of living – 30 points
Good medical care – 20 points
Warm – 15 points
Opportunity for investment, business, owner working – 15 points
Basic dependable utilities including Internet – 10 points
Availability of supplies – 5 points

Now, seven years later, I would say that were we doing the same exercise today . . . it would end up with pretty much the same results!

Taking a look at the overall ranking numbers and the weighted averages we had a better overall picture. Drum roll: here's what we ended up with . . .

Ventura - Overall 145 - Weighted 305
Panama - Overall 171 - Weighed 475

Costa Rica - Overall 112 - Weighted 305
St. Croix, USVI - Overall 124 - Weighted 195
St. Thomas, USVI - Overall 122 - Weighted 215

So we already lived in a near paradise – if you took away the traffic, the crime, and the high cost of living. But when you weighed in what was important to us – lower cost of living being the most important since we needed to afford to retire – Panama won hands down.

Now we knew where we wanted to end up! We'd found, at least on paper, our paradise, and its name was Panama.

Interacting

1. As of right now, what places would you include on an initial list of possibilities?

2. Think of the places on this list that you've already visited. As an exercise to start getting the hang of this, start thinking of what you remember of these places in terms of pros and cons. You may have only looked at them as a tourist. Think of them now as potential places to call home. Any difference in how you'd rate them from that perspective?

3. What are you going to do this week to start your research (aside from finishing this book)? This one is easy: head to Barnes & Noble, get a cup of coffee and start browsing!

4. How you do your analysis is up to you. Like me you may want to do charts and weighted averages and even more. (Give me credit: I didn't do an ROI ["return on investment'], but understand that when I was looking at things like government structure, economy, currency, inflation, stability and the like, I was definitely thinking investment and ROI.) You may just want to make a chart with checkmarks: fine, whatever works for you. The important thing is that you figure out a way to compare and analyze that works for you.

4. Visit A Leather Bar

OK, **I debated changing this title, but it really does say what I want to say, so stay with me!**

I know that this title may make some folk nervous, but nobody is going to change your sexual orientation. I just want to make a point about cultural differences.

So chill out!

I remember the first time a good friend "came out" to me and told me he was gay. And he wanted to take me to a gay bar, a very macho, gay leather bar. Fortunately I could come up with jeans and a white tee shirt so we got in, even although I didn't have a leather outfit with the seat of the pants missing.

If you live in or near a big city, the bar will probably have a name like The Corral, Spike, or Eagle. It probably won't look like much from the outside. It's not going to be next to the Mall or on the same street as the designer and boutique shops. It's probably on a back street. It may be hard to find and may not even have a sign. There may be bikes out front although this is not a biker bar. It may or may not have a rainbow flag. I suggest you leave your Hawaiian shirt and surfer shorts at home. Levis and a white or gray tee shirt (used, not new, best avoid any logos). A black leather vest would work nice, if you happen to have one tucked away. Leather boots if you've got them. No fragrances. Walk in, belly up to the bar, order a beer and soak up the ambiance.

If you can't find a leather bar, try any old gay bar. Looser dress code. Fragrances work here. Order whatever you like, preferably a martini, and soak up the ambiance. At least the dancing will be good.

If you happen to be into leather or gay bars then you'll want to find a very conservative, fundamentalist church. Dress code here is white shirt, tie, and jacket. Replace the red AIDS-awareness pin with an American flag. Tuck a Bible conspicuously under your arm and soak up the ambiance. Nothing against conservative fundamentalists, as some of my best friends are "fundies". And some of my best friends are gay, and some are theologically conservative and also gay, and I believe God loves them all! The point I'm trying to make is that you need to experience a culture radically different to the one to which you are accustomed. The point isn't for you to convert or change your lifestyle.

The point is to enter into and observe a culture that is different than your own.

Face it: if you are even considering relocating to another country, the culture, the customs, the language, the food, the mores, the laws – it's all going to be different. Some people do different well. Others are threatened by anything that's different.

This is a key point, key to your ultimate success and happiness in a new home. Do you find differences in culture and people fascinating, something you can't wait to experience and explore, or does it threaten who you are and what you believe? What is your level of tolerance? *Do you appreciate the broadness and color of the Kingdom of God, or do you just assume everyone should be like you?*

Now in our first experiment you visited a leather bar, a gay bar, or a church with a totally different "flavor" than you are used to, and at least tried to fit in. You kind of dressed down to look the part. Now imagine doing the same thing dressing and acting the way you normally dress and act. You walk into the leather bar in your Hawaiian shirt, surfer shorts and Teva sandals, or show up in church in your wildest Saturday-night-party-your-ass-off outfit. Imagine how you feel sticking out as a definite minority.

You can do the same thing in a lot of other ways. I am not a car racing fan. When I worked with 24 Hour Fitness someone in marketing got the brilliant idea for us to sponsor a race car. And so we found a car with the number "24" in the Winston Cup. So we had our 24 Hour Fitness car and team. Talk about expensive! Car racing really is the sport of kings! Not only did you need a car, you needed a huge van with 24 Hour Fitness painted all over it to cart the car around, and you needed a spare car, and another van, and a portable shop with extra engines and the list and expenses went on and on and on. So a bunch of us got to go to see our first race with VIP passes, a chance to see the race from the perspective of our pit crew and lots of gifts with NASCAR and our 24 Hour Fitness logo (which started to give me a clue as to why this was so expensive). I had never been to a car race before and I was awe-struck! There were thousands and thousands of people interested in Winston Cup racing and lined up to buy $500 leather NASCAR jackets, NASCAR underwear, you name it, they sold it! There was the even the Viagra car booth, I guess selling blue pills with the NASCAR logo. Here was this incredible subculture of which I was completely ignorant and with which I had no experience. But my marketing acumen was shrewd enough to look around at the decidedly overweight and out-of-shape crowd and knew that while these folks could certainly benefit from 24 Hour Fitness, these guys were not a very promising market. And eventually our marketing geniuses realized the same thing and we got out of racing. But NASCAR is one of those niche subcultures where, if you're not a NASCAR fan, you can feel very much like a minority.

Those of us who are white in America often have very little minority experience.

As I told you, my first church was an all-black congregation in the South Bronx of New York City in the late '60s, at the height of the Black Panther "Power to The People" era. Here I was, this white boy from Michigan who knew nothing about being black or being in the city, dropped into the South Bronx. I found out very quickly what it meant to be a minority! For a while it seemed like everywhere I turned there was a black fist in my white face, not literally, but certainly figuratively.

The head of my Usher Board was a lady by the name of Mary Ida Vandross[2]. Now the Usher Board is probably the most important organization and power in a black congregation. Mary Ida took pity on this single white boy and used to invite me over for Sunday afternoon dinners. I learned to love soul food! I mean that woman could cook!

Mary Ida had a teenage son who used to always be fooling around with music, singing, dancing, and doing awesome things with his voice. His name was Luther Vandross.

She had another son with serious drug problems who was in and out of jail. I hadn't been in the Bronx very long when Anthony got out of Riker's Island jail and ended up staying in the church's parish house while he got his life together. One night Anthony sat down with me and had a heart-to-heart talk. He said, "D, you have all these degrees, but you don't know shit about the street. You're not going to live long unless you start to learn. There are people out there who don't have any college degrees, but in terms of street-smarts they have Master's degrees and PhDs. I feel sorry for you, so I'm going to teach you and we're going to meet some of these people."

I'm alive today because of Anthony Vandross. He took me around the Bronx and Harlem and into bars and clubs. He'd say, "See that guy over there, he controls all the drugs in Harlem" and on and on. It took me a while, but I caught on[3].

---

[2] Mary Ida Vandross was an amazing woman. She is the only woman with whom I have been under live fire. I was driving her home at night from a church meeting in the church van when a group of kids on a roof top had been throwing rocks at the NYPD and the police were shooting at the kids. We would later spend a few hours at police headquarters trying to identify to officers shooting at kids only to realize that there is, maybe intentionally, no way to identify a middle aged cop from his Academy graduation photo.

Luther Vandross had an amazing talent and career that was cut short by diabetes. Mary Ida became a spokesperson for the Diabetes Association and along the way graduated from New York Theological Seminary and became an ordained evangelist. She later died of diabetes as did her daughter who was also a member of our church.

[3] Unfortunately I was unable to ever find out what happened to Anthony Vandross.

Preaching was another matter. I came out of seminary trained in expository preaching. Take a Biblical text, exegete it, discuss the Hebrew and Greek words and their meaning and the theological significance. It wasn't what they were looking for in a black church. They tried, and prayed a lot, and were very patient, and I tried. When I preached people would be yelling out, "Help him Jesus! Help him Jesus!"

One Sunday morning when I was finally getting the hang of preaching with a little more freedom and zing, Ms. Foreman got the Spirit. And she started jumping up and down, and crying, and shouting, "Thank you Jesus! Thank you Jesus! Praise you Jesus!" And I was so startled, I stopped!

After the service, Jack Evans, my Senior Elder, took me aside, put his arm around my shoulder and said, "Boy," – I used to hate it when they called me "boy"! – "Boy, let me tell you something about women. When they start shouting and moaning, whatever it is you're doing, don't stop!"

Well I learned a lot about being a minority. And I learned that the way we did things in Grand Rapids, Michigan, or in the white world, wasn't necessarily the only way or even the best way. I learned to appreciate being black. After a while people weren't black, or white, or Puerto Rican. It was Jeanine, Bats, Tito, Octavio, Eddie, Henry, Mary and Victor. Today I'd have to stop and think to remember if they were black, or brown, or white. They were just family and friends.

If you like where you live, if you're convinced it is the absolute best, the be all and end all, why even think about moving?

If you believe you have the best medical care, the fastest freeways, the greatest entertainment, a just justice system, the best shopping, and know what's best for the rest of the world, just stay where you are and keep exporting McDonald's, Subway and Kentucky Fried Chicken to the rest of the world. Pay your taxes and vote for the same folks the same way. Why change?

A friend of ours in Boquete was born in Panama, educated in the US and Europe and makes doors, cabinets and furniture. She knows wood. Wood is tricky in Panama. You don't go to Home Depot or Lowe's or someplace else and buy kiln-dried wood. You find someone who has trees to sell, size up the tree, buy it, chop it down when the moon is right, store it until it has properly dried and then make something out of it. A louvered door isn't made by some machine in North Carolina out of kiln-dried pine. It is hand crafted, piece by piece, out of *cedro*, teak or some other termite resistant wood. Michelle Brewer and her guys are artists in wood. It may take a while, but when it's finished it will be beautiful and worth the wait. The building boom in Boquete makes finding good woodworkers one of the most difficult things in building a home. And the wait can be frustrating.

Michelle was in her office at the shop and as she describes it, "This *gringo* came swaggering into the office. Military buzz cut, looking for all the world like a retired LAPD cop." Michelle is blonde, speaks three or four languages fluently, including English. He assumed she was a *gringa*. And he started unloading about being "sick and tired of these stupid, fucking Panamanians who can't do anything right." He was looking for woodworkers who could do things the "right" way, his American way. Michelle, who is this very gracious, gentle woman who's attended all the right schools in the US and Europe said, "Well I'm a 'fucking Panamanian' and this fucking Panamanian is throwing you out!" And she threw him out of her shop!

The same guy went down the road to another, American woodworker and started the same routine. Without knowing Michelle had just thrown him out, he said, "Sir, I'm a guest in this country and my workers are all Panamanians, so you can get out of my shop and don't come back!"

Who did this ugly American think he was? And why was he in Panama anyway?

Another sweet-looking little old lady in her seventies told a real estate agent she'd look at any property in Boquete, "Just as long as it wasn't next door to any people talking Mexican!" Did she realize she was in Panama, not Mexico? If she wanted only to hear English, why was she even considering living in Panama?

Don't go to another country wanting to change it or Americanize it or make it the way things were "back home."

If you want LA, stay in LA! The reason why you even consider another country or another culture is because you appreciate the difference!

I confess that I struggle with this every time I drive forty minutes to David and start shopping and get the typically lousy customer service that characterizes much business in Panama, or when I have a workman or service person scheduled to come to my house at, say, noon on Tuesday, and they don't show, don't call, but end up showing up Friday evening at dinner time.

People always ask me what the "toughest" thing is about living in Panama. It's not that we don't have Home Depot or Costco, although that IS tough, but it's the cultural differences that sneak up and grab you, sometimes when least expected.

Two examples . . .

First, *gringo* time and Panamanian time: totally different. Since time dominates the lives of most North Americans and Europeans, I guess this shouldn't be surprising, but it keeps "getting" me. If you are invited to a Panamanian's house for a party at 8 pm, and you show up at 8 pm the hostess will still be in the shower! 9:30 pm is a better time to show up and you'll catch the beginning of the party.

Second, Panamanians like to please. It's a way of life, an expression of good manners, and so they tell you what they think you want to hear which is not always what you need to hear. North Americans just want to hear it the way it is, straightforward and direct. Given my cultural mindset, it's easy to conclude that people are lying to me because they are not telling me what I consider to be "the truth", when in the reality of their culture they are just being polite.

Living abroad gives you the exciting opportunity to experience a totally new world usually including a new culture, a different language, and different ways of doing things, new foods, new friends, and new experiences. The reward is to embrace the differences and learn from them. The American way may be better, but you may just discover that others sometimes know more and have better ways that what you'd just assumed was the "best" way.

Return with me, if you will, to the dug out canoe, cruising up the river to visit my Embera friends. Understand that this was a surprise visit! They didn't know I was coming. Erito's wife had no idea he was bringing home a *gringo* for dinner and to spend the night. As far as I was concerned, I was just visiting a friend.

Naturally the village, which consists of around 10 family groups, about 20 individual families, and around 125 people, found this visit interesting.

It turns out that Erito is kind of the mayor of the village. His wife, the village preschool teacher is very protective of traditional Embera culture. Still nursing her baby, she was obviously embarrassed to be found by this *gringo* wearing a bra. She quickly slipped out of the bra to be culturally appropriately dressed for guests. She graciously whipped up a delicious dinner of fried, freshly speared tilapia right out of the river, plantains, fry bread, and thick, sweet coffee for this surprise Anglo guest.

Embera homes are built on stilts about six feet off the ground. The floors are strips of palms, the roofs are thatched, and the sides are all open. A log with notches provides stairs to the home from the jungle floor. After dinner we settled down. Erito, his wife, and two children were on one mat and I was on the other. Fires flickered from other homes in the village. And we talked. Talking was interesting because I knew only "*un pocito*" Spanish. Until the US turnover of the Canal, the Air Force had hired Embera to teach astronauts and pilots jungle survival. Several of Erito's people had worked for the US Air Force so he knew a few English words. Somehow, as we had when I first met Erito, we managed to talk into the night for hours. We discussed 9/11 and it's impact on the US and the world. We discussed Christianity. A movie company had filmed a movie about Nate Saint and missionaries who had been killed in the '50s by Indians in Ecuador, with the Embera playing the part of the Ecuadorian Indians[4]. We talked Southern California freeways. The concept of twelve and fourteen-lane highways was mind boggling sitting in the jungle, listening to tree frogs, and the village disc jockey providing entertainment. At about 9 pm the genre of the music changed to American love songs, presumably to encourage tribal expansion.

By midnight the entire village was asleep ... everyone but me. And the music was still playing. I was wrapped up in a sheet I had borrowed from the hotel to keep centipedes from crawling up my arms. About 4 am the damn music stopped and I thought, "Finally! I can get some sleep!" And at 4:30 am the roosters started crowing!

In addition to acting as mayor, Erito is also the village doctor. We discussed the whole range of illnesses and treatments. The Embera have plants for diarrhea, arthritis, heart problems, rashes, depression, even plants for venomous snake bites.

Have sexual problems? There are plants that act as aphrodisiacs. Cheaper than Viagra.

---

[4] The movie "End of The Spear" (2005) became one of the few independently released Christian movies to draw more than $1,000,000 in its first three weekends of release. By the time the film left the box office, it had made $12 million. It has since made over $20 million more in rentals and video sales, Some fundamentalist Christians had problems with the fact that Chad Allen, who plays the lead in the film, is openly gay.

Childbirth: "Well, there are women who understand that kind of thing." If the child is breached? "We take them down river to a town with road access and then get a cab or ambulance to the hospital."

Broken leg? It is set, bound with plants and sticks and allowed to heal.

Someone slices their arm with a machete? A plant helps stop the bleeding, the comb of a rooster is cut off and placed in the gaping wound, sutures are provided by a bug that has a jaw that clamps shut like a surgical clip, and the entire thing is bound up tightly with plants. The next day Erito showed me some of his handiwork. An ER doctor with the finest stitching technique couldn't have produced a less obvious scar.

First Erito talks about the problem. A lot of illnesses are "spiritual": a person is out-of-sorts with their spouse, or someone else in the village, and the physical symptoms are just manifestations of another kind of problem. Next in the line of treatment are various plants for various illnesses topically applied. Then come teas and brews made from various plants. If none of these treatments work, Erito has no problem transporting the person to the hospital in Panama City. There is no anti-medical attitude, it's just that it is cheaper, and often more efficient to use the remedies God has provided in the jungle.

The next day Erito and his grandfather, the senior medicine man, took me on a hike through the jungle, stopping to point out various plants and explain their use in treatment. Not surprisingly representatives of major drug companies have make this same trek.

I have a lecture I do on ships about the importance of rainforests. Did you know . . .

The US National Cancer Institute has identified 3,000 plants that are active against cancer cells and 70% of these plants are found in the rainforest?

Most medicine men and shamans remaining in the rainforests today are seventy years old or more?

When a medicine man dies without passing his arts on to the next generation, the tribe and the world loses thousands of years of irreplaceable knowledge about medicinal plants?

My point here is simply that often we just assume that we are the be-all and end-all and that because we're so modern, scientific and technological that we know it all and that our ways are the best and the only way. Folks, it just ain't so.

There is a vast world of people, and cultures, and knowledge just waiting to be explored! If we open ourselves, drop our ethnocentricities, have a humble attitude and listen, there is much that we can learn. That's what entering into a new culture is all about. If you can buy that, you're ready to think about actually making the move. If not, you're better to stay put.

* * * *

An interesting postscript to this story: After we'd moved to Panama, since I'd visited Erito in his home, I invited Erito and Zuleika to visit us in our home in Boquete. Much to my surprise they accepted and we enjoyed five days together in Boquete. They had never been across the Bridge of the Americas before or even visited Western Panama, much less Boquete. Since my Spanish is very limited, thinking and communicating in Spanish for five days left my brain feeling like mush, but we had a wonderful time. It was a thrill to show these people their country.

Erito and Zuleika and some of the other Embera have since visited us in Boquete several times. It's been fun! I served pancakes one morning and they were all eating them like *tortillas* until I explained the syrup routine. Fernando complained about how cold our shower water was until I explained both handles. These guys kept complaining about how cold they were at night and we kept adding blankets and they kept complaining. Finally I asked them to show me how they were sleeping. Then I explained you need to get under the blankets. Blankets aren't necessary in the Chagres jungle!

Interacting

1. Make a list of friends – acquaintances, if you need some help – who are different than you. The difference may be lifestyle, race, economic background, culture, sexual orientation, hobbies and interests, style, generation, whatever! Make it as complete and varied as possible. Then think of the things that you like and find interesting about the differences. Finally, list the ways in which you find the differences threatening. You may want to explore this further with your friends.

2. Make a list of at least four different cultural venues in your community that you could visit as a cross-cultural experience. It may be a church that's different than yours, a NASCAR race (only if you're not a fan), a gallery exhibition opening (again, only if that's not your normal thing), a different ethic area of your city, a restaurant of an ethnic variety of food that's totally different, or hang out with your grandkids and their friends and attempt to appreciate their music.

3. OK, now that you have the list, which one ARE you going to visit THIS week?

4. Go to Barnes & Noble or your local bookseller and browse through magazines designed to appeal to a different cultural or interest group than your own.

5. If you have tucked away a language course you've never used, or a Berlitz survival language handbook, or an old college language text, regardless of the language, pick it up and leaf through it. You may be surprised how much you remember! If you really wanted to communicate, and didn't give a rip what anyone thought, this language stuff might be easier than you think! The next time you see a Spanish-speaking person, maybe even your gardener or maid, try a few simple greetings in Spanish. Communication as a for-credit course is a bore, but when seen as a game it becomes challenging and fun!

5. Change Is Good

The Greek philosopher Heraclites observed that, "We are living in a world of constant change". Yet many of us, consciously or unconsciously, resist change, particularly when the change threatens familiar patterns in life.

Yet change happens. We look in the mirror and note how we've changed. We age. We move from one stage of life to another. Sometimes the events in life change us.

Sometimes we have a choice to change, and sometimes not.

Retirement looms as a major change in life. Will we be able to adapt? What will we do? How will we survive without the daily nine to five routine of work?

Pretty much how you look at change determines how flexible you are and how successful you can be at managing change in your life. The operative word here is managing. You have a choice to be the passive victim of change, or to manage change as it comes along. You can fight change, or you can embrace it. Change can be threatening or invigorating: the choice is really yours!

You can go through the changes in your life or you can grow through them.

Face it: most of us are going to live to be ninety. If you're thinking about retirement, you're probably at the age where you've already beat some of the odds. For most people life divides somewhat neatly into three segments:

Youth – Preparation. Roughly the first thirty years. Yes, I know that many of us who grew up in the '60s thought that life damn near ended at thirty – remember, not trusting anyone over thirty? But we know now that we were really just kids when we were in our twenties trying to figure out which end was up.

Responsibility – Roughly the second thirty years. I was tempted to call it "slavery", but that really would be a bit harsh. Thirty years of "getting ahead", building a "career", raising kids and pets, paying a mortgage, accumulating "stuff", and, hopefully, putting something away for retirement.

Your Time – Roughly the last thirty years. Now you could call this the traditional "retirement" period, or, in my mind worse yet, "maturity", but I prefer to think of it as your time.

You've paid your dues, you've worked your ass off, you've raised your kids and now it is time to enjoy life!

It's all a matter of how you choose to look at it! In many ways this last thirty years of "Your Time" should be the time of your life! Sometimes we get this incredibly negative attitude, usually starting around forty or fifty, that "it's all downhill from here." Bull! It's only downhill if that's what you choose. Just think of all you packed into the first thirty years – and you really didn't know which end was up! Or the second thirty years even with being a slave to a job and a career. Now, with all of that experience, just think what you can do with the next thirty years!

Like most people, as "kids" Nikki and I looked at growing old and decided it wasn't for us. We didn't want to grow old. Old, first defined as thirty, gradually got pushed to forty five, then fifty five, then sixty five . . .

Nikki was commiserating with her mom about growing old and said, rather flippantly, "I don't want to grow old and decrepit. If I do, I'm just going to walk in front of a bus."

Nikki's Mom said, "Oh, no, Nikki!" And Nikki glowed with her mother's care and concern until her Mom said, "Don't step in front of a bus, step in front of a train, it's much more effective!"

You have a choice to embrace change and grow through it or just endure. Growth is characteristic of all living things. Bob Dylan is supposed to have said, "A person is either being born, or he is dying"

When you retire, by choice or force, you leave behind a part of you. It may seem like a big part, but in the grand scheme of things it is just a part, nothing more, nothing less. That part is gone and it will never be the same. There is a loss and a natural grieving process over the loss of something that was very important in your life. You are forever changed. And in this fact lies both the crux of the problem and the opportunity. As with many changes in life, you can go through it or you can grow through it: the choice is yours!

I've always liked this poem by Gordon and Gladis DePree which, for me at least, captured the essence of growth.

Growing
is seldom a graceful process
it is shoots and half-formed leaves,
big teeth and bony knees.
Growing is the process of something
becoming larger, taller,
more mature.
And although growing
is not always a graceful process,
poised and polished and finished,
it is preferable to its alternative . . .
For when a plant or animal or person
or mind or spirit
stops growing,
it begins the process of dying.[5]

---

[5] THE GIFT by Gordon and Gladys DePree. Copyright 1976 by The Zondervan Corporation.

You are passing from one stage of life to another. Gail Sheehy in her book PASSAGES used the illustration of a lobster, which sheds its hard protective shell in order to grow as an example of the challenge of growth in the "passages" of our lives. During the period after the shedding of the shell, the lobster is exposed and vulnerable as a new covering grows to replace the one that was lost. Sheehy says, "With each passage from one stage of human growth to the next, we too, must shed a protective structure. We are left exposed and vulnerable – but also yeasty and embryonic again, capable of stretching in ways we hadn't known before."[6]

I like that – "yeasty and embryonic again, capable of stretching in ways we hadn't known before." When the kids were at home, when you had to be at work every day, when you had to struggle to make the mortgage, you didn't have the opportunities that you have now!

Sheehy observes that in each passage of life, in each change, "Some magic must be given up, some cherished illusion of safety and comfortably familiar sense of self must be cast off, to allow for the greater expansion of our own distinctiveness."[7]

She writes, ". . . we must be willing to change chairs if we want to grow. There is no permanent compatibility between a chair and a person. And there is no one right chair. What is right at one stage may be restricting at another or too soft. During the passage from one stage to another, we will be between two chairs. Wobbling no doubt, but developing . . . . Times of crisis, or disruption or constructive change, are not only predictable but desirable. They mean growth."[8]

So this is your time! Your time to grow!

---

[6] Gail Sheehy, PASSAGES. (New York, E. P. Dutton, 1976), pp.20-21.

[7] Ibid

[8] Ibid

When Nikki and I moved to Panama we both lost twenty pounds while eating better! Our blood pressures dropped to more acceptable levels. We started walking. Nikki left a high-stress job managing programs for the Ventura County Public Health Department. I tell her that the best thing she ever did for her health was to leave the health department!

Nikki faced such a round of pressure and deadlines and meetings getting ready to phase out of her responsibilities she said that when she came to Panama she didn't want to see anyone for three months. That only lasted a few weeks! She luxuriates in having three or four books in the process of being read, has become a really good coffee farmer and is active in several local community groups. I decided to start lecturing on luxury cruise ships and now spend half the year cruising around the world. I'm not ready to sit in the rocking chair, listen to the rain and watch the coffee grow, although, I confess, at times I do enjoy it!

When we first moved to Boquete we were, as the movie folk said back in LA, "on hiatus", not sure exactly what we would end up doing, but "yeasty and embryonic again, capable of stretching in ways we hadn't known before". We knew we were in a growth mode, just not sure where it was going to lead. For some people that is too challenging! They need a road map with detailed directions and mileage a 'la MapQuest.

We were challenged by feeling open and free to explore possibilities we hadn't had time to think of before because we were too busy with family and careers.

At first I thought I might stay in real estate, or open a business, but eventually I decided to enjoy the freedom of not being "locked in" or doing the things I've always done. We've developed our little coffee farm, found a beach house to someday fix up, and I've rediscovered my love of cruising and the sea and lecture on cruise ships about 50% of the time, allowing us to travel and meet people from all over the world. Life is good!

For me to switch from just going on ships occasionally for a week or two at a time to sailing on a contract for three to five months at a time was a big jump. One of the major cruise lines had offered me a five-month contract. I probably wouldn't have done it, except for the fact that my wife and kids said I would never last, so I had to prove them wrong. At the time I was reading a novel by Phillip Friedman and these words jumped off the page: "He was poised on the unforeseen cusp of his life. He could either leap into the unknown or slide back down to where he had been stagnating, where he would continue to stagnate, sustaining himself on illusions of renewal."[9]

I leaped and I love it!

Follow The String

I've always had a philosophy that you should "follow the string." I've taught this to my kids as they were growing up. You simply "follow the string" and see where it leads. If you don't, you'll never know what might have been. And if you follow the string and no longer like where it's leading, you simply stop following. That philosophy has led us as a family to many interesting discoveries, discoveries that would not have occurred had we not taken the first steps of following the string to see where it leads. And we're still following the string!

Now I will admit that there are can be limiting factors, If you haven't been climbing mountains all your life, it's unlikely, though not impossible, that in this stage of your life you'll scale Denali. This is where your gene pool and attention to your health and fitness all these years pays off. If you have serious health problems, they may be a limiting factor. As you get older the availability of good medical care becomes an issue, which is one of the reasons we ended up in Panama.

---

[9] Phillip Friedman, GRAND JURY

It's interesting in our society. We watch our grandson and we say, "My, isn't he growing!" We smile proudly and everyone is happy because the child is developing as he should. He is aging. We see that aging as growing and think it is great. People are supposed to grow.

But when you first saw gray hair, or faced a physical challenge or limitation brought on by aging, how did you look at aging? Did you feel good because you were getting older? Were you pleased that you were doing what people are supposed to do? Why are we so inconsistent? At one period of life we look on aging as something good and positive, and at another period of time the same process precipitates a crisis.

Would you really want to go back and relive your youth? I wouldn't! I thought I enjoyed it, Mario's observations about my pitiful youth lacking in sex, alcohol and drugs notwithstanding, but I wouldn't go back even if I could. Each period of life has its own unique opportunities for experience and growth. Having grown through one period of life I value and treasure it, but I'm anxious to go on and grow through the next period.

Douglas Macarthur said, "Nobody grows old by merely living a number of years. People grow old by deserting their ideals. Tears may wrinkle the skin, but to give up interest wrinkles the soul." He was right! More people die from hardening of the mind than from hardening of the arteries! The mind hardens when you give up on dreams and become rigid and inflexible. People who have a negative outlook on aging resist it and resent it. They see the changes in themselves but instead of accepting them they reject them. But the changes continue and they become bitter. Unable to accept the changes in themselves, they can't accept change in others or in society. They become very bitter and angry old people! Unless there is some radical surgery of negative ideas, these attitudes will kill them.

God made us and He made us to grow older. He designed the various stages of life, each with its own rewards and opportunities.

Part of living live abundantly as God intended, is for us to seize each stage and live it positively, fully and with enthusiasm!

I earlier mentioned Dr. Norman Vincent Peale. I remember getting into a hotel elevator in Milwaukee with Dr. Peale. He had just finished a rip-roaring speech to 9,000 prominent and successful sales people. He was in his late seventies and it was late at night, but he was still filled with vigor and enthusiasm. I asked him in amazement, "Dr. Peale, how do you keep going? How are you able to keep flying all over the country making three or four speeches a week, sometimes two in a day, and preaching in New York on Sunday?"

Dr. Peale cleared his voice and in his gravelly voice said, "Well, I'll tell you one thing: I don't eat the cold, rubbery chicken they serve at these gatherings. I go in, give my speech and I get out!"

I've always suspected there was more to it than that! Peale says, "Successful old-age is built on earlier years lived right." He said in old-age you'll be the same kind of person you were when you were younger, only more so. If you were positive and enthusiastic at thirty, you'll be that way at eighty. If you were a grouch and negative at thirty, just imagine what you'll be like at eighty!

Whatever your age it's not too early or too late to start loving life and approaching it positively and with enthusiasm.

Growing is a great adventure!

There is evidence that openness to new adventures can actually decrease stress and help you live longer. According to Dr. Norman Anderson coauthor of EMOTIONAL LONGEVTY: WHAT REALLY DETERMINES HOW LONG YOU LIVE, "People who successfully try new things develop a high sense of self-efficacy – 'a can do attitude' – which can lead to better health." Some studies have shown that this adventurous, positive attitude overrode other life-extenders like low blood pressure, low cholesterol, not smoking, low body-fat and even regular exercise.

There is evidence that continuing to learn, continuing to use and exercise your brain, actually lessens the chances of getting Alzheimer's disease. And there is no more strenuous and better way to exercise your brain and memory that learning a new language.

* * * *

Just a few words of caution here . . .

Sometimes people who are bored with their lives, or their relationships, or themselves, think that just changing location is the answer to their problems. When all you do is change location, generally you take all the underlying problems with you. You need to be basically happy with you before your think about changing location.

Take care of your business first: if you've got issues, deal with them. It's a lot easier to do it where you are, than to try and find a psychiatrist, counselor, or whatever, in a new country. If it's not working at home, just moving to a new country isn't going to "fix" things.

I was being driven in some country from the airport to the ship and I don't remember where. Working for a cruise line means you sit in the back of the plane and take the cheapest and most circuitous route the cruise line can find. After all the hours in airports and on planes the only thing I remember is a big bill board along the route to the ship that said . . .

"Amazing things happen when you say yes to life, with no strings attached!"

How true! Try it!

Interacting

1. In what ways has your life become predictable and, pardon me, boring?

2. If you could change three things about your life, what would they be?

3. In what ways is your life already changing?

4. If you could do anything, and nothing was impossible, what would you do?

6. Why Panama?

When I announced to my fellow REALTORS® in Ventura, **California that I was retiring early and moving to Panama the response was instantaneous and uniform: "Why Panama?"**

I'm probably the only *gringo* in Panama who ever moved here because of the Embera Indians.

I knew nothing about Panama. Yes I knew it had a Canal. I used to send people on cruises through the Canal and had been through twice on cruise ships during the Noriega years, or as the locals refer to it, "the dictatorship." As we slipped through the Canal the shore looked totally foreign, and threatening, evoking much the same feeling as Cuba is supposed to evoke with Americans today.

I had waded through David McCullough's book, THE PATH BETWEEN THE SEAS, about the Panama Canal. But in terms of modern Panama my only impressions had come from the movie "Tailor of Panama". Although the only major motion picture actually filmed in Panama, we would eventually come to realize its highly inaccurate depiction of Panama.

Not only was Panama not on our list, we'd never even thought of Panama!

I was serving as a Protestant Chaplain on a cruise ship that was cruising Caribbean and sailing into the Canal, turning around in Gatun Lake, and returning to Florida. The ship turned out to offer a stop in Panama providing opportunity for passengers to disembark in Gatun Lake if they were taking one of a handful of shore excursions. One of the shore excursions offered a trip in a dug out canoe to an "Authentic Embera Indian Village". My wife thought it sounded fantastic and jumped at the opportunity. At almost $100 a head I though it sounded expensive and I was sure it would be a hokey rip-off aimed at tourists, not that any cruise line would ever offer a "hokey rip-off" shore excursion! Nikki went on the tour and I took advantage of my chaplain status to go ashore to the "Gatun Lake Yacht Club" for the day – not a yacht or marina in sight, but it was a chance to actually set foot in Panama.

An Embera group from another village had been recruited by the tour operator to provide local, mostly naked, color. Bare-breasted girls and men in nothing but red loin cloths met the passengers disembarking the ship's tenders for the obligatory port disembarkation photos. To my knowledge this is the first time cruise ship photos had ever featured bare-breasted girls, so of course it was a big hit with the passengers, if exploitive.

There was nothing at the Gatun Lake Yacht Club. This truly was a hokey tourist rip-off. I guess to compensate the tour operator of the "yacht club tour" was offering free beer. There was a group of Embera women selling baskets. I looked at the baskets then walked across the lawn where the men were sprawled out. One young guy, whose name I later learned was Auselio, was sitting at a cement picnic table, all alone, and appeared to either be stoned, drunk or sleeping. Another Embera was sitting at another table watching me closely, since most of the ship's passengers were huddled together by the dock and the beer. He said something to me in Spanish, and I stumbled a reply, which pretty much exhausted my Spanish vocabulary. Somehow I managed to ask if this kid was drunk or stoned. He laughed, it was his brother, and he was just tired from the all-night trip in from their jungle village. He yelled for Auselio to come over and join us. Poor Auselio had obviously been in the middle of a very erotic dream, and he wandered across, half asleep but obviously aroused, not easy to hide in a loin cloth, and so this provoked a lot of good-natured laughter and teasing from his brothers.

So I met Erito and Auselio, then his brothers. It wasn't long until we are all sitting at a cement table deep into conversation. Amazing, especially given my halting and very limited Spanish.

Turns out that Erito was the head of the village. His uncles had worked for the US Army teaching the early astronauts and Green Berets jungle survival, so Erito knew a few words of English. About this time I got the idea of going over where the tour operator was serving free beer and bringing back beers for everyone. The group grew. I met Auselio and his girl friend, Erito's wife, and all his brothers. Auselio was in love and he wanted a picture taken of him and his beautiful bare-breasted girl friend. More beer. Auselio gave me a *"regala"* or gift of a beaded necklace, and I, with nothing else to give, gave him the 24 Hour Fitness shirt off my back.

Auselio couldn't wait to get back to the village to get his girl friend to put on the shirt so, as he put it, she'd "look sexy like American girls." Auselio had a one-track mind. I patiently explained that in the US the object was to get the T-shirt off the girl, not on.

They wanted to know what I did, and since I was doing the 24 Hour Fitness Web site at the time, I told them "Internet." Auselio's eyes lit up – he was a man of multiple interests – and he said, "Internet!" I thought to myself, "Oh, no, they have a Web site and he's the Webmaster!" That wasn't the case, but I began to realize that these guys, although committed to preserving a lifestyle, were very intelligent, articulate, and very aware of technology and what was happening in the rest of the world.

By this time, two hours into the conversation, we were attracting the notice of the tour operator's personnel. And, I guess, we were consuming a lot of beer. One of the tour operator's guys began serving the beer so I didn't have to keep jumping up for more, and bringing fruit punch for the Embera women. I wanted to take a swim in the Canal, but these guys who live in jungle huts, told me it was "too cold." I called them a "bunch of pussies" and then had to explain the term – gales of more laughter! I gave them my 24 Hour Fitness gym bag. They almost got my shorts too, which was all I had left, but I figured the sight of a drunken chaplain wearing a red loin cloth reboarding the ship might not go over too well with the captain, so I demurred. When it was time for the Embera culture and dance show for the passengers, I was escorted to a plastic chair in front of the ship's passengers and told that this performance was for me.

I was told by Erito, and this was later confirmed by the ship's staff, that I was the only *gringo* who'd ever really connected and entered into this kind of interaction with the Embera. Erito invited me to come back and visit his village and stay in his home. Five hours later, Nikki got off the motor coach from her trip to the Embera village (a nearer and different village than Erito's), and was greeted by her husband and all the Embera shouting, *"Esposa! Esposa!"* ("Wife!" Wife!")

Let it be said that the Embera Village trip was the highlight of Nikki's cruise. I have worked on ships transiting the Canal in the years since and I can tell you that every time we send groups out to the Embera village people come back to the ship saying, "Richard that was the best tour ever!"

Back on the ship the Shore Excursion Manager, who'd been observing this scene from a distance, commented on my unique experience. The Embera and passengers usually kept a discrete distance from one another. She promised that if I sent a package to the ship in Florida, she would see it got to Erito on the next Canal voyage.

I decided to send them a package that included a booklet of the pictures I had taken of our time together, along with pictures of my family and home in Ventura, California. I went to Joann Fabrics to buy the wildest fabrics I could find to send the guys for loin cloths. It was the first week of December and I was standing in a long line of women at Joann Fabrics waiting for my fabric to be cut and measured. I had a pile of wild fabric in my arms and this old lady in front was determined to make conversation. "My, what an interesting assortment of fabric. What are you making?"

Me, just wanting to escape Joann Fabrics, said, "Oh, you'd never guess."

"A clown costume?"

"Hardly. But, if you must know, loin cloths for Embera Indians in Panama!" That, I thought, would end the conversation.

To which she replied, "The Embera! My daughter lives in Panama City and knows the Embera and collects and sells their baskets." Now what were the chances?

So I sent the package to the ship and got an email back from the ship saying, "The guys loved the package! There was much laughter and celebration. Erito wants to know when you are coming to visit."

So that began the process. I began digging online for anything that I could find out about the Embera and Erito's village of San Juan de Pequini. It truly is a small world on the Internet. Online I found pictures that tourists had taken of Erito and his village. But the more I searched online for stuff about the Embera and Panama the more sites I discovered about retiring and moving and living in Panama. This was interesting! And the more I read about Panama, the more interested I became!

So, thanks to Erito, Auselio, and the Embera *de* San Juan de Pequini I discovered the real Panama. And Panama made it to our short list.

Many Latinos are very surprised at this story and our relationship with Erito and his family. Most Panamanians only know the Indians who work for them, generally not the Embera. Although they have considerable political power, on the Panamanian social structure the Indigenous are at the bottom of the totem pole, often treated as if they don't exist. We have been fortunate to continue our relationship with our Embera friends. Erito and his family have visited with us several times in Boquete and I have been fortunate enough to continue to visit their village with tours from the ships and with just my family.

A postscript about Auselio: today Auselio has "filled out" and looks like an ex-Marine. He has two lovely children and is a leader in his village. When I went to visit the Embera village Auselio was concerned that I not flash the picture around that I had taken of him at Gatun Lake. It seemed he'd fallen in love with and married another girl.

* * * *

So why Panama?

Diversity

Panama is known to the world for its Canal, being the flag of registry for many of the world's ships, an international banking and business center, and, increasingly the crossroads or hub of the Americas. Panama is emerging as "The Singapore of Latin America." Panama's population is around 3 million people, almost 2 million of whom live in and around Panama City.

Yet where we live, the province of Chiriqui, is far from the skyscrapers of Panama City. Chiriquí's main industry is agriculture. Chiriqui provides most of the country's dairy cattle, beef cattle, vegetables, citrus and bananas. Our particular town, Boquete, provides some of the world's finest high-altitude, shade-grown, Arabica coffee. Each year at this time there is a "cupping" where major coffee buyers come to sample and bid at auction for coffee supplies. The second most expensive coffee in the world is grown by our neighbor, Price Peterson. The most expensive coffee in the world is that stuff from Indonesia that's eaten by an animal, excreted; someone picks through the poop and sells it to you for $160 a pound. Price's Geisha coffee from Hacienda La Esmeralda is a bargain at only $120 a pound!

* * * *

Consider that in Panama there are:

• 1,800 miles of coastline
• 940 bird species
• 10,000 species of plants
• 200 species of mammals
• 200 species of reptiles
• Nesting home to four species of sea turtles
• Mountain peaks from which you can see both the Pacific and Caribbean
• Rivers where rafters can ride 20 sets of rapids in a single afternoon
• 1,518 islands

• More deep-sea fishing records off the Pacific cost of Panama than anywhere else in the world
• Seven Indigenous Indian cultures
• 30% of the country is set aside for conservation
• 125 animal species found nowhere else in the world
• Variety of ecosystems including tropical rain forests, grasslands, mountain forest, cloud forests, mangroves and deserts
• Two national marine parks, one of which – Parque Nacional Marino Golfo de Chiriqui– is just a short boat ride from Boca Brava, a tiny hamlet in Chiriqui

You can have a morning swim in the Pacific and the same afternoon sip cocktails in the Caribbean! How's that for diverse?

Because I'm on the ship half of the year, when I'm home in Boquete my idea of a good time is sitting by the fire with my wife and dogs, eating dinner on the couch and watching TV. Since I "eat out" every night on the ship, I'm not very interested in going out when I'm home. So I'm generally not really social, but this has been a busy week. Sunday we were invited to a potluck lunch and there were ex-pats (ex-patriots from other countries, usually retaining their own citizenship, just living abroad) from Canada, US, England, South Africa, Holland, Spain, Italy, France and Hong Kong, plus Panamanians! Fun afternoon with a neat and diverse group.

Thursday we had a bunch of people over for a wine & cheese party that went from 4:30 pm until 9 pm! One of our neighbors is a professional Poker player and his partner is from Taiwan. Friday we were invited over to a gay couple's house down the road for dinner. They've been together for 16 years (maybe a lot of straight couples could learn something from them about "family values"). Saturday night we went to a French restaurant in town for a 5-course dinner with 5 different French wines ($50 for two, including tax & tip) and at our table a retired race car driver, a horse trainer, a Canadian, a Brit, a Panamanian, and a few Americans like us. It is a VERY diverse, interesting and fun group!

Panamanians themselves are a historically diverse group with strains of Indigenous Indian cultures, and Spanish ancestry. There are many people in Boquete who have English surnames going back to early English settlers who intermarried with Panamanians. Jews, Greeks, Chinese, West Indian Africans, French, US and others all were involved in the Canal and entered into the mix. The result is that Panamanians are a mixed and beautiful group of people! When you throw an innate friendliness, politeness, and a lot of patience into the mix, you get a really great group of people!

Officially Panama is a Roman Catholic country, although religious freedom is encouraged. Catholicism is the largest religious group, but slowly declining. The fastest growing group is evangelical charismatic churches. "Hosanna!" is an Assembly of God church in Panama City that started 26 years ago in a storefront. Today the church has over 17,000 members, a medical clinic, TV station, and has planted numerous daughter churches around the country. The sanctuary only seats 5,000, so when they want to get the entire church together they rent a soccer stadium. I visited one Friday night and there were 5,000 people packed in!

You find Seventh Day Adventists, Mormons and Muslims. There are mosques in many of the larger cities, including David. My background with Muslims was largely influenced by Black Muslims in the US, so I'm often a bit taken back when I see a Panamanian Muslim woman, dressed modestly and appropriately, but looking like she just stepped off the runway of a Paris fashion show!

Again, in all ways, this is a very diverse country!

One of the things we've enjoyed over the years is just to jump in our 4X4 and explore. This weekend we headed off to Puerto Armuellas, formerly home to Chiquita Banana. Now it is an economically depressed area with nary a *gringo* in site. Yet everyone was friendly, eager to be helpful, even to two lost *gringos*.

* * * *

Beauty

Panama is a gorgeous country in addition to the beauty and diversity of the people.

"We've got everything God needed to make paradise. Great farming, beaches, mountains, wildlife you wouldn't believe, put a stick in the ground you get a fruit tree, people so beautiful you could cry." (John le Carre, TAILOR OF PANAMA)

Panama isn't yet overrun with tourists although the number of tourists is growing steadily. One statistic claims that Panama in an entire year gets fewer tourists than Disneyland in Anaheim gets on a single weekend! LONELY PLANET observes, "If you have ever found yourself saying, 'Oh, you should have seen this place 10 years ago, before it was overrun with tourists,' chances are you should leave Panama today feeling you'd visited at just the right time."[10]

Again, Lonely Planet, one of the few really good guidebooks on Panama, "Panama offers some of the finest birding, snorkeling and deep-sea fishing in the Americas, but most foreigners know the country only for its famous Canal . . . It's difficult to leave the country without feeling you're in on a secret the rest of the traveling world has yet to discover."[11]

Because the country isn't that big, in a single day you can drive from the Pacific to the Caribbean, from the *frontera* at the Costa Rican border to the edges of the Darien jungle, almost from one end of the country to the other. In a single afternoon you can pass through a half dozen eco systems. Coral reefs, deserted beaches, mangrove swamps, grasslands, ranches, pine-covered mountains where you feel like you've been dropped into the Alps, cloud forests, tropical rainforests, small Central American villages, and a vibrant Miami-like Central American city – it's all here, and it's all waiting to be discovered!

With over 1,500 islands, there is almost an island for everyone!

---

[10] Scott Doggett, LONELY PLANET PANAMA Melbourne, Lonely Planet, 2001, p. 11
[11] P. 12

And the weather is beautiful too! At nine degrees from the equator, yes, there are hot and humid regions, but there are also mountain towns like Boquete with the temperature, year round is a near-perfect 65-80 degrees. Even in many of the warmest areas there are ocean breezes that mitigate the temperatures.

In California we used to joke that we had four seasons: earthquake, fire, rain and mudslide – take your pick. Panama has three seasons: rain, rain and rain. Well, not really! Summer, the dry season is much like Southern California with little rain from mid-December to mid-April. Winter, the rainy season, or the "Green Season" as the tourist people prefer, runs from May to November. The months of June & July are kind of a Panamanian version of the US "Indian summer."

So, how much rain? How much rain depends on where you are at in Panama? Boquete gets moisture even in the "dry season." In the late afternoon a *bajareque* mist moves in over the mountains. Barely enough to wet the ground, it creates spectacular rainbows throughout the valley and the mountains. Boquete averages as much rain in a month as Ventura, California received in an average year. Even in the rainy season it rarely rains all day. Usually mornings are bright and pristine and everyone is up and out and taking care of business. About 2 pm the clouds start to move in and generally there will be an afternoon storm, sometimes continuing into the night. It can be a drizzle, or you can get five inches in a few hours in a tropical downpour. But, with the possible exception of October – the worst month of the rainy season, it never feels oppressive . . . like Seattle. (Sorry, Seattle!)

The Caribbean side, and the area around Bocas, receives the most rain, up to 3,500 millimeters year. That's about 10 feet, but who's counting? With that much water you can make your own wet tee shirt contests without even going to a bar.

Panama is not only beautiful, it is also clean!

Many Caribbean islands are gorgeous, if you can overlook overflowing, stinking trash bins, beaches littered with plastic bottles and bags, and roadsides covered with trash. Once you are away from the city, Panama is clean! People are proud and make a conscious effort to keep things nice and clean. You'll find less trash along major roads than in California. And because Panama doesn't have the US gang culture, there is very little graffiti! Where you do find graffiti it is mostly an expression of a current political grievance.

Economics

Panama's currency is called the "Balboa" but it is in fact the US Dollar. Since 1904 Panama, except for one week, has never printed money. Because the currency is the US Dollar you always know what something costs. You don't have to wonder, "How much is that in real money?" Panamanian coins are in the same denominations as US coins, in fact they have the same size and weight and coins are used interchangeably. You can put a Panamanian quarter in a vending machine in Miami just as you can put a US quarter in a Panamanian machine. Due to the short life-span of $1 paper bills and the high cost of shipping worn out bills back to the US Mint, Panama has introduced a 1 Balboa coin which is equal in value to the US dollar.

Because Panama's currency is the US Dollar, the rampant inflation that plagues many South and Central American countries and "Banana Republics" is not a problem. Panama's currency is as strong as the US dollar. When the US dollar is weak against major world currencies the price of many things we import goes up in Panama just like it does in the US.

Panama has a robust service industry. It is a major center for off-shore banking and corporations.

Many of the ships in the world fly the Panamanian flag, although Panama has no navy.

The Canal goes cha-ching, cha-ching, cha-ching 24 hours a day. Although it is an independent agency, it plows money into the country.

The Canal makes a direct contribution to the government of over $400-$700 million a year. Panama has begun to enlarge the Canal adding a "Third Lane", another set of locks that will accommodate ships larger than currently in existence. When completed the Canal will make a direct contribution of $1.25 Billion a year plus indirect contribution in the form of taxes, social security payments, etc. The Chinese are expanding their harbors at the ends of the Canal.

The Trans-Panama oil pipeline transports oil from Alaskan supertankers, who dock at Puerto Armuelles, across the Isthmus since the supertankers currently don't fit through the Canal. Plans are underway for a new oil refinery in Puerto Armuelles. The Japanese have just signed to build new docking facilities at Puerto Armuelles.

Panamanian coffee shows up in Starbucks and other coffee blends around the world and is exported to Japan, Scandinavia, Germany and Italy.

Bananas and beef are exported. Panama has one of the world's largest copper mines and a gold mine. With the high cost of gold the precious metal represents the highest dollar-value export of the country.

The Colon Free Zone is the second largest free zone in the world, second only to Hong Kong.

Additionally Panama has created a free zone at Panama Pacifico, the giant planned community being created on the site of the former Howard Air Force Base.

Unlike some of its neighbors, Panama has a comparatively diverse economy. The standard of living in Panama and the average income, although low by US standards, is the highest in Central America. And yet the cost of living in Panama is far less than in the US!

Depending on where in the US you are from you can live better for less in Panama. Our overall cost of living in Boquete is one third of what it was in Ventura, California! We'll talk more about this in "Running The Numbers", but it is amazing how much your money can buy in Panama!

Traditionally banking in Panama has been very private, although after a full court press by the US to break bank secrecy and holding a US Free Trade Agreement hostage, the US has managed to break down the secrecy the same way it did in Switzerland. Many major banks have branches in Panama, although because of Panama's banking laws, you need to open separate accounts in Panama. There are, of course, fees when you transfer money between countries, or currencies and it's not quite as simple as it looks in movies, but it does work. With the new US Panama Free Trade Agreement the US has imposed a lot of additional book keeping and reporting duties on Panamanian banks, so you may find banks who don't want to be bothered with new US clients.

A lot of people assume that Panama is a "tax-free" haven; not exactly. There is no tax on resident's income that is earned outside Panama. And there is no tax on interest earned from bank deposits in Panama. Panama's laws for anonymous corporations and foundations do provide opportunities for international sheltering that can offer legal tax advantages for other than US citizens. If you are US you owe the government a "pound of flesh" regardless of where you live or where your money comes from. If you have questions you will need to talk to a Panamanian and US tax attorney. The US now has 10 IRS agents at the Embassy in Panama City and only 2 FBI agents which pretty much tells you the priorities.

Panama is certainly not a "tax-free" haven for US citizens, but it still does offer some unique tax advantages. Generally if your permanent residence is outside the US, and you are not in the US more than 30 calendar days (very strictly counted including US air space and territorial waters), you can deduct up to $92,900 per person of *earned* income from outside the US. Ask your accountant or tax attorney for details.

Location

Panama's location, the isthmus bridging north and South America, nine degrees north of the Equator, is one of the ideal locations in the world, not just because of the ideal weather, but also because of its strategic location.

Even if it wasn't home to the Canal, Panama would be a strategic center of world commerce. Vasco Nunez de Balboa and Christopher Columbus both put into Panama long before a Canal was even conceived. Sir Frances Drake and Henry Morgan both sacked Panama, proving that piracy in Panama is nothing new except that today's pirates are more likely to be fly-by-night, mostly US, real estate developers than sea-farers.

Panama is quickly becoming the legitimate "Crossroads of the Americas" as more and more airlines use Panama City as a hub for South and Central American flights, as well as flights to the Orient. Panama City's modern Tocumen International Airport provides convenient access to most of the world.

One of the major benefits of Panama's location is that it lies outside the hurricane belt. Anyone who has witness the devastation of South Florida or the Caribbean by a hurricane will immediately appreciate the importance of living outside of the hurricane belt. Tropical depressions can cause lots of rain, particularly on the Caribbean side, which can produce local flooding at times.

Panama has no active volcanoes unlike other Central American countries. Volcan Baru last had any activity 500 years ago. Volcan Baru towers above my home town of Boquete rising 11,407 feet [3,478 meters] above sea level. It doesn't "look" like a volcano because, like Mount St. Helens it blew its top off some five thousand years ago. It has not just one, but seven craters. On a clear day from its summit you can see both the Pacific and Caribbean.

In Panama, like California, we occasionally do rock & roll. Although near the intersection of several major tectonic plates, unlike California, we do not sit on top of the major fault.

Largely as a result of fairly recent quakes – a 6.3 quake on Christmas Day in 2003 killed two people in Puerto Armuelles – seismic building codes have been updated and careful attention to seismic engineering is an essential part of building a home in Panama. Like California, tremblers rarely happen and when they do you hang on and ride it out, then talk about it for days to come.

Infrastructure

Panama, in part due to US influence through the Canal years, has the best infrastructure of any Central American or Caribbean nation. And face it, no matter how romantic your dreams, if you're going to live someplace, infrastructure is important!

Water

Panama has tons of fresh water! Coming from Southern California, where my water/sewer bill ran as high as $90 a month, I still find it disconcerting to pay only $5 a month for water, no matter how much I use. Where we live in Palmira our water is piped down from high up on the volcano. Plus I have my own well which taps into an underground stream flowing from way up on the volcano, the kind of water we used to buy in bottles in Southern California! It is delicious! In most of Panama you can drink the water, although, particularly when you are acclimating to a new area, it might be advisable to boil your water initially.

Sewage

Most homes in Panama use septic tanks. In Panama City and Colon, where 80% of the people live, because of the heavy rains sewer systems often overflow and raw sewage makes its way into the bays or oceans. For this reason Panama City is now building a major new sewer system. Many of the coastal Indians have traditionally used the ocean as a sewer. In rural areas people frequently just throw trash in the rivers, counting on the river to carry their garbage into someone else's backyard.

Roads

Panama has some of the best roads in Central America. In Panama much of the Pan American Highway is already four lanes, and most will be when the current construction is completed. Main roads in Panama are generally quite good. When you get off the beaten track, however, as we frequently do while exploring, anything goes! On side roads and out-of-the-way places it can get quite rough. It used to be that unless a former politician happened to live in the area the road would remain rough. Now with money flowing in from the Canal and a government attempting to root out corruption, even rural roads are being paved.

Panamanian drivers aren't quite as good as the roads! Driving in Panama City is a never-to-be-forgotten experience! Many expats will not drive in Panama City and instead hire drivers when they go to town. As an ex-New Yorker I find driving in Panama City chaotic, but a challenge and refreshing in the sense that other drivers do not use the standard, offensive New Yorker hand signals, and people actually will let you into a stream of traffic, particularly if you close your eyes and just go! Panama has virtually no street signs, nor one-way signs. Everyone generally knows which streets are one-way and which way they go, and if you don't, lots of people on the sidewalks will remind you.

Apart from the Pan American Highway almost all roads are two lanes, so you need to brush up on your passing skills. The rules here, in practice at least, are different. A double yellow line means that you should at least look before passing. Fortunately (and sometimes unfortunately) as the money flows in Panama things are becoming more and more regulated. Tránsitos, the traffic police, now have radar guns that work. Laws regarding speed, use of seat belts, and non use of cell phones are increasingly being enforced.

Our friend, and the builder of our first house, Jeff Daugherty, has lived all over the world building for Chevron. When we came to Panama he advised me that no matter where in the world you live, even if it is infested with terrorists, the single most dangerous thing for Americans abroad is driving. Folks will stop or pull into traffic without warning, and make left hand turns without signaling, which is especially fun if you've just pulled out to pass!

The key to driving and surviving in Panama is to expect the unexpected. Driving on California freeways may seem a nightmare to non-Californians, but basically you either sit bumper-to-bumper and creep, or you zoom along at 90 miles an hour bumper-to-bumper. Both are hazardous but you know what to expect. In Panama a horse, cow, or Indian, may suddenly appear in the road. The guy with his right turn signal on may end up turning left. Or the truck full of cows up ahead may be stopping without any lights. In rural areas like Chiriqui, old farm pickups may or may not have working brakes. Driving in Panama you always need to be alert.

Phones

Panama thinks it has reasonably good telephone service but based on my personal experience I would disagree. It has become increasingly hard to get a land line so you are largely dependent on cellular service. There are several cellular services that spend a great deal splashing their colors of paint all over the country and advertising signals they claim to be fantastic. We find it necessary to have two of the three services, separate phones, and even then calls are continually dropped and often we cannot get a decent signal.

Monthly cellular plans seem much more expensive than in the States, so most people use pre-paid phone cards. To call our families in the US from Panama costs about the same as it did from California, but like most folks we use Skype and call for free. Often I will have to use Skype to even call at a small cost within Panama because the cell signals are so poor.

Mail

Mail service in Panama is nothing like the US. For one thing we don't have addresses. Really! Even in Panama city addresses will describe an area, and the name of the street, and the name of a building, and if necessary where that building is in relation to a larger, better-known building. People who demand my street address and don't understand that we don't have such a thing, at least as they expect, look bewildered when I tell them, "Palmira Centro on the road to the cemetery the driveway before Carlos Uriola's *beneficio*"! Alternatively, you can just ask for "The gringos with the two Dalmatians." So without addresses and no mail deliver you pick up your mail at the post office in town. When we first came to Panama there weren't enough mail boxes to go around so we had to use general delivery. Every time we saw a funeral procession we'd rush to the post office to see if we could get the postal box of the deceased!

Some expats from the US use a Miami post office box and a courier-forwarding service. It is expensive, particularly when the credit card providers and other junk mail producers get your Miami PO Box address and all the junk mail comes to Panama! I pay a small monthly subscription to such a service, although I never use it and probably should cancel.

I regularly order books from Amazon or my publisher and have had them sent by regular mail without problem. Generally an order takes twelve to seventeen days to arrive by regular mail. The catch is if the Panamanian customs people decide to check the package and hold it in David at the main post office. To retrieve it requires a trip to David, standing in line, and paying a few cents a day "storage" fee because you didn't drop everything and run into David. With a book, and books are exempt from duty, it is a real pain driving to David, signing forms and getting them rubber stamped (two different windows and two different stamps of course!) and then paying storage fees for a book on which there is no duty anyway. But, as we often say to one another, "Welcome to Panama!"

Internet

Panama for the most part is wired. There are Internet cafes everywhere, with rates ranging from $.60-1.00 an hour. Internet has been a nightmare! When we first moved to Valle Escondido they promised "high speed Internet" which it never was until we moved to our farm and then Valle Escondido got cable TV and the fastest Internet in town. But where we are living now we have no choice but to use a wireless service charges $65 for .5 Mg and horrible service.

The current President, Ricardo Martinelli has promised free Internet connectivity for the entire country, and if you take your laptop to the plaza in Boquete you can generally get a free signal.

Supplies

It's important to be able to have a good source of supplies wherever you choose to live. As a general rule in Panama we have found that, "You can find anything you want in Panama City, anything you need in David." Find is the operative word. You're going to have to look for things and learn, largely from others, where to find certain things, but for the most part, it's here. You may not find the brand you are used to, and it may be packaged differently, but in all likelihood it's available somewhere in Panama City.

In the eight years we have been in Panama we have seen huge changes in David. Anything you need is pretty much available in David. We've seen new malls with department stores and home improvement stores. No Home Depot, Bed, Bath & Beyond or Wal-Mart – yet. But we do have Price Smart, from the folks who brought you the original Price Club in California. They have hot dogs for $1.65, although the drink isn't included and they're not Hebrew National, but it looks and feels the same, although much smaller. The variety and prices aren't nearly as advantageous as Price Club/Costco and there isn't something new to tempt you every time you visit, but for us there's a certain comfort in shopping at Price Smart. There are three huge supermarkets in David, and three smaller ones in Boquete.

When we came down we brought a forty foot container because we had a lot of furniture we liked and things that were important and meaningful to us, like my wife's grand piano! But we know other folks who sold everything before leaving the States, came down with a suitcase, and furnished their entire homes very nicely with what they purchased in Panama. So it's really a matter of choice. If you have a lot of patience you can get wood, metal and rattan furniture hand-crafted – all you need is a photo or sketch of what you want! It's easier to get old overstuffed furniture re-upholstered, provided you can find fabric you like, than it is to find new overstuffed furniture that suits American preferences for style and comfort.

"Propane"

Like most of the world there is no natural gas, so you have to adjust to living with propane. It's easy to get propane but "developing nation" propane tends to be dirtier and not as hot or efficient as propane in the US. Many Panamanians do not have hot water heaters or use so-called "suicide" shower heads – plug in electrical units attached to the shower head! The "dirty" propane is hard on traditional tank water heaters, so most expats are going to on-demand hot water systems, either electric or propane. Yet the propane on-demand hot water systems, most of which are made in China, don't work after two years either and need replaced.

Electricity

Beware of property that doesn't have electrical service. Putting in electrical lines can cost a small fortune! Considering all the hydroelectric power generated in Panama, particularly in Chiriqui, you'd think electricity would be a bargain. It should be, but it isn't. Private companies provide electricity and happily sell the surplus to Costa Rica while charging customers more than in most Latin American countries. In Boquete we don't need air conditioning or heating, but during the rainy season dehumidifiers can consume a lot of power. Electrical service is generally reliable . . . most of the time. There are outages which usually are only a few minutes or a few hours. Some people have put in back up generators but generally we don't mind burgers on the grill with a romantic candlelight dinner.

In the rainy season when the hot air blowing up from the lowlands meets the cold air off the mountains we do get some rip roaring electrical storms which can produce electrical outages.

Medical

If you are going to live someplace, particularly as you get older, good medical care is important. Many Panamanian doctors are trained in the US and a good many speak some English. There are four large hospitals in David, forty minutes drive from where we live. There are excellent, large hospitals and specialists in Panama City, about an hour's flying time from David. And Miami is just three hours flying time from Panama City. But medical practice in Panama is very different than the US. The cost of medical care in Panama is a fraction of what it is in the US.

When we first visited Boquete my wife wanted to check out the doctor. So she went, without an appointment, to see a local doctor who at that time served many of the expats in Boquete. He was American-trained and spoke fluent English. My wife had to wait a little longer than usual because the doctor was out making a house call: our first clue as to just how different medical practice is in Panama!

He examined her and ran an EKG to check out how she was doing at the altitude in Boquete. She asked, "What happens if one of us has a heart attack?" The doctor said, "Well, you call me. I call the ambulance and ride with you to the hospital in David. We get you stabilized, and if it requires invasive surgery we'd probably fly you to Panama City where the best cardiologist is located." He picked up his phone and said, "Let me see if I can get him on his cell." He chatted with the specialist for a while, handed the phone to Nikki and said, "Here, you talk to him." Unfortunately that doctor moved to Panama City and we've never found a doctor quite so good in Boquete, so now end up going to David.

We needed some prescriptions filled so we went to the pharmacy in town. It cost me $85 after my 20% retiree discount. I was grousing because if repeated regularly, this would break the budget, when my wife asked, "Well, how many prescriptions were there?" Five. "So, at home, five prescriptions with our co pay would have cost us $50. You paid $35 more for the full cost without any insurance." We've found drugs to be more expensive than we budgeted.

Medical insurance is of course an issue. Depending on your age, and that's a key factor, it can be relatively inexpensive. However, the bug-a-boo is "preexisting conditions. One local hospital offered a very attractive, rather inexpensive plan that covers you for up to $18,000 a year, but didn't cover pre-existing conditions for the first two years. It looked like a good deal and we've been enrolled for about 7 years depending that now our pre-existing conditions would be covered.   We noticed that some of the terms of the plan, which was really more of a major medical scheme than actual insurance, changed over the years and that the hospital offering the insurance upped its charges, but . . . compared to the US, still a good deal. The deal must have been too good, or the actuaries didn't really consider that they were selling mostly to retired and aging folks, because now it appears that the plan is supposedly merging into another plan with a larger and more diverse risk pool. Of course this kind of thing happens here as well as in the US.

When we came to Panama it was our intention to basically self-insure and use our US Medicare as a fail-safe, last resort back up plan. I didn't take the optional parts of Medicare because when I looked at the total costs of treatments in Panama and compared them to the out-of-pocket costs in the US, even with the optional Medicare coverage, it still worked out to be cheaper in Panama.

What we have noticed through the years is that the cost of medical services, at least for expats, has slowly been increasing.

There are a number of reasons for this. First the cost of everything has been increasing in Panama, just like in the US. Since Panama uses the US dollar as the dollar devalues a dollar in Panama buys less just like in the US. Plus Panama imports most things besides food, so as the value of the US dollar drops and the cost of oil increases, prices go up, including costs of medical supplies and equipment. And, doctors realize that with *gringos* they can charge more.

The cost of medical care in Panama is still a fraction of what it is in the US.

What is lacking, at least in Chiriqui where we live and particularly in Boquete is emergency response. Ambulances are primarily used as transportation and we don't have an American-like 911system or equipped ambulances staffed by EMTs. It's pretty much get yourself to the hospital and good luck! There are two emergency rooms in Boquete, one in the national heath clinic designed to serve mostly the Indigenous and the Social Security clinic designed to serve workers who are covered by Social Security. Both emergency rooms are closed at night so you need to plan your emergencies accordingly. There are trade offs, and this is one. I guess we feel that the overall quality of life and medical service in Panama offsets the lack of good emergency service.

A few years ago we did have a company that came in with a medivac helicopter that was well equipped and staffed with emergency room physicians. Like a lot of other expats we subscribed. The company went belly up before it even started, but they did refund everyone's subscription fee. [Recall that all purpose phrase of explanation and acceptance: "This is Panama".]

Lifestyle

One of the things I like best about Panama is that we enjoy a better lifestyle for a lot less money.

Living in Panama is for the most part far healthier. Traffic accidents are probably a push. But the air in Boquete is crisp and clean and unpolluted. And you should see the stars at night! The food is far better. Meat is all locally grown in Chiriqui province and is not force-fed on feedlots or loaded with hormones. Vegetables and fruits are locally grown on small family farms, many of which, as yet, have either not discovered or can't afford chemicals. And there are several organic growers. Carrots, potatoes, onions are fresh from the farm, and haven't been around for months in warehouses being treated with who-knows-what to keep them looking eatable. We don't have the temptation of fast food. Yes, there is a McDonald's and Kentucky Fried Chicken, Subway, Pizza Hut and TGIF Friday's in David, if you get desperate, but for the most part we eat healthier. The bread is freshly baked. The water is like what we bought in bottles for $1.40 a liter back in California.

The forty minute trip to David once a week used to be trying at times, but now with a new four lane highway it is a lot easier and less frustrating, but at its worst it was nothing like the 101 Freeway! I'm not spending 10% of my life stuck in Southern California traffic.

In many ways life in Boquete is like life in the States in the '50s. Real family values dominate. The family is all-important. The work week is Monday through Saturday at noon. Saturday evenings and Sunday afternoons you will see entire families, dressed in their best, coming to town to shop, treat everyone to an ice cream cone and go to church. Many of the Indians live in what we in the States would, in exercise of our cultural imperialism, term "hovels", yet when they come to town they are wearing spotless clothing, their hair is slicked back, and the children walk obediently with their parents. All children go to school in the morning and all wear uniforms. There is little smoking in Panama. The government has outlawed smoking in all public buildings, restaurants and bars, but even at 15 cents a cigarette, it is an expensive habit for people who may only make $10 a day.

Aside from occasional political comment, there is no graffiti. Outside of the big cities trash isn't strewn about. There is no prevalent gang culture. There isn't the same oppressive police presence or climate of fear as in the US. Police are being better paid, trained and more effective. National Police, like city cops in the US, now carry little hand-held computers which link them immediately not only into national computers, but into Interpol as well. So if you are on the lam from the law in the US, don't even bother to think about coming to Panama because you will get caught!

Even the "Tránsitos", the traffic police, similar to CHP, operate in a very civilized manor. Their cars and motorcycles are well marked and always park very visibly next to the highway in the same way. To make it even easier, all the Tránsitos wear fluorescent red reflective vests, good for safety and also Tránsito-spotting. Yes, a few do have radar, but not to worry – a dozen motorists coming the opposite direction will flash their lights indicating you should slow down either for an accident ahead or a Tránsitos. Most Tránsitos seem preoccupied on their cell phones and the hassle of hanging up on their girlfriends, putting on helmets, and hopping on motorcycles, well, it's a lot of hassle when the Tránsitos role seems mostly to remind good people by their presence to slow down and obey the law.

Occasionally you will run into an entrepreneurial Tránsito who needs your help with shoes for his kids or lingerie for his mistress. but as Panama becomes more organized and computerized the is more likely to have a working radar gun, a computerized ticket machine, and a hand-held computer to see if you have any outstanding warrants in Panama or anywhere else in the world!

The incessant US demand for illicit drugs and Panama's proximity to Colombia creates an enormous problem. Weekly you read about huge seizures of literally tons and tons of cocaine that the Colombian drug cartels are trying to smuggle through Panama. We don't, yet at least, have the violence of Mexico, but until the US takes the profit incentive out of the drug trade by decriminalizing and regulating all drugs, this problem will continue throughout Latin America. The drug cartels have seemingly unlimited amounts of money. Recently a joint US and Panamanian operation busted a surplus Russian submarine that the cartels were using to transport drugs.

Alcohol is local and cheap and it is a problem for some. Monday morning after payday it's not all that unusual to see an Indian sleeping it off in the street. When the sun comes up the police rouse them awake and send them home. I see lots of young people wearing caps and shirts with pot leaves, but this may be more an aping of US culture, which Panamanians love to do, rather than a commitment to being a "pot head." I don't see a lot of stoned kids or obvious stoned-kid behavior. Some of my expat contemporaries, products of the '60s . . . well, you gotta wonder. I suspect that the biggest consumers of marijuana in Boquete are sixty-something US expats.

But, unlike the Ventura-Oxnard area of Southern California, you don't open the paper every other day to read about kids killing kids because they wear the wrong color shirts, or just to prove they can kill someone, or cops killing suspects because they are suspects and the cops can, or gangbangers shooting cops because they are cops. In fact in our area there seems to be very little killing, which is refreshing.

Panama isn't perfect and like any place else it struggles with problems.

Long noted for corruption, the present government struggles to create an environment with "0% Corruption" as did the previous government.

Is there injustice in Panama? Certainly, but nothing like the injustice in California where Brandon Hein [brandonhein.com] has spent sixteen years in prison for a crime nobody says he committed! Panama is more honest and has a better self-understanding than the US, maybe because of having lived through those agonizing years of "the dictatorship." Panama doesn't pretend to be the "shining light" and has never set itself up as the be-all and end-all and the ultimate standard of a just society. Panama doesn't pretend to know what's best for the rest of the world, and even if it did, doesn't have a military to impose itself on the rest of the world.

Panamanians have a laid-back and hassle free attitude towards life, which taken on the whole leads to a more relaxed life. Adjusting to "Panamanian time" is difficult, but not impossible. Things will get done, it just might take longer than you would expect or like. When I first came to Panama and was being frustrated by the seemingly impossible task of getting things finished I received two words of advice. One, from a *gringo* who had happily adjusted. His advice, one word: "Surrender!" If you don't worry about it, it's not a problem. And the other, from my banker, "Don't stress: live long!"

Overall the cost of living in Panama is far less than in the US. How much less will depend on you, what your standard of living was in the US, and what you want your standard of living to be in Panama. In our case, our overall cost of living in Panama is 35% of what it was in the US, and we're living better!

Some of that is because we "cashed out" when we sold our home in California, and purchased our home in Boquete for cash, so we don't have to cope with a mortgage. One of our retirement goals was not to have a mortgage. Now my Social Security combined with my wife's pension is about one-third what our income was in California, but in Panama we can live comfortably with that. The net result is that we have a much better lifestyle, without having to work, without the stress of Southern California life, albeit still with nothing left over at the end of the year.

Prices have increased in Panama, no question, but they have also dramatically increased in the US as well. So our cost of living with today's dollars and costs is still about 35% of what it would be in the US, and we live better.

One of the unfortunate things about the Web is that a lot of people accept anything they read online as the gospel truth. Not so! Another unfortunate thing is that stuff on the Web is not dated, so there is a lot of outdated cost information on the Web about Panama. A lot of real estate listings, still on the Web as if they were current, were sold years ago. The fact that Panama would give you a "*Pensionado*" or retirement visa if you could prove you have $600 per month pension, implied that you can live on $600 a month in Panama. Truth is: you can! You can certainly live on $600 a month, and maybe less, IF you want to live like a Panamanian. But when push comes to shove, that's not what most Americans have in mind.

Bananas, should you not be growing your own, are three for 10 cents. Fresh bread is 35 cents a baguette. A deliciously ripe pineapple is $1.50 *gringo* price, 75 cents for Panamanians. But cereals, Pam, Kleenex and all the other "essentials" of American life cost about the same as or slightly more than they do in the US.

We discovered that we don't really pay that much less for food partly because we still like some of the stuff we enjoyed in the US and like to buy some things that are partially prepared. Eating out, because the cost of labor is so low in Panama, is a real bargain compared to Southern California. $4 for a haircut and under $35 for my wife to have her hair cut and colored – those are real bargains compared to California. Locals get massages for $35 midweek when the tourists aren't here, and a manicure and pedicure runs $13-$26.

How much can you live on? Well, how much can you live on in Southern California? It depends! Less if you live in Bakersfield, more if you live in Beverly Hills. It just depends. There is no hard and fast rule. To find out what you can live on, you'll need to do your homework on both ends, spend time, and do your own research or work with a consultant.

Incentives

Panama offers many of the *Pensionado* or retiree benefits that Costa Rica used to offer as encouragement to *gringos* to retire in Panama. Why? A few years back Valle Escondido estimated that each *gringo* who retired to Boquete spent about $250,000, including land, home, car, furnishings and legal fees for immigration. According to Valle Escondido, "Because the amount of money is significant and coming from a foreign source, the expat also becomes a foreign investor. These additional foreign investors become very significant in financial terms. In the case of Valle Escondido they alone represent about $50 million in initial investment. The average retiree has about $2,000 a month in expendable income. This represents another $6 million a year in spending on food, maintenance, and travel. In addition to these expenditures, each retiree has an average of three visitors per year who come as guests and consequently tourists."

Pensionado Visa

The big benefit of a *Pensionado* visa is the right to permanently live in Panama and the right to come and go from Panama. The *Pensionado* visa represents a big welcome mat! You can't work for anyone with a *Pensionado* visa, but you can invest in your own business or consult.

Other benefits to *Pensionados* include:

Import tax exemption of up to $10,000 US on household goods
Discounts on many services, such as:
Movies, recreational, and sports events: 50% off
Public buses and trains: 30% off
Boat and ship transportation: 30% off
National airline flights: 25% off
Hotels: Monday – Thursday 50% off; Friday – Sunday 30% off
Regular restaurants: 25% off
Fast food: 15% off
Hospitals (without insurance): 15% off
Prescription drugs: 20% off
Doctor visits and surgery: 20% off
Dental work: 15% off

Optometrist visits: 15% off
Electricity (if under $50 per month): 25% off
Telephone/water: 25% off

That sounds great, but often actually getting the discounts is another story. It's the law, yes, but there are a lot of restaurants and others who simply don't choose to offer the discounts. Some restaurants seem to work overtime to avoid giving the *descuento*. The Thursday night all-you-can-eat rib special is a "special" so no discount. Some drugs which have a minimal mark up: no discount. Book your hotel online, no discount. Have a special rate, other than the "rack rate", no discount. So you see how the game is played. A few of my expat friends who have been here a long time and speak fluent Spanish can pull out a copy of the law and argue their case in Spanish, but for most of us . . . if you happen to get the discount, nice, but . . .

In my opinion the *Pensionado* discounts are highly over promoted and overrated.

Supposedly an additional *Pensionado* benefit is tax exemption to import a car every two years. On the surface this looks good, but in some cases it's cheaper, and far easier, just to buy a car in Panama. Everyone knows car importing horror stories. One couple brought in a Mitsubishi that they could have purchased in Panama for $15,000. Even after the *Pensionado* tax benefit, they ended up paying other taxes and duty amounting to $10,000. So the car they'd paid $15,000 for in the States, and could have purchased in Panama for $15,000 now cost them $25,000!

Foreign Ownership of Real Property

There is no problem with foreigners owning property in Panama, a big benefit compared to some other Central American countries.

In the past in most cases land was purchased using an "S.A." or *sociedad anónima* corporation. Here the corporation owns the land and the actual owners of the corporation, the holders of the stock, are anonymous in the public record. This is one way of protecting and shielding assets, and was all very legal. Whoever actually has the shares in their hand, owns the company, which owns the land, making it simple and easy to pass on assets to your heirs or transfer property. Now Panama wants more "transparency" of ownership so they can collect taxes on transfers. And the US which wants to control all information in the 21st century world and doesn't like anything they can't "see" is pushing Panama to end SA corporations.

Property Tax Exemption

As an incentive to develop property, Panama has granted various real estate tax exemptions depending on the value of the property. Originally these were for twenty years of no property tax, and those benefits are transferred when a property is sold. So there are still properties on the market with portions of the twenty-year exemption. Under the new law there is still a property tax exemption for new construction, but it is not as generous and decreases as the cost of construction increases, thus offering the greatest exemption to the least expensive properties of the poorest people which probably makes sense.

Not Taxed

Panama has a territorial tax code, meaning only income generated in Panama is taxed. Income from foreign sources is not taxed, and filing income tax forms for income earned outside of Panama is not required. So if you are a *Pensionado* and receive Social Security and/or other income from the U.S., this income is not taxed in Panama. You do, however, have to file U.S. income taxes if you are a US citizen. Interestingly interest from deposits in a Panamanian bank is not taxable in Panama. Historically Panama did not report such interest although if you were a U.S. taxpayer it was your responsibility to report all income worldwide regardless. Now the US has full access to your financial information in Panama.

As mentioned earlier, if you live permanently outside the U.S. (and you have to prove you've not been in the US more than thirty days a year) you can exempt around $92,900 per person of your earned foreign income. (Check with your accountant.)

Foreign Investment

Panama offers numerous schemes to encourage foreign investment including tax concessions and even, under certain scenarios, Panamanian passports. There are incentives for starting businesses, for tourist business is certain designated areas, for reforestation projects, and the like. Panama has several free zones to encourage manufacturing activity.

Interacting

1. Which benefits of Panama do you find interesting and why?

2. What are the elements of your current lifestyle that you like and what are the elements you dislike?

3. What is your current medical insurance situation? What will it be when you retire? What are your pre-existing conditions that would create problems in getting insurance?

7. How Stable Is It?

Let's face it: before you go running off to live in another country, you need to know something about the history and the stability of government.

You don't want to move to "paradise" only to find yourself in the midst of endless demonstrations, a coup d'état, or left holding a fist full of devalued money.

Panama is one of those countries which owes its very existence to the long-term US world view that it has a Divine mandate (although the "Divine" is more and more tucked in the closet as a mater of political correctness) to manipulate the world in it's own interests. Although archeological evidence shows people living in Panama for some 11,000 years, the current Panamanian history begins in 1821 when Colombia, including the Colombian "department" of Panama, gained independence from Spain. By 1889 the French attempt at a Canal had failed, but the US was very interested in the Canal concept and sought to buy out the French franchise through a treaty with Colombia. Colombia said, "No way, José!" So the US encouraged anti-Colombian sentiment in Panama and supported the declaration of Panamanian independence issued by a revolutionary junta. Conveniently the US immediately recognized the status of the Republic of Panama, and when Colombia sent troops to quell the rebellion, the US just happened to have warships sitting off Panama to repel the Colombians.

Fifteen days later the US had negotiated a treaty giving the US "sovereign rights in perpetuity over the Canal Zone" and further broad rights of intervention into the affairs of the newly created Republic.   Interestingly no Panamanian ever signed the treaty! The treaty was ratified despite Panamanian complaints. And the Canal was built and opened in 1914.

[If you want more about the fascinating history of the Panama and the Canal, or if you are ever contemplating a cruise through the Panama Canal, be sure and get my book, CRUISING THE PANAMA CANAL, available at RichardDetrich.com, Amazon, Kindle or your local bookstore.]

.

Lest those of us accustomed to US manipulation of international affairs just assume Panama was solely created at the convenience of Washington, R. M. Koster and Guillermo Sanchez point out, "Panama was always a separate national entity [and] was never organically integrated into Colombia. The chief reason why was that Panama achieved independence from Spain on her own. The authors of this independence, perhaps frightened by their own audacity, then began to fear a Spanish reconquest of the Isthmus . . . Panama was both small and thinly populated, with no troops and few weapons. That is when the idea came up for Panama to join with a larger nation . . . [Colombia] then governed by Simón Bolívar in a confederation called Gran Colombia. Bolivar was almost a mythological figure, almost a divinity. His prestige drew Panama into a union with Colombia. In no one's mind in Panama, however was this union intended to be permanent. When the danger of Spanish reconquest was over, Panama would return to independence."[12]

Panamanians grew tired of being taxed by Colombia and being asked to send their sons to fight Colombia's wars. "By the time Bunau-Varilla, Cromwell, and Teddy Roosevelt came on the scene, a revolutionary conspiracy was already in progress. But those directing it were realists. They knew Panama's weakness and the strength of Colombia's veteran army. They seized the moment when a coincidence of interests presented the best chance for independence. Here it is that Panama's national aspirations became bound up with the irresistible expansionism of the United States, the political ambitions of Theodore Roosevelt, and the turbulent intriguing of Bunau-Varilla.

---

[12] R.M. Koster and Guillermon Sanchez, IN THE TIME OF THE TYRANTS: PANAMA 1968-1990. New York, W.W. Nortonn & Company, 1990. p 390

"But the principal separatist impulse came from within Panama . . .
[Other countries achieved their independence with help from other
nations] and Panama's founding fathers were no less brave,
generous, far-seeing, or fallible than those of any other country."[13]

Colombia did not recognize the Republic of Panama until 1921 when
the US paid Colombia $21 million in "compensation" to buy a kind
of Colombian recognition of legitimacy. The US would continue to
intervene in Panama's political affairs until 1936 when the US
agreed to limit the use of its troops to the Canal Zone and the annual
rent on the Canal was increased.

The absence of US troops led to an increasing role for the
Panamanian military. Some three decades later, by 1968 the Guardia
Nacional had become powerful enough to depose the elected
president and take Control of the country. The Guardia's General
Omar Torrijos emerged as the new leader, a "military strongman."
Torrijos undertook a program of reform and public works and
modernized Panama City, while incurring a huge debt.

It was Torrijos, much to the delight of Panamanians, who negotiated
the 1977 Canal Treaty, signed by Jimmy Carter, that would
eventually turn the Canal over to Panama in 1999.

The CIA was concerned over the role General Torrijos was playing
in Latin America. Torrijos, although not the feared Communist and
socialist reformer Fidel Castro, was seeking similar reforms in
Panama and Latin America. Torrijos' image and friendliness with
Cuba and Castro caused the US concern. So the CIA nurtured a CIA
operative within the Torrijos government named Manuel Noriega.

Noriega would turn out to be a Frankenstein-like monster.

Noriega, a member of Torrijos party, became head of the secret
police. When the enormously popular Omar Torrijos was killed in a
plane crash in 1981, the power of Noriega was coalesced. Noriega
leveraged his secret police to close down all opposition.

---

[13] pp 30—392

The cause of the crash that killed Torrijos was never determined, although conspiracy theories involving Noriega and/or the CIA abound. Most likely the plane crash was caused by the violent weather that frequently builds up in the mountains of Panama.

Panamanians don't like to talk about "the dictatorship" just like most Americans don't like to talk about Spiro Agnew, the Nixon presidency and Watergate or the McCarthy era witch hunts. It was a dark period when anyone who criticized was likely to be beaten or disappear. You will find that a number of Panamanians will have a four or five-year period of their history where they worked abroad.

Relations between Noriega and his former US spy-masters went from bad to worse. Noriega murdered opponents, rigged elections, and, the cardinal sin, disrupted the US ill-advised and long-failed "War on Drugs" by becoming involved with drug trafficking. [Never mind that the CIA was running its own dirty drug trafficking operations.] Noriega raped and pillaged Panama economically and in the process shipped millions of Panamanian dollars to his accounts in Europe. Noriega became the military dictator and loudly taunted his former CIA spy master, now President, George H. W. Bush.

Bush, running for President, attempted to pass off his relationships with Noriega claiming the last seven American administrations had paid Noriega. Retired Navy Admiral Stanford Turner, who took over the CIA from George Bush in 1977, said, "Bush is in the government during the Ford administration and Noriega is on the payroll. Bush is out of the government during the Carter years and Noriega is off the payroll. Bush comes back and so does Noriega. Those are the facts, and you have to figure out for yourself what they mean."[14]

The US instituted sanctions against Panama and that, plus Noriega's corruption left Panama in economic shambles.

---

[14] Frederick Kemp, DIVORCING THE DICTATOR: AMERICA'S BUNGLED AFFAIR WITH NORIEGA New York, G.P. Putnam's Sons, 1990 p. 29

The US had agreed to turnover the Canal just before the Millennium. Panamanians were ready for change and fully expected that eventually the US would negotiate Noriega's retirement. To add to the US embarrassment an unarmed US Marine in civilian clothes was killed by Panamanian soldiers.

Instead of the negotiation Panamanians expected, operation "Just Cause" was launched with 26,000 troops invading tiny Panama, attacking with tanks and aircraft. At least six times as many civilians as Panamanian military died in the December 1989 U.S. invasion, according to Physicians for Human Rights. The exact numbers are still being argued, but Physicians for Human Rights estimated 300 civilians and 50 military were killed, another 3,000 injured and 15,000 left homeless. It is said that in this nation of less than 3 million people, where everyone is related, almost everyone has a family member or knows someone who was killed or injured by the US invasion. Most Americans like to think that Panama, like the rest of the countries the US invades, is grateful for US intervention. Although most Panamanians ape any US fashion or brand and genuinely like the US and Americans, and although they were happy to be rid of Noriega, the violence with which it was accomplished remains a sore spot.

Many Panamanians lost everything as a result of the invasion. After the invasion Panama was in chaos; the US had no plan. The old police force was in hiding and there was no law. The US had "liberated" Panama only to bring incredible hardship, chaos, and anarchy in the streets. There was wide-spread looting. Many small businesses were destroyed. Larger business, unable to collect, went bankrupt.

For twenty years Noriega languished in prison in Miami. After a lengthy legal fight, in April 2010 Noriega was extradited to France. TV cameras caught glimpses of a frail, old man being escorted onto an Air France jet.

In the US, because he was a "war criminal" Noriega continued in prison to be addressed as "general" (even though Panama no longer had a military) and was given the prison perks of a POW general. In France he was treated as a common criminal without the perks or rank of "general."

In December 2011 Noriega was extradited from France to Panama and currently resides in El Renacer Prison (interestingly meaning "rebirth") which is located right beside the Panama Canal just South of where the Chagres River flows into the Canal. It is a simple, nondescript Panamanian prison and Noriega has a simple cell with some accommodation made due to his poor health and to protect his security. Some of his friends and family would like to see him under house arrest due to his age and infirmity, but that is unlikely since he faces additional very serious charges and sentences already handed down for multiple murders, kidnapping, and corruption.

The former Panamanian President, Martin Torrijos, is the illegitimate son of former military strongman Omar Torrijos. Martin was raised in the US, worked in McDonald's, and graduated from Texas A&M. Torrijos did a lot of the right things: cracking down on corruption, talking about accountability, initiating various reforms, and struggling for a strict accounting of money.

Panama's current President, Ricardo Martinelli, is a no-nonsense businessman who owns the largest chain of supermarkets in the country. Martinelli has a business degree from the University of Arkansas as well as an MBA from the INCAE Business School (founded 1964 by the Central American private sector, Harvard Business School, and USAID). Martinelli still goes back to Arkansas to watch the Razorbacks play.

In his inaugural address Martinelli laid out his no nonsense approach to governance saying, "In my administration it's OK to put your foot in your mouth, but not to put your hand in the till."

When a nephew was involved in a drug deal in another Latin American country, Martinelli went to the airport to personally arrest him when he returned to Panama. Martinelli is running the country like a business and has made major reforms. He donates his entire salary to various orphanages and charities, which he fully discloses, and has already said he won't run again for President since he "can't put up with all this crap." My kind of guy, and since he has a high approval rating, obviously lots of folks agree.

I met him by accident at the airport in David where I had gone to pick up my wife. He was an underdog candidate and had just arrived to lead a rag-tag "parade" of supporters and old cars and banners out of the airport. He was on foot with his supporters and I was stuck in my car, waiting for them to get out of the way. He walked over to the open car window, obviously recognizing me as a *gringo* who couldn't vote, shook hands and asked in perfect English how we liked Panama and if things were going well for us. Impressed me!

The Canal is operating more safely and efficiently than ever before, making more money. The "third lane" expansion program is well underway and more-or-less on schedule. As a result of the lessons learned in "the dictatorship", Panama, like Costa Rica, has abolished the military. Money that was once used for the military is now used for universal education and social programs. Panama has torn a page from the Swiss play book, knowing that if you have their money – and offshore corporations – their hearts and minds will follow and they won't attack you and their money. Of course Panama can afford not to have an army since, although the Canal must remain open and neutral for all nations in both peacetime and wartime, the US has the right to protect the neutrality of the Canal.

The relationship between Panama and the US strikes me somewhat as the relationship between an older and younger brother. The younger brother obviously wants to strike out on his own and not be ordered about, but if you get in a jam, it's nice to know you have back up from your older brother. This gives Panama a stability that goes beyond its borders and own political system.

A word about red tape: Panama has no more red tape than the US, and maybe less. Government workers and bureaucracies are pretty much the same the world over, except Panama uses a lot more rubber stamps. One difference: because Panama has a smaller percentage of government workers who are part of an entrenched bureaucracy, so when the government changes (a new President is elected every five years) there is almost a complete turnover and a lot of confusion during the transition.

Interacting

1. What do you know about the history and political stability of the new places you are considering?

2. What should you know about the history and political stability of the new places you are considering?

8. Running The Numbers

Most of us avoid numbers

Few of us know exactly where we spend our money, or exactly how much we will have for retirement. We like to think we know and deal in generalities, but we don't know exactly.

If you're going to think about escaping. now or in the future, you have to "run the numbers" and know exactly how you spend your money now, how much money you can depend on in retirement, and how much money life is going to cost.

When we began this process, we quickly realized how little we knew. Money came in, money went out, and generally at the end of the year, it was all gone. Sometimes more went out than came in, so like most Americans, we depended on credit cards to tide us over. Our household income generally ran between $150-200K. You'd think we would have had lots of money! We thought so too! When I did my taxes I could never quite understand: if we made this much, why wasn't there anything left? I'd see folks who I know made a lot less than we did, and they had pick ups loaded down with adult toys, and we didn't have any toys. They ate out all the time and we seldom ate out. I'm still not sure exactly what I did wrong. We were convinced that we could never afford to retire. But then we never really ran the numbers, so we didn't know for sure.

There is no way around it. You have to run the numbers. And you have to start by analyzing your current spending. You need to know exactly what's coming in, and exactly how it is being spent. I know, it is very anal and if you're not an anal person, this will be a real struggle.

Craig Hay has been my friend since we were in high school. In New York we shared an apartment. In Littleton we lived down the street from each other and our wives and kids were best friends. And Craig has been my accountant and more than anyone else he knows how "numerically challenged" I am. He would look at my tax scratching and just shake his head. And when I got my MBA and became a "bean counter" he really shook his head! But no matter how much it violates your sense of who you are, you need to run the numbers!

When we actually recorded and looked at our spending in Ventura, it broke down like this:

Housing 29%
Enjoyment 6%
Food & Clothing 8%
Medical 3%
Transportation 8%
Taxes 36%
Children, gifts, donations 10%

The single biggest percentage of our money was going to pay off Uncle Sam and his various cronies! And, frankly, I didn't like what he was doing with my money.

The second biggest chunk was going for housing. Most Californians spend a much larger percentage of their income on housing than typical Americans. It used to be a kind of forced investment and in our case our major, and at times only, investment. One of our goals was not to have a mortgage when we retired, so we had a 15-year loan which required larger payments.

So what will it cost when you retire? A lot of the conventional wisdom is that with inflation factored in, to retire comfortably you will need 50-70% of your current income, and I think it's more like 70%. In our case using $150K for example, that would mean we would need retirement income of about $105K a year.

Every year the Social Security Administration mails contributors an estimate of what your Social Security payments would be if your retire at various ages. In my case, if I retired at roughly 62.5 I would get around $15,200 a year. There's a big gap between $15,200 and $105,000!!! If I waited until 66 to start collecting, I would get Social Security payments of about $22,000 – still a big gap! To fill that gap with investments, at a 5% annual return, we would need about $1.7M, which we definitely did not have! And history has proved that my assumption of 5% annual return was far too optimistic!

Now, understand this: unless you run the numbers you really have no idea where you are at!!

So we kept looking at the numbers. We hadn't factored in various IRAs. We didn't have a lot of IRA investment, but we had some, but these weren't really going to kick in until later in life. I had a small Reformed Church pension, but over the years it had been mismanaged by ministers and with so much of it sucked up in fees, I knew that it wouldn't amount to much, if and when I was old enough to get at it. I think the strategy was that you were supposed to go to your eternal reward first. Unlike most pension funds, this one seemed designed so that the principal never increased.

I was a REALTOR® in Ventura County and watched the value of real estate soar back in the good old days when you wrote out offers on the hood of your car for more than the asking price. So, what if we were to "cash out"? I'd been worrying about the value of everyone else's home: what about mine? Well, it turned out we had about $400-500K equity in our home even although we'd owned it for less than six years. (Meanwhile the value of my Reformed Church In America pension was roughly the same as it was six years previously.) $400-500K cash made the idea of cashing out, selling our house and retiring early more interesting.

Although I'd never been a gambler, I had the sense to know that there comes a time when you need to cash in your chips and get out of the casino.

I began to ask some questions.

What if we didn't have a mortgage to worry about?

What if we weren't paying 36% of our income in taxes?

What if we could find a place that we both liked, that fit our "dream" specifications and still had a lower cost of living?

Could it be possible?

We started looking in earnest at my wife's retirement possibilities. She'd been with the County almost seventeen years. She was fully vested and could retire whenever she wanted, she just had never thought about retiring. California lives in a state of perpetual budget crisis, but the last one Nikki endured was kind of the straw that broke the camel's back. Nikki was dedicated to her programs working with teen mothers, teen dads, and "at risk" kids with real needs – about 1,000 kids at any one time. To the State her programs were just another budget line item to be retained or eliminated based on political benefit, not the needs of kids.

So my Excel spread sheets and budget analysis started in earnest. And we started making the lists and analyzing them. When we finally settled on Panama as our first choice, we began collecting everything we could, talking to anyone who would listen, scouring the Web, seeking out information about costs in Panama.

When thinking about a budget for retirement, you need to budget for you.

If you eat out every night, don't expect to change once you retire. If you require first class accommodations, don't plan on living in a thatched roof hut. Make a budget that reflects your lifestyle and the lifestyle you want in retirement.

By the time we actually moved to Panama we had a pretty good budget worked out, based on our understanding of how we spent money and our understanding of the cost of items in Panama. We knew health care and health insurance would be a killer (Isn't that a telling line!) and we budgeted accordingly.

The only area we were really off on was the cost of food. Our actual food cost is about twice what we budgeted, and most of that difference is in the cost of prepared food items, like Cheerios, Diet Coke (the rum is only slightly more expensive than the Coke!), paper goods, and the like. Strictly food, we'd have probably been very close.

Here's a quick comparison:

Item	California	Panama
Housing	29%	17%
Enjoyment	6%	13%
Food & Clothing	8%	18%
Medical	3%	19%
Transportation	8%	8%
Taxes	36%	20%
Children, Gifts & Donations	10%	5%

The comparison should indicate that not everything is cheaper in Panama and a lot depends on you and how you choose to live. We were able to pay off our mortgage in California and still have enough money to pay cash for a very nice home in Boquete. We're not paying a mortgage, but we do have a 4.5 acre farm to maintain. Because I work on cruise ships we don't spend as much on the travel aspect of "enjoyment" as others might.

For our first few years in Panama I was a stickler for recording everything we spent because I needed to know if this was working and if it would continue to work. When we drew all this up I didn't know that I would continue working part time with the cruise lines, so that has made things a little easier.

I've done spread sheets showing how much money we will make until we have both reached 98 as we start drawing down various pensions and IRAs. If – and let's accept it, life is always an IF!! – If all goes according to plan, we will live comfortably in our retirement and hopefully leave some money to provide for the education of our grandchildren.

As a *Pensionado* I cannot work for anyone in Panama. I can, however, consult or have my own business and, in my case, work on cruise ships. Since our permanent residence is outside of the US (meaning we are not in the US, or in US waters or airspace more than 30 days a year) my wife and I can each make up to $92,900 earned income without paying US taxes on that amount. Until you reach "full retirement age" you're Social Security check is penalized if you earn over the Social Security limits. While Panama taxes expats for income earned within Panama it does not tax you on income earned outside Panama, like Social Security, pensions and the money I earn internationally on ships.

Now that I'm past my full retire age, and working on cruise ships six months a year, I really do have the best of all worlds!

I carefully watch my time in the US or in US waters. For example, I can't work ships when they are doing Alaska or Canada & New England since that, plus visiting my kids in the US, would put me over the thirty day limit, and to retain my outside US permanent residency status I can't be in the US more than 30 days a calendar year.

These are big decisions, decisions that you don't want to make blindly. They are decisions which could be very costly if they are the wrong decisions. Don't be afraid to seek out professional help as it will save you money in the long run.

People sometimes ask, "Won't all the *gringos* moving to Boquete drive up the cost of living?" That's exactly the kind of question you need to be asking. The answer is, yes, and no.

The cost of land had already been driven up, some would say "through the roof", by the time we got here, particularly in Boquete. The town is changing. Old buildings are being replaced. There is now a four-lane highway between Boquete and David. We even have Mail Boxes, Etc.: can Kentucky Fried Chicken be far behind? In some ways it reminds me of the transformation we saw when we lived outside Breckenridge, Colorado.

Is it good for investment? Absolutely. Is something valuable also lost along the way? Absolutely. Yet construction is booming in Boquete. Anyone who wants to work can work. When we came there were two banks, now we have seven to choose from. The local Romero supermarket is open 24 hours.

As Panama moves forward and enjoys one of the few booming economies in the world, the cost of living is going up, not just in Boquete, but all over the country. In Boquete at the same time you have almost two economies developing. For example: Romero is the *gringo* store of choice and it looks and feels somewhat familiar. Mandrian and Baru are grocery stores that cater more towards Indians and Panamanians, and often have lower prices for the same goods. You can have breakfast (eggs, local fry bread, a corn tortilla, juice and coffee) at Central Park Cafe for $4.25. (The same breakfast at Central Park when we came six years ago was $1.75). Or you can have the same breakfast at one of the *gringo* restaurants with a flower on the plate for $9.00. Your choice.

There is no question that the economic growth in Panama, driven mostly by expansion in Panama City, the Canal Expansion and other major projects, is driving up the cost of living. Because Panama uses the US dollar, the dollar takes a hit here just as in the US. When the dollar drops against world currencies, inflation is inevitable. If the cost of oil goes up in the world, the cost of diesel goes up here as well. The haircut that used to cost $2 now costs $4. A maid that used to run $8 a day is now $15. A gardener used to get $8 a day, and now gets $10-15. So, yes, costs have gone up here, but they have elsewhere as well. I'm shocked when I go back to the States by the cost of everything! So although costs have increased in Panama, compared to Southern California at least, Panama is still a whole lot cheaper.

It's not just about the cost of living; it's also about the quality of life our quality of life is better in Panama, and for less money.

* * * *

So now that house values have plummeted in many parts of the world, is moving to Panama still an option?

For many people I would emphatically answer, "Yes!" You may have to scale back your expectations. Maybe you won't go the "dream house" route, which frankly many folks end up regretting. But the cost of living in Panama is STILL a whole lot less than it is in many places in the US! And the quality of life is better in many ways.

Let me give you a few examples of "affordable" living in Boquete even if your house equity in the US has mostly disappeared. I built a nice 1,100 square foot casita or little house for my brother: two bedrooms, comfortable, cute and nice. Including the cost of land $50,000. When I go to David I drive by a guy's home made of two 40 foot containers (about $4,000 each delivered), nicely painted with windows and doors, both covered along with the center section. The space in between is an open living area, which makes a lot of sense in a place like Boquete. It's creative, comfortable and funky and I'll bet he has less than $30,000 in the project, including the fancy Chinese front door.

Another friend of ours bought a small coffee *finca*, took what had been run-down Indian housing and turned it into the cutest little cottage you can imagine. This gal is super creative and she basically renovated the place using scrap construction, hard work and a ton of imagination and creativity!

Or you can just rent a decent place in Boquete for $700 to $2,500 a month depending on your wants. But you don't need a million dollars or to have cashed in your chips before the crash to take advantage of moving to Paradise!

Interacting

1. So what do you know, REALLY (and be honest!) about your current spending? Everything, including both partners' "cookie jar" accounts!

2. If you don't know, and most people don't, what are you going to do about it this week? Don't cut back anywhere, just record what you're spending so you have something with which to work.

3. What do you anticipate to be your Social Security payments?

4. Using the 70% rule, what would you need in investments to retire now?

5. What sources of income would you have after retirement, and how much could you anticipate from each?

6. Looking at your current costs of living, if you removed certain categories (like mortgage expenses), or reduced some (like taxes), how much would you need for retirement?

7. What's really important?

9. Getting Off The Hamster Wheel

Not only had I never planned to retire, I'd never even thought of retiring early.

Retirement means different things to different people. For me it has never meant sitting in a rocking chair! Forget shuffle board. Retirement hasn't even meant not working.

I guess for me retirement means not having to work.

Retirement means not being locked in or tied down and having the freedom to do what you want, when you want.

When I sold real estate in Ventura I sold a lot of "coaches" – never call them "mobile homes" – and "manufactured homes" in "Senior Parks" or, as the Boomer's preferred, "Over 55 Parks". I noticed an interesting phenomenon. The people who left the "Over 55 Parks" were mostly in their 80s. As one elderly lady told me in Lemonwood Senior Park, "This is God's waiting room." People left either to be cared for by children, to move to an assisted living center, or by hearse. So I was selling homes owned by older people, complete with sculptured shag carpeting, and tangerine and avocado kitchens. A lot of young people I knew in their mid-20s would have killed for this retro look!

The people who were buying in the "Over 55 Parks" were for the most part younger people, who were just counting the days until they turned 55 and could get in. They'd buy the older units and either totally refurbish them or pull them out and put in a modern, manufactured home.

These younger newcomers weren't interested in the indoor shuffleboard courts. They were making the move because: they could "cash out" of their traditional homes, buy something for cash, and ditch the mortgage and the parks and "coaches" had virtually no maintenance. In an adult community they didn't have the noise and hassle of kids, skateboards, teenagers, and cars with subsonic boom boxes. They could invest their some of their equity for retirement income, and the remainder went into the home and travel. Most of the parks had parking areas where they could park their mobile homes and when they went on the road or traveled abroad, there was high security primarily provided by with lots of close, and even nosy, neighbors.

Interestingly, when we made the decision to move to Panama, the cost of a new manufactured home in Lemonwood Senior Park in Ventura was just about the same as the cost of a new, 3,000 square foot [279 square meter] home overlooking a golf course in Boquete, Panama! Plus the monthly "space rent" in Lemonwood was over $600 a month, forever! The homeowner dues in Valle Escondido were less than $100 per month.

* * * *

I loved life in Ventura. It was the stuff of dreams and movies. We lived on the hillside overlooking Ventura, the Marina and the beach. I could watch the sun rise over the Santa Monica Mountains and see the ocean waves breaking onto the beach. Had I been a surfer, I would have immediately known if the surf was up. It was ten minutes drive down the hill to beautiful beach. I could walk down the hill to the old downtown of Ventura, filled with trendy restaurants, a movie theater and two live venues, antique shops, and tons of funky, trending upscale charm. It was Santa Barbara without the tourists, with better beaches, fewer transients, and without the attitude.

Our home was perfect for the two of us. We bought it from the old man who had built it in the '50s and it still had sculptured shag carpeting over virgin hardwood floors. The house had minus seventy curb appeal when we bought it, but it had a killer view! We had a pool, huge avocado trees (I do miss the endless supply of guacamole!), orange, lemon, peach, and apple trees. We had great neighbors. I could sit in my spa and during the day see the famed arch on Anacapa Island, and at night see the lighthouse light. We had tons of birds, could hear the foghorn at the harbor, and even on rare occasions the sounds of seals barking out in the ocean. Selling real estate was a job I enjoyed and I was good at it.

Life was good! Who would want to give this up?

But life was also very expensive.

Increasingly I felt like the hamster running on the cage wheel, constantly running, and getting nowhere!

Following 9/11 life in the US seemed to be getting increasingly oppressive, not necessarily from the threat of terrorism, but from the talk of terrorism which seemed to be providing opportunity for more and more governmental intrusion and the chipping away of rights which, once lost, would never be regained.

I'm not sure the traffic became worse, but I became increasingly frustrated by the hassle and waste of time sitting on the Freeway at a dead stop.

I was also getting increasing fed up with gang culture in the Oxnard/Ventura area, the crime and the drugs that lurked beneath the tinsel-town-like, Santa-Barbara-want-be surface. I was tired of kids shooting kids, and cops shooting kids. I was tired of excessive and oppressive policing, the injustice of the so-called "justice system", the hypocrisy of the "War on Drugs", and the California prison industry.

You say, "Gee, what do you want? You bitch about the gangs and crime, and then about cops, the justice system and prisons! Why do you think we have cops, the justice system and prisons? To deal with the gangs and crime, stupid!"

Yeah, and unfortunately that's what a lot of people think in the US. The truth is it's the same problem: the drug lords, the gangs, the justice system and the prisons are all sucking at the same teat! All of these institutions have a common interest, keeping the "War on Drugs" going so they can reap the huge profits and keep their jobs.

As long as the citizens live in fear of the drug lords, and the cops, keep telling kids to "Just Say 'No'" while "Just Saying 'Yes'" to every request for more police, more courts, more prisons, the system can continue. Using drugs is stupid: you can kill yourself and others using drugs. Abusing alcohol is very legal, and very chic AND you can kill yourself and others abusing alcohol. Smoking cigarettes is not only legal, it is also subsidized by the US taxpayer AND you can kill yourself and others smoking cigarettes.

Dah? But I realize most of the country doesn't get it.

When I was an Associate Pastor at the United Methodist Church in Westlake Village and the Senior Pastor was away, I received a prayer request dropped in the offering plate: "Please pray for our son, Brandon Hein, who is facing life in prison without possibility of parole for a crime he didn't commit." In a nutshell Brandon, just 18 at the time, was with a group of five other boys who went to buy marijuana from a boy who sold it out of his backyard "fort" in Agoura Hills, California. A fight broke out with the boy who was selling drugs, his friend and so-called "bodyguard", and one of the boys who went to buy marijuana. Fists flew. When it was over one of the boys with whom Brandon went to the "fort" had stabbed the drug dealer and his "bodyguard" friend. One of the stab wounds to the "bodyguard" friend went directly to the heart and he died.

The combination of teenage testosterone, alcohol, drugs, bravado and stupidity is not unusual, but on this day it ended tragically for everyone involved.   The boy who died also happened to be the son of an LAPD detective. Although the boy who actually did the stabbing confessed, under the Felony Murder Rule[15] all of the boys were charged with Felony Murder and received sentences of life without possibility of parole, including Brandon whose only "crime" aside from using alcohol and pot was to be at the wrong place at the wrong time.

That prayer request came over SIXTEEN years ago, while Brandon was still at LA Central Jail, not yet "State Property #K24820". When no one else could get a face-to-face visit, I went to see him, exercising my clergy privileges. Because he was "LWOP" (Life Without Possibility of Parole) and a "High Power" prisoner (i.e. convicted of murder) he was brought in chains and shackles, and shackled to the floor and table. Brandon has always looked younger than his years, and that day he looked all of sixteen. At first I was skeptical, but the more I studied the case, the more I became absolutely convinced that this is one of the worst miscarriages of justice in US history and an embarrassment and affront to all the honest, law-abiding Californians who believe in justice.

It has been over SIXTEEN YEARS and Brandon still sits in prison.[16] The case has made its way through the appeals process without remedy. Former California Governor Arnold Schwarzenegger did see fit to take the first step toward justice and remove the "without possibility of parole" from the sentence, but in the end pardoned the son of a political crony, a guy who really did kill somebody.

---

[15] The concept of Felony Murder, that everyone involved in the underlying crime, regardless of their intent or if they had any knowledge of the murder before, during or after, can be convicted of murder using the "legal fiction" of the Felony Murder rule goes back to English law. England has had the good sense to abolish the law but California has not. Prosecutors love it because it is an easy way to get convictions without having to prove anything.

[16] Conservatively the cost of keeping Brandon in a high security California prison is about $60,000 a year, not counting the loss to taxpayers of Brandon being a productive, tax-paying citizen. For a cash-strapped State like California, Brandon's incarceration has cost the taxpayers almost $1 million! Aside from the gross injustice, this is fiscal stupidity.

Hopefully the present Governor will have the moral courage to right this wrong and give Brandon a complete pardon.

No one has ever said that Brandon killed anyone, that he had a knife, or that he knew anybody had a knife, or even knew that anyone had been stabbed until after the fact. Yet he remains in prison. There have been articles in newspapers, magazines like ROLLING STONE, segments on 60 Minutes II, two documentaries, even a play by Charles Grodin. His case is known and provoked outrage around the world, yet Brandon still sits in prison. Over the past sixteen years, in half a dozen depressing California towns where the only industry is the prison, in maximum security prisons that look like your worst nightmare, I've visited with Brandon. He has become a great friend. I am amazed at his maturity, his ability to adapt and survive, and his enduring belief that somehow, someway God has a purpose for all of this hell. He can sit calmly and talk with other Level IV prisoners who really have done some very bad things, or he can sit down for a 60 Minutes interview with Dan Rather, equally poised and calm. He is also a fantastic artist with some of his best artwork being on the only canvas he had available, his body. One day, when this is all over – pray to God! – we have promised to relax on the beach in Panama.

More than anything else, Brandon's case[17] has caused me to question the fundamental principals of liberty and justice upon which we claim the US is founded.

My great, great, way-back-great grandfather came to the US from Bavaria on a ship called the MINERVA, landing in Philadelphia in 1767. He married the girl he had fallen in love with on the crossing and they settled in Pennsylvania on the banks of the Conococheague River. When the Revolutionary War broke out he joined the Lancaster County Militia and became known as the "Drummer Boy of the Conococheague."

---

[17] For more on Brandon's case visit BrandonHein.com, a Web site maintained by Friends of Brandon Hein.

I have no doubt of the principals of liberty and justice upon which the US was founded. I just question the ways in which those principals are or are not being applied in the present moment. I confess I had similar questions in the South Bronx in the late '60s. I didn't drop out then, but, damn it, I'm dropping out now.

I haven't "left" the US, it has left me.

Except for a brief stint as an Independent in New York, which allowed such a thing, I have always been a Republican. My maternal grandmother was a big shot in the local Republican party and very proud of her collection of elephants. On my paternal grandmother's side, President Herbert Hoover is a distant relative. I even liked Reagan, although his economic theories have come home to roost with vengeance. During the Bush era I was appalled at the ways in which Republican principals were twisted and the government was allowed to intrude more and more in individual lives and freedoms. I will always remain a US citizen and I'll keep voting irrationally dreaming that my one vote counts, but until the US recaptures its vision and renews it's commitment to the freedoms and principals that made it great, I will happily live in exile.

9/11 forever changed both the US and the world.

It is ironic that the terrorists, by creating a climate in which liberties are gradually being chipped away by something ironically called "The Patriot Act", have achieved something more devastating to the US than the terrorists could ever have dreamed.

The result of 9/11 has been the US government taking away basic freedoms and liberties of American citizens destroying key elements and freedoms of American life. Ironically under a Republican president, the central government intruded into all areas of your life – family life, schools, snooping into the books you borrow, your Internet use, and even your phone conversations. We have gone from the "land of the free and home of the brave" to a nation living in fear. It is fear that breeds dictatorships and a climate passively accepting the loss of liberties. FDR was spot on when he said, "The only thing we have to fear is fear itself."

The borders are being squeezed closed and it's only a matter of time until Americans are required to carry identity cards, something most of the world already requires, but that, until now, most US citizens, almost with the cachet of Roman citizens, have not been required to carry. No longer can as a US citizen move freely, without Passport, between our closest neighbors, Canada and Mexico. In the climate of fear created post 9/11, it is just another step to close down the borders to outgoing as well as incoming traffic. Already the Obama administration has said, "We know that you think it's your money and while we know that you earned it and paid taxes on it, we don't think you should be able to take all of it out of the country if you want."

"But it's my money!"

"Correction, pilgrim, it's our money."

Not surprisingly more Americans than ever before are "escaping" while the borders remain open.

All of these factors began to coalesce together, and I began to think, "Now is the time for a change." Both my wife and I were still in relatively good health, so why push it? Why not relax and enjoy life without the unnecessary pressure? It's not about how much you make, it's how much you keep.

We knew we'd make much less in retirement, but in Panama at the end of the day we'd end up keeping just as much, and with a better lifestyle. The little benefit advantage I would gain by working in the US until "full retirement age", for me 65 years and 10 months, would be more than offset by being able to enjoy life together and preserving our health.

Panama was ripe for investment and we were still young enough, adventurous enough, and flexible enough to opt for a new challenge.

When I moved to Panama in 2004 I had looked into my crystal ball. As a REALTOR® I looked at what was going on, and while I loved writing offers on the hood of my car, I realized that there comes a time when you need to cash in your chips and get out of the casino. I saw the US lurching away from traditional freedoms . . . and it wasn't just changing the color of money, "greenbacks" to a rainbow Currency, or changing the name of the country from the "United States of America" to "The Homeland" [that just sounds so Third Reich to me!] . . . but it was foreseeing the time when US citizens were no longer allowed to freely leave the country and take their possessions, and their money, with them.

At least for the moment, although you can no longer take all the money and assets that you worked to produce, that you saved, and that you've already paid taxes on . . . you can still physically leave the US.

Interestingly more and more US citizens are looking to relocate abroad and for the first time people are openly discussing the option of relinquishing their US citizenship. Personally, I'm not ready for such a drastic step, hoping, maybe against hope that the US eventually will get back on track. And I'm pragmatic enough to know that a US Passport is still the most convenient passport for international travel. But, I think significantly, traffic is spiking to Web pages about giving up your US passport, or getting second and third passports. If that sounds tempting, I'd take a good, long and hard look at those passports and how readily they are accepted as you travel around the world.

* * * *

Lecturing on cruise ships, I travel a lot, and frequently need to depart, arrive or connect through the US.

Returning to the US after you've been away for a while is a strange and scary experience.

Compared to entering Panama, or most nations in the world, returning to the US is like returning to a police state. You have to run a gauntlet of frequently rude uniformed officers and authorities to get in and out of the US. Coming back I almost had to take off my pants to get through security because the zipper on my fly was setting off the security scanner. How many men do you think have zippers on their pants? And how many airlines are hijacked by the zippers on men's pants? It has gotten ridiculous. And is the US any safer? Do you really feel any safer?

Unfortunately the terrorists have already won.

With the help of our government we've created a climate of fear in which Americans are standing by watching rights which have endured over two hundred years being steadily whittled away. Yes, unemployment and under-employment are huge problems in the US, and I suppose TSA is keeping a lot of marginal workers off unemployment and welfare, so maybe this really has nothing to do with security. Or maybe we all secretly want to pose for naked pictures that the TSA employees can laugh at. Who knows? But I'm always glad to escape back to Panama!

And let me say that I am NOT "anti-American": I am SAR-certifiable[18] since my family has been in the US since before the American Revolution. But I am fed up and I see nothing wrong with people who aren't commentators or talking heads on FOX also being concerned and critical about the way the country is heading. We do still have the freedom in the US to think and speak – at least for the moment..

* * * *

---

[18] Sons of The American Revolution

An interesting postscript to life in Boquete; when we moved to Panama many of the US people who were choosing to live here were coming in part because they were unhappy with the direction the US was taking under Bush-Cheney. Many of the US folks who are coming down now are unhappy with the direction the US is taking under Obama! Hopefully we can all get together in Panama, forget US politics, celebrate our life in Paradise and sing "Kum By Ka" together!

Interacting

1. What are your personal arguments for doing it NOW as opposed to later?

2. What are your personal arguments for waiting?

3. What are your own thoughts about the direction the country is taking?

10. You're Not In Kansas Anymore

One **of the real problems many Americans face is the challenge of finding and buying real estate in the land they've chosen to call their new home.** This is particularly true in Central America, and especially in Costa Rica and Panama.

"Professional Real Estate"

The real estate market in the US is largely influenced by, and some would say "controlled" by professional real estate. Real estate in the US is highly regulated, compared to most places in the world. In California the real estate business is very regulated by the Department of Real Estate (DRE) and has a strong infrastructure of title companies, escrow services, inspection services, multiple listing services (MLS), and local real estate associations.

If you want to become a real estate agent in California you first take a real estate course. This can be either in a class room setting, on line, or by home study. You then must pass a written exam administered periodically by the DRE. Then you are fingerprinted, you are checked for any police record, and given a provisional license. To get a regular license you must take additional courses. Licenses are renewed every four years and you must continue to take professional development courses mandated by the DRE. Most importantly, the DRE is always looking over your broker's shoulder, who is always looking over your shoulder as an agent. Most, but not all, real estate agents in the US are REALTORS®. REALTORS® are very particular about that trademark – that it always is in all caps, with the registered trademark behind it. This designation means the agent is a member of the American Association of REALTORS® and has subscribed to a very detailed Code of Ethics. Additionally REALTORS® are usually a member of their local Real Estate Board and the local Multiple Listing Service (MLS).

Once in a while a REALTOR® does get out of line. If it is a question of violating the Code of Ethics usually the local Real Estate Board steps in and peer pressure alone leads to a change in behavior. If the infraction is a violation of California Real Estate Law the DRE steps in and puts the violator on probation or yanks their license. It is against the law in California to sell or represent the sale of any property other than your own if you are not licensed. This is why when you call a California broker in response to an ad in Sunday's paper, and just want a quick answer about a property, the receptionist cannot by law give you the answer, but must transfer you to a licensed real estate agent.

Most Americans are used to a real estate market that has a strong MLS or multiple listing services. Professional real estate in the US is set up with one goal in mind: to get the highest and best price for the seller.

This is why the wise buyer will sign an Exclusive Buyer Broker Agreement which means that the real estate agent is working only for them, and not for the seller. All the brokers who list their properties on the MLS agree that they will share their commission with whatever broker actually brings the buyer. This gives properties the widest exposure in order to achieve the highest possible selling price in an open market. As I used to constantly tell my clients, "It doesn't make any difference whose name is on the sign. I can show you any property!"

- So most Americans come from a real estate environment that is:
- Highly regulated
- Professional
- Has a strong infrastructure of related services – finance, title,
- escrow, inspection
- Has a strong MLS system.

But come to Panama and "You're not in Kansas anymore!"

When you choose to purchase property in another country you are suddenly confronted with a real estate environment that is nothing like what you've always known.

There is little effective regulation. Panama has increasingly given lip service to regulation and does technically require real estate sales people to be licensed. Slowly, very slowly since this is Panama, things are changing, but you will still find everyone and his brother selling real estate – the dentist, the hairdresser, the taxi driver – everyone!

There is almost no infrastructure of related services.

There is no MLS so every agent is only showing you properties on which he makes a commission, i.e. his listings and without an MLS there is no truly effective way to develop "comps".

Throw into this mix real estate laws that are very different than those in the US, dealing with square meters and hectares instead of square feet and acres, then add the fact that not all real estate in Panama is actually owned by title – well, you can understand why many Americans are confused and, sometimes, swindled.

* * * *

Consider these events, all similar to actual events, any one of which would have caused the perpetrators to have, at the very least, their licenses yanked in California.

Affordable Ocean Front Lots!

The lots were small, but drop dead gorgeous! Bordered on one side by a not-bad-by-Panama standards road and sandy beaches with coconut palms on the other side, it was the stuff of dreams! Azure-blue waters and great fishing. You could pull your own boat right up on the beach and drift of to sleep with the sound of waves. And the price was fantastic!

Problem: Despite the signs, the flags, and the lot markers, the property between the road and the beach was actually owned by the Republic of Panama and by law wasn't for sale by anyone at any price.

Mountain Paradise!

"Spectacular mountain views in this alpine paradise. American builder will construct your dream home in this alpine paradise for 20% less. Using a streamlined US approach to building development, we can give you greater building quality for less money. We guarantee to have your home completed in eight months without the usual Panamanian delays. Top quality!"

Problem: The builder required 80% of the cost of the construction up front. Although apparently well-intentioned the builder had never built in Panama before, got in over his head, and went belly up taking the dreams of several dozen unsuspecting families with him. Interestingly these people were mostly back in the US, assuming their homes were progressing as promised. They accepted at face value glowing emailed "progress reports" only to find they had nothing but cement slabs for the 80% they'd paid up front.

Caribbean Island Dreams

"Spectacular sun sets, coral reefs, turquoise-blue waters, Captain Kidd's Fancy has it all! Live on your own private island with only thirty others and enjoy your own marina and 8-hole golf course. Only ten beautiful sites remain! Hurry!"

Problem: Although the development was spectacular, and the homes already built were really nice, everyone was in for a big surprise, including Captain Kidd. The developer had purchased and sold "rights of possession" that were acquired from an American company. Unknown to the developer or the American company a Panamanian family had acquired prior rights of possession twenty years earlier, and had maintained a tiny, rundown wooden house on one tiny point of the island where members of the family occasionally visited to relax and fish. Enter lots of lawyers, long litigation, and major uncertainty for everyone involved.

When you don't know the "system" . . . *"Cuidado!"*

Pacific Sunsets

"Pacific island property, just meters away from a marine reserve. Spectacular views, palm-fringed beaches, protected anchorage, and just off shore some of the most spectacular fishing in the Pacific. Twenty hectares, $7 per square meter."

Problem: The American expat knew paradise when he saw it, and began negotiations with the real estate sales person who had showed him the property. He was ready and anxious. The agent came back and said that there was a slight problem. It seemed another unknown buyer had come in at the last moment and snapped up ten of the twenty hectares and the seller had now raised the price on the remaining ten hectares to $14 per square meter. The price had doubled overnight! The prospective buyer walked away. In the meantime the seller, who knew nothing about "the last minute unknown buyer" and still had twenty hectares to sell, contacted the prospective buyer directly asking, "What happened?" When buyer and seller compared notes, it turned out that the real estate agent was carving off ten hectares for herself, as additional "commission", while the prospective buyers was to pay for the whole thing!

* * * *

Understand that this does not apply to all real estate sales people in Panama! There are real estate firms and sales people who are professional, dedicated, have great integrity, and who will bend over backwards to steer their clients through waters sometimes infested with sharks. There are Panamanian real estate firms who have been in business for many years and have a long and enviable history of servicing their clients. But there are also folks who've been kicked out of one country or another and who've left a trail of disillusioned and "taken" clients.

The point is: be careful! You are not operating under the same assumptions and rules that applied in the US. Take your time. Talk to people.

Don't believe everything you hear, but if you talk to enough people the same names will come up again and again, both in terms of recommendation and caution.

I think the "Buyer Broker" concept, where the agent is hired by you to work for you and to negotiate the best deal for you, makes a lot of sense, particularly in Panama. If your agent knows that he is going to be paid a certain percentage by you regardless of what you purchase, it opens the door for your agent to go out and beat the bushes and find the property that meets your needs at the price you want to pay.

Because Panamanian real estate is not as developed and organized as real estate n the US, many sellers question what, if anything, they are getting for their commission. So "for sale by owner" offerings are very common. Drive into Boquete from David and you'll see tons of "*Se Vende*" signs with the owner's phone number. When owners are setting the prices without consultation they may be asking too little or, in some cases, far too much. "*Gringos* will pay anything," also known as "*Gringo Bingo*", may be the key pricing consideration.

In the US, with organized real estate, MLS, and local real estate boards, an agent with a few computer strokes can give you reliable "comps", i.e. the exact price of comparable properties and when they sold. This is critical when a market is going rapidly up or down. You can't depend on what people say they paid or what sellers say they got. Everyone wants to look good, so the actual prices tend to be adjusted accordingly. Again, this is an argument for hiring your own "Buyer Broker" who will work for you, scout the territory, and negotiate realistically on your behalf with "for sale by owner" sellers.

Don't think "for sale by owner" offerings are shark-free either! Sometimes sellers just don't actually own what they're trying to sell! Or they want to play games. I was very interested in a property listed online for $399K for a nice coffee farm. I emailed back and forth with the owner in the States and went out to see the property several times. It was a nice property, attractively priced, and we were very interested only to discover that once he knew of our interest he jacked the price up to $600K! I told him I was always interested in negotiating the asking price downward, not upward! Thanks, but no thanks! It is fairly common with "for sale by owner" properties to find the seller jacking up the price at the last minute figuring that either that *gringos* have tons of money, or are stupid, or are both! This has happened to us again and again!

* * * *

Who owns what?

Traditionally there have been two types of property in Panama: titled property and rights of possession.

Titled Property

Titled property is similar to what we understand in the US, except for the fact that there are no title companies to research the title and insure the title. In Panama your attorney will do a title search and confirm that the title or "*escritura*" is registered in the public registry. This includes verifying that there are no encumbrances on the property and that the property has been surveyed. And you should have the property surveyed by your own surveyor to verify the accuracy.

Rights of way are very tricky in Panama. Every piece of property must have access to the public, at least by a walking path and the access must remain public even if the ownership of the property changes hands. Once a right of way has been granted it must continue in perpetuity if it is regularly used, and regularly can be as infrequently as once a year. When property is subdivided the original owner must provide access from a public road and sometimes, over the years, these rights of way have not always been duly recorded and yet they still exist.

Often developers in Panama will hang onto the title until your home is actually completed and you receive a certificate of occupancy. However, if the developer suddenly goes south after you've almost completed your home, but before you get your certificate of occupancy, you can either be out of luck or find yourself tied up in court for years.

Rights of Possession

Rights of possession are a type of ownership in Panama but do not constitute titled property.

To acquire rights of possession a Panamanian citizen files an application to the government including a survey and statements and agreements from the neighbors. He then has possessory rights. Hanging onto those rights requires that the "possessor" actually use the property and make improvements.

Improvements can be buildings, or something as simple as planting grass, palm trees, or fencing in the property. The "possessor" can then sell his rights of possession to you, after which you need to actually buy the property from the government. If you skip this important step, you have the right to use the property – sometimes referred to as "The right to pick fruit" – but you do not actually own it. Fortunately this is changing in Panama as the government seeks to have all property titled. Why? The government can't collect taxes on rights of possession property.

Ways to Own Property

When you purchase property in Panama you can purchase it in the name of a real person (your own name), or in the name of a corporation, or in the name of a Private Interest Foundation. Panama does not recognize joint ownership by husband and wife. If one dies, property is not automatically transferred to the other. Most expats choose to own property in the name of an S.A. corporation for various legal and confidentiality advantages. The owners of the corporation own the shares and the corporation owns the real property. Usually these S.A. corporations are bearer bond entities where whoever physically holds the bonds, owns the company. So if you or your spouse dies, the survivor has the bonds, so owns the property.

Some people, in order to protect assets and easily transfer assets to heirs, create something called a Private Interest Foundation (PIF). This is a relatively new entity in Panama, but one which has been used in other countries specializing in off shore corporate business. The Private Interest Foundation has no shares, and no owners, but there are beneficiaries. When the founder of Foundation dies, in theory the PIF and its assets pass automatically to the beneficiaries. There is no public record of the real owners or beneficiaries, so in theory at least it provides a high level of confidentiality.

The US, obviously wanting a slice of any foreign pie, now requires US citizens to disclose these entities and any profits, insuring continued employment for US accountants. Before you jump into a Private Interest Foundation you need to decide if it solves or creates problems. The US IRS has now decided that a Panama Private Interest Foundation is the same as a Trust. So there is now way to escape the long arm of the IRS or the US pile of onerous paperwork.[19]

Signing on the Dotted Line

Say you actually find a piece of property and you and the seller agree on a price, then what? This is where you're really not in Kansas . . . or California any longer!

---

[19] I've never minded paying my taxes as much as the incomprehensible labyrinth of paperwork.

As a REALTOR® in California I used to chafe over the length and complexity of the California Association of REALTORS® residential purchase agreement. But it was a standard agreement that applied to the purchase of all real estate in California, and it prevented a lot of problems by clearly defining everything and anticipating problems in advance and indicating how these problems would be resolved should they occur. In Panama there are no "offer" and "acceptance" documents, no standard contract and no deposit or earnest money. Having reached agreement, the "intending" seller and "intending" buyer sign a "Promise-to-Sell" agreement and the intending buyer makes a down payment. The agreement is amazingly simple and doesn't anticipate problems opening the door in my opinion for misunderstandings and conflict. Once the contract is signed, the intending buyer makes a usually sizable down payment. The "Promise-to-Sell" agreement is then recorded in the Public Registry to prevent the seller from selling to someone else.

Say what?!?

There is no escrow. There is no neutral third party to hold the money in a trust account, be sure the terms of the contract are fulfilled, and parcel out the money at closing according to the contract. (For this reason, real estate agents can often find themselves stiffed on their commission.) Funds are sometimes held by the lawyer, assuming the parties are using the same lawyer or can agree on whose lawyer will hold the money, a bank, and in some cases the real estate agent. If this sounds dicey . . . well, coming from California, it is! It seems to me there is a lot of trust involved. Trust, when you're the new kid on the block and may not know who to trust. We were lucky: our builder and his attorney not only were honorable and trustworthy, but they have also become our friends. But . . .

When the title is actually registered at the Public Registry the money changes hands. If you've bought property held by a corporation you'll also receive the bearer shares for the corporation that owns the property.

You'll want to put these bearer shares in your safe deposit box . . . except for one problem, Panama banks don't the safe deposit boxes we're accustomed to in the US. So when you pack your container bring along a good safe. Unless you're loaded down with the family jewels, a good fire rating is the most important thing in selecting a safe.

Panama has several advantages over some of the other Central American countries retirees may consider. Foreigners can own property in Panama, which is not always the case in other countries. And Panama does not have the problems of squatters and squatter's rights as in Costa Rica.

Location! Location! Location!

Anywhere in the world, these are still the three most important words in real estate! To really understand the differences in location, you need to do your homework, ask around and spend some time in an area before you commit.

Shopping Online

Funny thing, when the Boeing 707 made Trans-Atlantic travel comfortable and fast, people said the age of passenger ships was over, yet today the cruise industry is booming! When DVDs first came out, people said movie theaters were finished, yet today where there was once a ratty little theater you'll find a 20-screen movie theater with lines at the box office! When Amazon was launched people predicted the death of bookstores, yet today Barnes & Noble and Borders have become vast emporiums of literature and community centers! When the Internet first started showing real estate listings many brokers were wringing their hands, yet today the Internet is the single biggest marketing tool for REALTORS®.

Using sites like EscapeArtist.com, Viviun.com and others, you can dream about properties all over the world. Goggle and other search engines have made it relatively easy to ferret out properties for sale anywhere in the world.

But like anything else, the Web can be abused. Have you ever noticed how REALTORS® in the US generally leave up the "For Sale" sign until the new owners are threatening to bring the sign to the broker's office and hit him over the head with it? Why? It's great and free advertising! I once took a listing for a home on the busiest street in Ventura, right by a freeway entrance. I thought to myself, this will take forever to sell, but what a great advertising opportunity. Fortunately for the seller, unfortunately for me, I sold it in two days!

Unfortunately the same thing happens on line. Either intentionally, or just because they don't know how to get the damn page down, properties remain "for sale" online long after they are sold. Aside from being very frustrating to Internet shoppers, this adds to the confusion.

For example, I was looking for property on a certain Panamanian island. I found what appeared to be the ideal property, titled, partially developed, listed by a real estate broker at a whale of a good price. When I actually cruised by the property I discovered the development had long since been finished and the property had in fact been sold years ago, which is why it was priced so low. It's probably still online! After inquiring about two or three more properties listed by the same agent, and never receiving any response, I've concluded that those properties have probably been long since sold as well. So I just ignore her site.

There are sites where sellers can pay a monthly or flat fee to showcase their property for sale. Some of these are realistic sellers: others are people who've said, "Well, if we could get X dollars, sure, we'd sell." So they're not really looking to sell, unless some fool happens along who is willing to pay their "dream" price. Sometimes there are hotels, B&Bs and small businesses where the owner is tired of being an indentured servant, and would like to cash out, if they could get a price that really doesn't make sense if a prospective buyer runs the numbers.

Keep checking the same sites regularly. Notice how long some homes remain for sale. Because they drop off the listing doesn't necessarily mean they've sold: the sellers may just have given up, for the moment. It's amazing how some of the same properties keep cycling back onto the popular international real estate sites. Interestingly sometimes the price keeps inflating, as the seller keeps dreaming.

As you scour the Internet for properties you will notice the identical property being "offered for sale" on various sites at wildly different asking prices. This is because a seller is looking for a "net sale price" and various authorized and non-authorized agents and promoters are trying to sell the property, jacking up the price to cover their profit.

Interacting

1. How is buying property going to be different than the experiences you've had in the US?

2. Assuming by now you've identified some areas you might like to call home, start following the real estate market in those areas online. Do some comparisons.

11. Our Experience A to Z

Here's an A to Z of some of our experiences living in Panama.
This is our experience, much of it based on living in Boquete in
Chiriqui province.   I don't pretend that the experience is the same
for everyone.

ATMs – Ubiquitous in Panama, as in the rest of the world. And
since Panama's Balboa is in fact the US dollar, it makes life quite
simple. Cost to withdraw from another bank is generally moderate.
Although a US dollar should be a US dollar anywhere in the world,
if you deposit a check for US dollars from a US bank in Panama the
Panamanian Bank may charge you a fee to "convert" US dollars to
US dollars! For a while I got around this by withdrawing money
from my HSBC-US account at the ATM at my HSBC-Panama bank,
then walking inside and depositing the cash in my Panamanian
account. Then HSBC decided it would gratuitously charge 1% for
every withdrawal so I found a new bank, Banistmo, which got
bought out by HSBC. Such is life.

Attitude towards Americans – Panamanians like anything
American and that includes Americans. I'd love to escape
McDonald's, but Panamanians think it is wonderful. They love
American products. You'll see Indians wandering around with all
sorts of prestige American logos and university and school wear,
most of which came to Panama as one or two of a kind, remainders,
and sold for about $3 a shirt. (Of course all those shirts with US
logos were probably made in the Asia.) I think Panamanians come
out of the womb with a cell phone! Everyone has one! Panamanian
kids ape American styles. At school everyone wears uniforms, but
when they get dressed up to come to town they look as "hip" as teens
anywhere.

Many Panamanians have someone in their family or circle of friends who either worked for the Canal or the US military. And many Panamanians have dual US/Panama citizenship because someone worked for the US military or Canal. Panama is one of the countries in the world that likes the US even although its history might have given cause to feel differently.

It is important to note that there are cultural differences which must be taken into account. Panamanians are "pleasers" and they are eager to please so they tend to tell you what they believe you want to hear. This is a frequent source of confusion and frustration. You can ask your builder, "Can you finish this project in four months?" and he will probably tell you he can, because that's what he knows you want to hear, while all the while he knows the project will take at least nine months.

A friend of ours, Maria Ruiz, of the Ruiz coffee family, has a Ph.D. in how business organizations communicate and function. She points out that the US as a nation exhibits more traditional "masculine" tendencies, more aggressive behavior, higher national testosterone and a John-Wayne-like directness, whereas Panama as a nation exhibits more traditional "feminine" or maternal tendencies, is more nurturing, less aggressive and more patient. So just based on our differing cultures, the *gringo* way of doing things is much different than the Panamanian and this can create misunderstanding and conflict.

Friends of ours who lived through Noriega and the US Invasion tell us that Panamanians never expected the US to invade. The Panamanian way would have been do discuss and attempt to mediate the conflict, even if the discussion were still continuing to this day!

We heard of another expat who retired from the US as a fire chief. He looked at our fledgling "*bomberos*" and their lack of equipment and saw a need that he could fill. He rounded up donations and equipment from the US, but it seemed to him that one of the major problems was organization. A fire department simply could not function as a "democracy" where everyone decided together how to respond.

He knew the fire department could function better with an organizational hierarchy. Someone needed to be chief and issue commands. Knowing that equipment alone wouldn't solve the problems, he made the contributions of needed equipment and resources contingent on reorganization: take it or leave it. The *bomberos* left it.

Balboa – The "Balboa" is the official currency of Panama, but exists in coinage form only. Balboa coins are identical in size and weight to US coins so can be used interchangeably. The only paper money is the US dollar; therefore the Balboa is automatically at par with the US dollar because it is the US dollar. This makes it easy to know exactly what things cost in "real money" and provides stability to the currency that is rare in Latin American countries. Because of the relatively short life of US paper dollar bills and the high cost of storing worn out bills and then shipping them back to the US Mint, Panama has recently issued a 1 Balboa coin which is equal in value to the US dollar.

Banking – There were ten banks in Panama in 1959 when Panama's legislature adopted provision for numbered bank accounts and banking privacy. Today there are over seventy banks and Panama has become a safe international haven for money attracted by the privacy and absence of exchange restrictions. Unlike the US, where you show up, open an account and deposit money, establishing an account in Panama requires tons of additional paperwork and hassle in an attempt to discourage money laundering. Like banks everywhere there are lots of additional fees, and since you likely can't read the multipage small print agreement you sign, many of the fees will come as a surprise.

Bullied by the US, in order to secure US approval of a Free Trade Agreement, Panama has now bent over to allow the US "to have its way" with the country's traditional banking privacy. It remains to be seen what effect this capitulation has on Panama's banking business, but the good news for US citizens is that the US now has complete access to your banking records in Panama and the IRS has opened an office in Panama City! Now ten IRS agents can give you ten different answers to your tax questions without even leaving Panama, but if you're looking to hide money look elsewhere.

"Bars" – Bars on the windows of homes are as much of a decorative and architectural feature in Central America as a security measure. Where they are a security measure they are just like alarm systems in the States. Sometimes people use bars on their windows to imply to their neighbors that they have enough valuable stuff inside that they need bars, in other words as a status symbol. We have seen Panamanian homes with bars on the windows but without front doors, just a bead curtain or fabric curtain or "Dutch door" – go figure!

Locals in Chiriqui, who lived through the Noriega years, tell us that many of the older homes installed bars because of concern that Noriega's thugs would invade their homes. And in Panama City and surrounds there have been a rash of home invasions.

Bocas del Toro – Bocas del Toro is the name given to the province adjoining Chiriqui on the Caribbean side. It's where we thought we might like to retire, before discovering Boquete. The mainland of Bocas del Toro is prime banana growing territory. "Bocas" generally refers to the island archipelago of six large islands and many smaller ones, and specifically the Bocas Town on Isla Colon. Columbus visited the area and named several of the islands, and it was a haunt for pirates, and many believe it is still a haunt for real estate pirates. The population is heavily West Indian, people who originally came to work on the Canal or on banana plantations. Bocas Town is popular with young people and has a reputation as a laid-back party town. The town is the jumping off place for many of the stereotypical Caribbean-type islands with clear blue water, great diving, and palm-fringed white sandy beaches. Bocas Town is accessible by air from Panama City and also by bus and ferry.

Lots of expats like Bocas and have retired there, but for me it is too hot and noisy. My idea of a Caribbean island paradise is not hearing the boom-boom of the disco on the island across the water.

Boca Chica – Boca Chica is a tiny fishing village on the Pacific side, about 40 minutes from David and the jumping off point for Boca Brava Island and Parque Nacional Marino Golfo de Chiriqui, a 57 square mile [14,740 hectare] national marine park that protects 25 islands and 19 coral reefs. Now that the road has been redone it's not a bad trip. We bought a waterfront property in Boca Chica with a tiny little casita that I eventually want to make into an overnight getaway. There are now developments around Boca Chica with million dollar beachfront homes.

Boquete – Boquete is actually a district (something like a US county) in the province of Chiriqui. In addition there is a town of Boquete, which is where we live. Boquete is set in a beautiful valley surrounded by mountains, and is reminiscent of the Swiss Alps in many ways. It is a small town, a Panamanian jewel prized by Panamanians from around the country. It is a favorite vacation spot for Panamanians who want to escape the heat and humidity of other areas of the country. Boquete is known as "the land of eternal spring" because of its year-round pleasant, spring-like climate. Boquete is known for its flowers and coffee and every year holds a Coffee & Flower Fair.

Indians settled in the highlands of Chiriqui and Boquete long before Columbus arrived in Panama. The Indians of Chiriqui never surrendered to the Spanish. The first settlers came in the late 1800s when Boquete was still jungle. The present town was founded in 1911 and many of the early pioneers were expats from Europe attracted by the rich volcanic soil and abundant water. Some of the early settlers were disenchanted gold seekers who left California after the gold rush. Teddy Roosevelt, Richard Nixon, Charles Lindberg, Admiral Richard Byrd, Ingrid Bergman, John Wayne, William Holden, Clark Gable, Sean Connery, Mel Gibson and the Shah of Iran, Reza Pahlavi, all found their way to Boquete through the years. Several former Presidents of the Republic of Panama live in Boquete.

The word "*boquete*" actually means "hole" which explains the unusual variety of pictures you will turn up if you do a Google image search without a censoring filter turned on! And it means something else altogether in Brazilian Portuguese.

Our home and farm is just up the mountain from Boquete in a crossroads known as Palmira Centro.

Builders – There are reputable Panamanian and American builders in Boquete, and there are some who may not be so reputable or experienced. And a few who may just be crooks! You need to be careful! Builders should be licensed, but even that is no guarantee. Plans must be approved and in compliance with building codes of Panama, Chiriqui and Boquete. Much of Central America, Boquete included, is in a seismic zone and this must be taken into consideration when designing a home.

The traditional, time-honored method of construction is concrete block with poured, reinforced concrete. Some newer construction is using structural skin panels with Styrofoam core insulation sold under the trade names of Covintec and M2 which I tend to think of as Styrofoam and chicken wire. The claim is that construction is faster and that the Styrofoam has insulating properties. The manufacturers of M2 (*"M -y- dos"*) also claim seismic advantages. The technology is too new to have lived through a serious Panamanian quake, and no one knows for sure the long-term effects of living in what essentially is a Styrofoam cup. Yet to be addressed is the disposal of all the left over waste since Styrofoam is not biodegradable.

Because of termites, wood is generally used only for doors and cabinetry, although many of the old Boquete homes were built of now very expensive wood naturally resistant to termites. Labor costs are considerably lower than in the States which means that you can build more for less. Most *gringo*-style construction is running from $80-140 a square foot. [Panama measures all of the space covered by roof when determining structure size, so this would include areas such as patios and garage/car port, which are not included in the US.] World-wide costs of cement and steel have been increasing, pushing up building costs. The Canal expansion will create even greater demand for cement and steel.

A typical American attitude is that an American builder must be better than a Panamanian builder. Not necessarily. An American builder may be building the way houses are built in America, which may, or may not, work well in Panama. When we chose to build on our farm we chose a Panamanian. We were impressed with the uniform quality of his work. He only built two or three houses a year with a small crew, but he seemed to have pride in his work, and without a lot of overhead, was very competitive . . . and he turned out to be a crook. He took 97% of my money, having only finished 70% of my house before I fired his ass, kicked him off the property and finished it myself.   I now know that he, like a lot of Panamanian contractors, underbid to get the job, took all of his profit upfront and then pleaded poverty planning that I would keep giving him money. I still see him driving around town in his dark windowed green Toyota truck that he bought with my money!

Buy vs. Build – We bought our first house completely finished. We lucked out. The builder was reliable, honest, a civil engineer by training, and became a friend. That isn't always the story unfortunately. One American came to Panama to build homes and charged people 80% up front. He was new to building in Panama, and soon he was upside down, and went under, taking the dreams of a lot of people along with him. Who would put 80% up front anyway? Many of these owners, still in the States, just accepted glowing email reports of the progress being made and assumed their homes were nearing completion. Ooops! If you are going to build throw all time estimates to the winds. I'd advise against building long distance! I'd spend the money, take the time, come down and rent a place, and be on site every other day and know exactly what is going on. And, even then, it's a crap shoot.

If you are thinking about building you simply must accept that you cannot, CANNOT build long distance, and end up with what you want and expect. It's just not possible: deal with it! Even with the best builders, you need to be on site. Plans here are sometimes more "guidelines" than specifications.

If you are even thinking about building, read **chapter 13 "Building In Panama"** very carefully.

Canopy Tour – Boquete Tree Trek offers an almost two-mile zip line canopy tour traversing a cloud forest of century-old trees and waterfalls. The tour is divided into eleven different zip-line cables. The cables will support 10,000 pounds [4,536 kilo], and the harness will support 2,000 pounds [907 kilo], so no matter what your size you can enjoy making a controlled cable flight 100 to 200 feet [30 to 60 meter] off the ground through the forest canopy. For the timid, a guide will hang on with you for the duration of the tour. One single expat woman gushed that the "hunky guide" was one of the best parts of the tour.

Cars – As in most of Latin America, Japanese cars seem to be preferred. Toyota is the preferred brand, mostly because Toyota has the strongest franchise in Panama and parts are readily available. If you have some brands of American and European cars, you car may sit in the garage for months while a part makes its way from across the world. Compared to much of Central and Latin America, cars are relatively inexpensive. Registration must be renewed yearly and there is a concentrated effort to get unsafe vehicles off the road. Initially we went from a two-car couple to one car for a while, but preserving our marriage seemed to require going back to two cars even if I'm gone half of the time. Gas is a little more expensive than in California, and so a lot of folks use diesel to get more mileage and since diesel is subsidized. Car maintenance and service is a lot cheaper, but whether at a "shade-tree mechanic" or the dealership, isn't always very reliable.

Casco Viejo Panama –The older section of Panama City juts out into the Bay and has narrow streets, balconies, and a French and Spanish influence reminiscent of New Orleans and Old San Juan. The French influence dates back to the original French attempt to create the Canal. Some areas were heavily destroyed during the US invasion. Panama is attempting to restore much of the area and it is becoming a very neat, and expensive, area with night clubs, boutiques, and small hotels.

Casinos – Panama has had casinos since the days of the pirates – hmmm, makes you wonder! Las Vegas-style casinos are located in some hotels and shopping centers. There are three in David.

146

Chiriqui– There are nine provinces in Panama of which Chiriqui and Bocas del Toro are the Western most, bordering Costa Rica. Yes, the length of Panama runs West to East, which means the Canal runs North to South. Chiriqui is by far the most independent of the provinces, and Chiricanos take great pride in their flag and identity. Chiriqui feeds much of the rest of Panama. The mountain towns of Boquete and Cerro Punta are favorite get away vacation spots of Panamanians.

Church – Boquete has a large Roman Catholic church in the center of town, and several smaller parishes in outlying areas. There are Christian churches of all varieties including a thriving Assemblies of God congregation. All of these are local churches so, naturally, have services in Spanish. There are a number of small interdenominational groups in Boquete with services in English that, like restaurants, seem to come and go. Although Panama is officially a Roman Catholic country it is very multi-cultural, and accepting and tolerant of all religions.

Coffee – This is as close to coffee heaven as you can get! We're surrounded by coffee farms producing some of the finest coffee in the world. Even within Boquete, different *fincas* produce different tasting beans, just like vineyards in Napa or Sonoma produce slightly different tasting wines. Coffee connoisseurs all have their favorite *fincas* and blends. Coffee trees have beautiful white flowers and can produce several harvests a year. The Indians climb the steep valley trails harvesting coffee. Since we have a small coffee farm we enjoy our own home grown coffee, but sell most of it to one of the large *beneficios* in town.

Coffee Flies – The only disadvantage of coffee plants are that they attract a tiny gnat locally called a "coffee fly". The pesky tiny fly bites much like a "no-see-um" at the beach. Expats who have been here a while tell us that eventually you are no longer "fresh blood" and the coffee flies no longer bother you. The theory is that at this altitude your blood eventually thins and you are no longer quite as tasty. My problem is that every time I go away to do a contract on board ship I'm "fresh meat" when I come back.

Corruption – Unfortunately Panama, like many Latin countries, has a long history of corruption. You could write a book with just the stories Panamanians tell about former presidents! The current President, Ricardo Martinelli, famously stated in his inaugural address, "In my administration it's OK to put your foot in your mouth, but not to put your hand in the till." And it would seem for the most part this anti-corruption effort is making a difference. Martinelli isn't taking any crap from anyone and his administration doesn't seem to be hesitating in going after officials from past administrations who allegedly were on the take.

Although Martinelli increased police pay in an attempt to create a more professional force that didn't have to take bribes to make ends meet, the Transito who pulled me over for passing in the wrong spot obviously hadn't gotten the message. I played "dumb" as he tried to threaten me with a ticket. I figured he'd get frustrated and go away, but he didn't. It was a friendly encounter but eventually we both got tired of the game so he took out his ticket book and wrote "$50", the price of a ticket. Then he crossed out the "$50" since this dumb *gringo* obviously wasn't getting it and wrote "$20." I said, *"Por usted?"* and he smiled, so I gave him the $20. Friends tell me I should have bargained him down to $10. Now days if the Transito is looking for cash, I give him a lecture in my halting Spanish about "0 corruption" and warm him that he is risking his job and hurting his family and tell him if he really thinks I deserve a ticket to go ahead and write it. Usually I end up with a warning and he hastens off to pull over the next guy. There is a famous YouTube video about one such encounter, but as Panama moves to first world status the cop is more likely to have pulled out his computer and entered your license plate number before he gets to the car, and at that point there is no going back.

"Customer Service" – Non-existent. Panama is for the most part a non-competitive business environment. Prices are regulated. A store is doing you a favor by allowing you inside and selling you merchandise. Employees are there to take your money and put in their eight hours.

There is no sense of valuing the customer or wanting to serve the customer or gaining a repeat customer, probably partly because there is no sense of valuing the employee. From the top down the customer is viewed as a necessary evil of doing business. Don't expect anyone to stand by their work or merchandise if there is a problem. It's one of the things North Americans have to get used to when dealing in Panama. Not pleasant, or logical, but reality.

When I come back from a ship, after spending three months in an environment where everyone is bending over backwards to provide excellent service, doing any business in Panama is like running into a brick wall. Panama over the next few years will add about 20,000 new hotel rooms including some of the finest hotel brands in the world. It will be interesting to see what happens! I can't imagine someone used to Four Seasons hospitality putting up with a surly desk clerk who is just putting in time! On a positive note I did enjoy what could be billed as the most expensive hamburger in Panama City at the Trump Ocean Club and both food and service were as impeccable as the design.

Customs - Residents, and permanent residents like *Pensionados*, can bring $2,000 worth of goods back into Panama so most expats take a big suitcase when they leave with a smaller suitcase inside. That extra suitcase is packed to the brim when returning.

Packages mailed to Panama depend pretty much on size and what custom inspectors think might be inside. If customs wants to inspect your package it is held in David (rental charge 25 cents a day) until you come down so it can be opened and you can pay any customs duty required. So if I get a proof copy of a book from my publisher it may require a 40 minute drive each way to David, standing in line at the customs window at the post office, so the package can be opened. Since there is no duty on books, all I have to do is pay the 25 cents a day or so for the time the package has been "in storage." Welcome to Panama!"

David – Is the third largest city in Panama, with about 150,000 people, and the provincial capital of Chiriqui and located right on the Pan American Highway, about 34 miles from the Costa Rican border.

David has a small airport with daily service to Panama City and Bocas del Toro and several flights a week to San Jose, Costa Rica. It's a forty minute drive from Boquete to David and David is where we go for hospitals, Price Smart, and major shopping.

Decameron – The Royal Decameron Beach Resort is the first major, all-inclusive destination resort in Panama. With 600 rooms, golf, spa, casino, and seven restaurants, it is popular with international and local tourists. Midweek rates seem attractive for locals, but it's hard to get past the horde of time-share-type hyped sales kids to even take a look to see if you might want to pay a visit. Other newer projects include the Sheraton Bijao Resort, an all-inclusive we have used on the Panama Relocation Tours.

Dentists – There are several dentists in Boquete and David, some who speak English. Dental practice here is different that Southern California in that many dentists are just generalists who know how to fill and pull teeth. It took me quite a while and about $1,200 in dental work by poor dentists, work that either fell out or needed replaced, to find a really good and qualified dentist,. A tooth extraction which would have cost $400 to $800 in Ventura County cost me $80. It was no more or less uncomfortable. Crowns and bridgework cost less than what they do in the States. An implant runs about $1,500 here. Dental insurance is virtually unknown, but at these prices, who needs it?

Developers – Buyer beware!! You could write a "Northern Exposure"-type TV show based on life in Boquete, just with the various developers as characters and the true and imagined stories about them. We have all kinds! We have some who embody Boy Scout virtues of honesty, character, integrity, etc., etc. They do their homework and do it right. But we also have others who . . . well one was hunted down and deported to face rape charges in the US. Unfortunately some folks come to Panama to try to reinvent themselves. One, supposedly, was chased out of a neighboring country and came to discover paradise. Another charged folks 80% upfront to build their retirement dream homes and unfortunately went belly up taking dreams with him. Some fancy themselves "lord of the manor" and a law unto themselves.

How do you sort through the cast of characters?

First, don't believe all the PR and hype. All the PR and hype tell you are how good a developer is at marketing, not how good he is as a developer. Take everything with a grain of salt. The promised "high speed Internet" may not exit . . . or may be years away. Half of the promised amenities may only be the developer's wet dream and may never happen, or may cost an extra fortune to use even after you've plunked down a pretty penny for a lot. If the developer ends up belly up so do your dreams. Listen, but don't jump! Rarely does property, and especially building lots, sell instantly. Unlike hot real estate markets, like the one we had when I was a REALTOR® in California, you don't need to write contracts on the hood of a car or lose a property!

Second, ask around. Do your due diligence. Talk to people who already own and live in the development. Don't just talk to the people the developer suggests . . . dah! Go ahead, knock on doors! After all, these folks might just be your neighbors. If the developer has nothing to hide he won't mind. Talk to the locals, but understand developers control jobs and have considerable clout. People aren't going to come right out and say it, but you can often read between the lines. Sometimes a local may be praising the developer, for whom a relative works, while at the same time rolling their eyes. Watch the eyes! Ask around about locals who used to work for the developer. Talk to people who used to live in a development and have moved out. What are their stories? Again, take everything with a grain of salt. There are folks who make a hobby trashing one developer or another . . . but where there's smoke, there is often fire. There is a natural tension between developers/builders and the folks who buy from them. No developer or builder is perfect or will win a popularity contest. That's the way it is: just accept it. But you're looking for the overall picture. On the whole are people speaking well of the project, the developer, or the builder, or have there been problems and unresolved issues? How does the developer relate to the people who have become his customers, his staff, and the community?

Third, shop around. There isn't one paradise. In a place like Boquete there are many developments. Some will make it: some won't. Take your time. Check them out. Don't jump at the first one. If the first one turns out to be the right one, it will still be there. And it takes time. You probably won't find your particular "paradise" in a single trip to Panama.

Fourth, look at the reality . . . not the promise! What has been accomplished? Is any part of this reality, or is it all just pretty renderings . . . and hopes . . . if the money holds out.

Diving – Panama offers the best of two oceans! Panama has two marine national parks, one in each ocean, coral reefs on both sides, and dive shops near the best areas. From Boquete you can be in the Caribbean in three hours and in the Pacific in two hours. Carlos Spragge, who's dived both oceans and has a dive shop in Boca Chica, says the Pacific diving is just "wilder" with "bigger fish."

Driver's Licenses – You can drive on your US license for 30-60 days, depending on your tourist visa. After that, if you're staying on in Panama, you're supposed to get a Panamanian license, although many expats keep on driving with their US license. As of this writing, and this being Panama policies change regularly, you need your passport, documentation from Immigration that you can remain permanently in Panama, a blood test (to be certain you know the right blood type), and a photo. Under the newest rules you have to take a driver course and driving test of sorts, but that's today, and our experience in Panama is that licensing requirements seem to change monthly. And there are frequent check points to inspect driver's licenses.

Drugs – Prescription drugs are easy to come by. Unlike the US, for most drugs you don't necessarily need a prescription to get what you want. Forget about refills, etc., just take in the box and tell them what you need. They don't compound prescriptions, but sell pills, usually by the pill. The person behind the counter isn't necessarily a licensed pharmacist as in the US.

Except for narcotics, there is little regulation or record keeping. The *Pensionado* visa does give you a discount on most drugs. Panama doesn't really have the generic/brand differentiation that you have in the US. In many cases the brand drug may not be available, so what you are getting is the Latin American version of the brand drug which may be licensed or a generic. We've found that overall we're spending a more for medicine than we planned and since we self insure it's a big hit on the budget.

Illegal drugs exist all over the world, just as in the US. There is drug use here, but I don't find the drug use or the drug culture to be as all-pervasive as it is in the US. If you go looking for it, you will find it. It is illegal, more so for foreigners, but there is not the oppressive and ineffective "law enforcement" policing or foolish "War on Drugs" hype as in the US.

Because of Panama's proximity to Colombia, and its role as the land bridge between the continents, there is a constant fight with folks who want to bring drugs bound for the US through Panama. Until the US wises up and decriminalizes drug use and controls distribution, thus removing the profit incentive, the problem will continue. It is an unpleasant reality, but most of the violence associated with drug trafficking is amongst the criminal element involved.

Panama is far more concerned with seizing and destroying the tons of cocaine in the pipeline for US distribution than they are with the occasional pot plant.

My wife happened to attend a meeting with other expats and afterward many of them ended up in the same little restaurant. Little groups were seated at different tables, but the conversation went back and forth between tables. Somehow the subject of drinking too much alcohol came up and one retired expat piped up, "I don't drink anymore", she said, "It's just not healthy. I just toke!" There was a lot of laughter and then the gal said, "Come on, you guys, fess up, how many of you smoke pot?" About 60% of the hands went up! Go figure.

Many of the retirees coming to Panama are "baby boomers" and children of Woodstock and the '60s. Unlike Bill Clinton, they did inhale . . . and some still are inhaling. However, it is illegal here too. And one *gringo*, who apparently started growing weed wholesale in his backyard, must have angered his partners or the local competition because someone broke in and killed him. Moral: play with fire and get burned. I suspect there are expats here who quietly grow their own and smoke it.

Dry Season/Wet Season – Weather in Panama depends somewhat on which side you are on. The Pacific slope has a different climate than the Caribbean slope. The Caribbean slope gets a lot more rain than the Pacific slope. Generally Panama has two seasons. On the Caribbean side they are "Wet" and "Wetter." On the Pacific side they are "Dry" and "Rainy", or as the tourist people prefer: "Dry" and "Green".

Summer, the dry season, runs roughly from December to April, and the rainy season from May to November, although Boquete has had some of the heaviest rains ever in January. Rarely does it rain all day, or for days on end. Even in the rainy season mornings in Boquete are usually crystal clear and sunny, with showers in the afternoons. The "showers" can get quite heavy; sometimes feeling like someone is dumping buckets of water from above.

In a little town like Boquete we have many microclimates. One side of town gets rain constantly, while the other side may be dry. This is a good reason to spend some time before buying property and find out what it's like before you jump.

The only really bad month – Seattle-like if you will – is October. Good time to take a vacation or be on a cruise ship in the Med.

Emergency – Panama is trying to implement a 911 system for road accident emergencies in and around Panama City, assuming your cell phone works and doesn't drop the call. But a 911 system like in the US is nonexistent.

Boquete does have a fire department. Since most structures are concrete and steel there isn't quite the same fire problem as in the US. Our forests are primarily rain forest jungles so wildfires aren't a big problem. The police department has limited resources and can't always respond to emergencies. The ambulance is mainly a vehicle for transport. There are no paramedics. Most of all you pray a lot and handle things yourself.

One of the fun things about living in Boquete is seeing people respond in various ways to needs. Realizing that there was a serious communication problem for English-speaking *gringos* in an emergency, working with the emergency services the community has come up with a unique solution. We now have an emergency number which is manned by a bilingual person totally confined in a wheelchair. He takes the calls 24 hours a day and contacts the appropriate emergency service.

When we first came to Boquete my wife had a severe allergic reaction to a drug she was taking and we had some personal experience using the ambulance. I rushed her to the doctor's office where she was stabilized and the doctor called for the fire department's "new" ambulance donated by the community with a lot of expat support. They said they'd come if I gave them some money for gas. No problem! They struggled to get her onto the gurney and she held her own IV bag until they could hook it onto the ceiling light. That didn't work, so she just held it all the way to David. Nikki's a bit taller than most Panamanians, so the rear door wouldn't close all the way, and the gurney didn't lock into position. The kid who was the attendant scrunched up his knees and pushed on the gurney all the way to David to keep it in place so Nikki didn't roll out the back door! It wasn't raining that hard, but her feet did get wet. I was riding in the front. The kid who was driving was a good driver, but Panamanians generally ignore sirens, so it was an interesting, and at times hairy, drive down the mountain to David. We did get to the hospital in one piece and they efficiently and accurately diagnosed the problem, treated her, and kept her overnight. And I did give the ambulance driver $30 "for gas". But it worked. It's not the States by any means, but it works . . . at least going down hill. It's funny now, but it wasn't at the time.

Fishing – There are still trout in the streams high above Boquete but once you get below the coffee *fincas* leaching from the hulls of the coffee fruit does something to the oxygen in the water that has destroyed the trout. Many coffee *beneficios* are trying ways to deal with the problem and there is hope that eventually the rivers can be restocked. But with two oceans to choose from, Panama is home to some of the world's greatest sport fishing. Marlin, sailfish, dorado, tuna, wahoo and a myriad of other game fish roam the continental shelf and islands on the Pacific side making this a fisherman's paradise.

For Fun – For me, walking. Gardening: during the rainy season just stick it in and it grows! Driving two hours to the Pacific to pick up shells and sand dollars, swim, kayak, dream of our beach-house getaway. Unfortunately the latest developer to try and build a project on this beach has now blocked off access. There have been three or four previous development attempts and all have failed, so who knows. Our favorite thing used to be to hop in our 4-wheel drive SUV and explore Panama! We'd head down "roads" we would never have thought of as other than cow paths, just to see where we end up. Now with all our projects . . . gee, it hurts to say this, but we're too busy to explore every back road.

For The Birds – We're not bird-watcher types, but some of our friends are and the birds in Panama are amazing! Every time we drive to Boca Chica we hear, then see, flocks of green parrots. In our yard we've counted different kinds of birds, including at least five species of humming birds. We joke about putting up a sign in our car port, Watch For Low Flying Hummingbirds". We haven't gotten impaled – yet. Put out an overripe banana and you are guaranteed 15 different species of red, yellow, green and blue-colored birds within half an hour.

Frustrations – The most frustrating adjustment for me has been very unexpected!

I thought I could deal with laid back, heck, it's one of the reasons I came here. But there is a fundamental different understanding of the meaning and value of time. *Gringos* come here with a US understanding of the value of time – "Time is money! Steal my time and you steal from me!" In my case this is overlaid with a Calvinist/Protestant work ethic which means seizing every moment because each moment is a gift from God to be used and invested. At 24 Hour Fitness I worked for a boss who was a time fanatic! If a meeting was to start at 10 am it was to start at 10 am not 10:05 am. Now I come to a country where the dominant attitude is "*Mañana!*" The accepted excuse for everything is, "This is Panama!" (Implied, "And what did you expect?") And, amazingly, that's OK!

Originally it took four months for me to get Internet service that was supposed to have been there all along. [Now Internet is readily available, even cable Internet in some areas of Boquete.] Bookcases I'd ordered three months before I arrived, so that they would be ready when I got here, took five months after I got here. Everything takes much longer. Some folks say: "Rant and rave if you want to get anywhere!" Unfortunately, as in Asia, ranting and raving just causes you to lose "face" and doesn't get anywhere, which has been tough for me to learn. Others say, "Be friendly! Try friendship and sugar." Others, "Just wait." Probably the best advice I've received was one word: "Surrender! You can't control it, so surrender. Don't get all worked up. In a year it will be done, and you'll look back and will have forgotten the hassle."

If you go to a Panamanian party announced for, say, 7 pm, expect to find your hosts in the shower. 7 pm Panamanian time is not the same as 7 pm *gringo* time. So you learn to ask, "Is this Panamanian time or *gringo* time?" If someone is gong to stop by at 11 am, they most certainly won't be there at 11 am, but you don't know if it will be 12 noon, 3 pm or not at all – and it's not rude, or inconsiderate, or a snub or anything else: it's just the way it is.

I remember rushing around in the States, working sixty to seventy hours a week and still, at the end of the day, after taxes, not having a lot to show for it but indigestion. That was my understanding of the value of time. Then in Panama I see a guy by the side of the road in a little hut selling coconuts. He's sitting in a hammock all day watching the cars go by. All he probably needs is to sell a few coconuts each day. He's happy. He's satisfied. And who's to say the guy in the hammock selling coconuts is wrong? It took me sixty years of hard work to get to Panama and sit in my hammock!

The other BIG frustration revolves around a different cultural concept of truth and honesty and the value of someone's promise and "word." North Americans are by nature more trusting people than folks in many parts of the world, including Latin America. We have been far too trusting and it has cost us money . . . lots of it! . . . and hurt feelings all around. Unfortunately we've had to learn not to trust people, which, although it goes against my grain, is a cultural reality.

Furniture – You can get most anything if you know where to look. Ask enough people, look long enough, and if you are willing to pay the price you can find it or have it made.

We bought vinyl, all-weather, imitation wicker furniture for our patio at Home Depot before we left the States and had it shipped down in our container. The complete set cost us around $1,200. I've seen the identical furniture in several stores in Panama for three times the price. Yet I probably could have gotten real wicker furniture in certain areas in Panama City for just a little more than what I paid for the imitation.

I designed an armoire for our TV that was hand-made locally out of a very hard, durable *cedro* with louvered doors that would have cost $2,900 in Santa Barbara: it cost me $800. We had beautiful custom-made bookshelves made for our living room and bedroom incorporating some old, hand-carved Mexican drawers fronts salvaged from furniture I bought when I graduated. It took five months longer than scheduled to complete, but they are gorgeous and match the rest of the woodwork in our home.

I designed wrought iron chairs, a coffee table and chandeliers that a local iron artisan made for me. The chairs were $75 each, the coffee table $110, the chandeliers $130 and they are beautiful!

Garden – Wow! You just stick it in the ground and it grows! Really! It's amazing! I have a tree covered with orchids I've collected or bought, most of them wild varieties of local orchids. Panama actually has 1,000 varieties of orchids! There are thousands of "Angel's Trumpet" trees in Boquete and when they bloom with their drooping ten-inch trumpet-like flowers in pink, yellow and white the roads are spectacular. The fragrant smell is supposedly an aphrodisiac. The "Angel's Trumpet" like many garden favorites is supposedly poisonous, but if you carefully break off a branch and stick it in the ground – voila! you have another tree! Stick the trimmings of hibiscus bushes into the ground, water them, watch the leaves die off until you have dead-looking twigs, and in a couple weeks they spring to life! It's really quite incredible. Unfortunately weeds also flourish. A gardener costs $1 to $1.25 (*gringo* inflation) an hour, but full-time gardeners are easier to find than someone who only works a few hours a week.

For gardening inspiration in Boquete there is *"Mi Jardín Es Su Jardín"*, a sprawling, magnificent and at times funky gardens of a private home. The gardens are open to the public for free during daylight hours. It's just outside town, up the road from Cafe Ruiz, a delightful spot for a cup of coffee.

Getting to Boquete –Panama Arrival: International flights arrive at Tocumen, north east of Panama City. Taxis to the city or the national airport run around $30, plus tolls, or whatever more that that you are willing to pay.

By Air: National flights leave from Gelabert Airport or Albrook in the old Canal Zone. A taxi from Tocumen to Albrook runs about $35. Because of the flight schedules from the US you usually need to spend a night in Panama City. There are lots of good hotels with rooms for around $85 and up. There are some cute B&Bs that will run you $50-85.

Air Panama has three flights a day between Panama City and David. You can rent a car a David airport from a half dozen car rental companies or take a cab to Boquete for about $35. There are a few local car rental places in Boquete where you can rent a car for a day or two.

By Car: You can also rent a car at Tocumen and drive to Boquete via David, about seven hours. Driving is a nice way to see the country, the roads are good, and during the daytime it is an interesting drive. The toughest part will be getting out of Panama City. I usually leave at 5:30 am to avoid "rush hour". You may find it helpful to hire a taxi just to lead the way through Panama City.

By Bus: There is also express bus service to David from the Panama City bus terminal, which is near Albrook Airport, and it takes about seven hours, costs $15. The school bus from David to Boquete costs $2 and runs hourly.

We're still waiting for someone to start flying from David to the US direct.

Golden Altar – One of the best stories I know of is about the Golden Altar of St. Joseph Church in the Casco Viejo area of Panama City. The origins of the altar go back to colonial times in the original city of Panama, the ruins of which can still be seen in the "Old City." The city of Portobelo near Colon was a major transshipment point for Central American gold to Spain. In June 1668 the English pirate Henry Morgan sailed into Portobelo with nine ships and took the city by surprise, robbing, plundering, killing and burning everything in sight. News spread across the Isthmus to Panama City, and the word spread, "Morgan is coming!" And Morgan was indeed hacking his way through the jungle across the Isthmus.

The main altar in Panama City was made of solid gold. Not gold leaf, solid gold. A layman, Brother John, hatched a plan to preserve the altar of gold. The main parts of the altar were disassembled, and the golden columns and altar tables were taken out into the Bay and submerged. The rest of the altar could not be moved so Brother John painted it with white wash, hoping to hide the great treasure beneath.

As Morgan entered Panama City plundering, pillaging and burning, the inhabitants fled into the jungle, but Brother John remained behind, determined to protect the church. When Morgan arrived at the church Brother John received him courteously and gave him everything he demanded. When they entered the church, John reputedly said, "Sir, now we are in the presence of a great work, but you can see that we are a poor and humble church and that we've already fallen behind in finishing the altar. I have given you whatever you asked, and now you are obliged to give me a favor, is this not right?" Impressed, Morgan asked what Brother John wished. "That you give me alms of a thousand ducats to finish the wood of the altar."

Morgan laughed, handed over the money and exclaimed, "This brother is more of a pirate than I am!" The pirate never realized that the white washed "plaster" altar was actually solid gold!

And the altar was spared, and moved to the new city which is today Casco Viejo and where you can see the golden altar.

Happiness – I think we are happier than we've been in a long time. Relaxed. Not pressured. At ease. Able to enjoy life. We love Panama, as if you hadn't already guessed. Is it perfect? Not by a long-shot, but it suits us. People are friendly, patient, and good natured. At peace. For a long time it really bothered me that the church had rejected me. Now, I don't care. Life is good!

Health – Our health has improved dramatically since moving to Panama. The best thing my wife did for her health was to leave the Health Department! Both of our blood pressures have dropped considerably, just getting rid of the stress. We've both lost twenty pounds without any diet regimen. We walk daily. We breathe crystal clean air. The water is pure and tastes good. The food is farm fresh every morning, largely pesticide-free, and the meat is free of hormones and additives. Our medical care has been adequate.

Holidays – There are 21 paid public holidays! Workers also get 18 sick days and 30 days of vacation!

Nothing happens on holidays, or around holidays. Holy week, or *"Santo Semana"*, is a week when nothing happens, as is the week between Christmas and New Year's. Nothing happens around Carnival and in Boquete the week of the *"Feria"* is another week when it's tough to get anything done.

With all these holidays it's a wonder anything gets done!

The good news: fireworks seem an essential part of any celebration especially at Christmas. Christmas Eve at midnight the sky explodes in Panama!.

Horses – Horses are a big part of life in Panama, especially in Chiriqui! In Boquete there is even a development that centers around an equestrian center. In Volcan there are beautiful horse farms that are visited by wealthy sheiks looking for prize horses. For many rural Panamanians horses are still the primary means of transport. As you drive along the roads you will often pass folks on horseback and see horses tied up besides the road grazing.

Boarding a horse costs around $250 a month. My horsey-set friends tell me that a good Western horse runs around $700. Peruvians, which are bred in Chiriqui, they tell me start at around $2,500. There are places where you can rent horses for $5 to $10 an hour.

Hospitals – Chiriqui Hospital and Mae Lewis are two private hospitals located in David, forty minutes drive from where we live in Boquete and are the preferred hospital for expats. Major procedures are usually done in Panama City at Punta Pacifica, a hospital in affiliated with John's Hopkins or Paitilla Medical Center in Panama City Additionally there is a large Maternal & Child Health hospital run by the national health service and a Social Security Hospital for Panamanians who are part of the national Social Security program which is supposed to service all Panamanians who work and a part of the Social Security program.

Humidity – When we were in the cruise business and clients inquired about Canal cruises during the summer, I'd tell them that the ships didn't do Canal cruises in the summer because it was "too hot and humid." At the time it didn't dawn on me that nine degrees from the equator it was always hot and humid. Fact was that the cruise ships didn't do the Canal in the summer because they made a whole lot more money in Alaska and Europe!

There are areas of Panama that are usually hot and humid. But there are areas like Boquete where the temperature is usually cool. Particularly in the rainy season you will need a sweater and blankets at night. And the higher you go, the cooler it gets. It is sometimes humid in Boquete, and during the rainy season you'll probably need a dehumidifier, but it is not the oppressive hot humidity you find in lower altitudes along the coast.

Hurricanes – Having seen first hand the devastation a hurricane can do in the Caribbean, an important factor in my choice of Panama as a place to live was that it is outside the hurricane belt. The Caribbean side, particularly Bocas del Toro, can feel the effects of tropical depressions, mostly in terms of heavy rain and flooding, but no full force hurricane winds.

Insurance – Car insurance is about the same as in the US and even although required not all Panamanians have insurance, so it's imperative that your protect yourself with adequate insurance. And if you are in an accident getting paid for repairs is time consuming and complex and designed with the hope that you will just give up and forget it. Homeowner insurance is similar to the US. Our standard homeowner's policy, including earthquake insurance is just a little less than what we paid in California without earthquake insurance..

John Wayne – Yes, Panama's the kind of place that would appeal to "The Duke". Wayne came to Panama in the late '70s on the recommendation of President Jimmy Carter. Wayne became friends with then strong-man General Omar Torrijos and informally helped the two leaders reach agreement on the turnover of the Canal. In gratitude, Torrijos gave Wayne the little island of Taborcillo, now touted as "John Wayne's Island."

Jungle – Yes, it really is a jungle out there! You name it, we got it. Panama has one of the richest varieties of ecosystems on the planet! Tropical rainforests, cloud forests, savannah, mangrove swamps, and coral reefs – this is one fantastic country, and it's all within a few hours drive!

Kids – People always ask me, "Well, what do your kids think?" The answer is simple: they see Panama as a low-cost resort destination!

Increasingly we are seeing young families with kids relocating to Panama from the US and Canada, many times because of their kids. Some are home schooling, but many are putting their kids into private or public Panamanian schools. Some of our long-time *gringo* friends, whose children grew up here in Panamanian schools, have had their kids go on to top US universities, sometimes benefiting from scholarship opportunities because they brought with them a cross-cultural perspective that the university valued.

Kilometers & Other Metrics – It's intimidating, particularly at first, but after a while you start thinking in kilometers, hectares, square meters, and centigrade. You come up with a few basic conversions to help you get a handle on the new metric measurements and after a while start thinking metric. Interestingly in building both systems are used. The plans will be in metric, but the workers will be measuring in feet and inches as well as meters. Gasoline is served up in gallons. Panama is supposed to shift to all metric . . . but of course so was the US.

Land – When we left California my son-in-law gave me a Tee shirt with the Will Rogers quote, "Buy land they aren't making any more of it." I hope Will was right! Land in Panama is priced by the square meter, which is about ten square feet. The larger the parcel, generally the cheaper the cost per square meter.

Until the recent world-wide economic downturn, real estate in Boquete has been going up at something like 15% a year as more and more expats want "their piece of the rock."

This kind of escalation in price can have serious social consequences as locals, after celebrating the price their land is bringing, realize that their children and grandchildren are being priced out of their home town. Asking price for land on Central Street is as high as $300 a square meter, but you can still find land up in the mountains overlooking Boquete for $10- 20 a square meter. Go east to the little town of Caldera and you can still find land for under $5 a square meter. Caldera is much hotter, but, who knows, if you like Palm Springs, you may enjoy Caldera.

Lawyers – For a non-litigious society there are tons of lawyers in Panama, almost as many lawyers as people selling real estate! The S.A. or *Sociedad Anónima* corporation makes it difficult to sue. There are not a lot of personal injury or medical malpractice suits, which is one reason why the cost of health care is so low. Yet there is tons of paperwork and loads of regulations, so lawyers are essential. Your lawyer generally handles the S.A. corporation through which you own property, handles visas and immigration, and offers essential advice if you even think of hiring anyone or going into business. Finding a good lawyer who follows up and does what he says in a reasonable time frame is one of the biggest challenges in Panama.

Panama as yet does not have a "Bar Exam" so you can have lawyers who have gone to school and end up being lawyers without really "knowing" the law. The best way to find a lawyer is to talk to a lot of people and get their recommendations.

Liquor – Panama grows lots of sugar and produces lots of local rum and something called "*seco*". Seco Herrerano is triple distilled from sugarcane, sold at seventy proof and used straight or in mixed drinks as a replacement for rum or vodka. Since I suspect *seco* could also be used as jet fuel, I stick with Panamanian rum at about $8 a bottle, some of it made in David.

Other liquors are imported and prices are similar to what you'd pay in a US liquor store. Generally the drinking age is supposed to be eighteen, but at least with beer it doesn't seem to be rigidly enforced (by whom?) and therefore doesn't seem to be much of a problem. Panama has four local beers, Panama, Atlas, Balboa and Soberana, which run about 85 cents a can. Corona, Heineken, Miller, Budweiser and others are all available at higher prices.

My favorite spiced rum used to be "Panama Jack" Island Spiced Rum, as good as Captain Morgan at a fraction of the price. $8 at Romero's in town. When "Panama Jack" disappeared, I was forced to invent my own. And it is easy to make . . . and good.

Here's my recipe for spiced rum, saving you more than the cost of this book:

1 liter golden rum or dark rum
1 vanilla bean cut up or ½ teaspoon vanilla
3 cinnamon sticks (3")
4 whole allspice or a pinch of ground
1 whole nutmeg crushed
3 star anise
pinch anise seed

Let sit one week more or less, depending on strength of flavor desired. You can experiment and get exactly what you like.

Mail – There are various mail service which allow you to have a Miami post office box and then forward your mail to Panama where you pick it up at a local merchant. The catch is you pay by weight and volume, so it can get very expensive – like $50 a month expensive. We dutifully cancelled catalogs and opted out of every list we knew we were on. We begged alumni associations to let us ride off peacefully into the sunset. And although we told the US Post Office only to forward first class mail, we forgot that they cooperatively inform all the junk mailers of your new address, so all the junk followed us to Panama, at great expense. It took us several years to get a mail box at the post office: someone had to die so we could get their box.

Actually we have had very good luck, as far as we know, with mail both to and from Panama. Nikki's alumni association and AARP send us their magazines, and I get my California ballot (since it was the last place I lived in the States), and it doesn't cost much more to send a letter to the States from Panama than it does within the States.

If you go to the post office in the US and ask what it costs to send something to Panama it will cost more, than just sticking a regular stamp on it and mailing it. Go figure! Maybe the same folks at the US post office, who think "New Mexico" is a foreign country, think that Panama is one of the US States. Who knows? Figure out the US Postal Service and you'll have a pretty good shot at figuring out the meaning of life. Most expats have a couple of rolls of US stamps and when one of us is going to the US they take along everyone's really important letters and mail them when they get to the States.

The biggest mail challenge in a humid environment is finding envelopes that aren't already sealed shut! You'd think the self seal envelopes would be easy to find: not so, pilgrim!

"*Mañana*" – My high school Spanish really failed me on this one! I learned that "*mañana*" meant "tomorrow." In fact that's the meaning you'll find in most English-Spanish dictionaries, BUT it's not what the word means in Panama! It took me a lot of frustration to come to the realization that in Panama "*mañana*" really means "Not today." It's important that you understand that the implied additional meaning is "Not today, some unspecified time in the future." We kept thinking "*mañana*" meant the day after today and couldn't understand why things promised "*mañana*" kept dragging on for weeks or months.

Massage – Boquete is a tourist destination for Panamanians on weekends and holidays, as well as backpackers and increasingly people from abroad thinking of moving to Panama. There are a growing number of spas in Boquete offering a wide variety of spa treatments. Massage runs about $60 an hour, about the same as the States, but far less than on cruise ships. Most of the spas have midweek rates for locals that run about $35 an hour. Of course on the ship it runs about $125 an hour plus tip.

Mold – Mold was a surprise! It shouldn't have been when you combine 80-90% humidity in the rainy season with warmer temperatures. We were caught unawares when I started sneezing like crazy and mold started appearing on book covers and clothing. The secret to combat mold is dehumidifiers, and lots and lots of air circulation (ceiling fans, free-standing fans, all windows open). You may want to consider air conditioning, not so much in Boquete for cooling the air as for dehumidifying the entire house.

Our new house is very open and has a high ceiling and an exhaust fan so we're able to keep the air moving. Traditional Panamanian houses don't have glass windows, so with the air circulating have fewer problems with mold. *Gringo* houses are built like *gringo* houses, all sealed up with no fresh air constantly circulating, so *gringos* have mold problems. In the rainiest times of the year mold is a challenge.

Mosquitoes – Actually we had more mosquito bites in Ventura, where there really weren't that many mosquitoes - not if you'd ever spent a summer in Wisconsin! Although Ventura did have West Nile virus, so mosquitoes were always a concern. Although Boquete is wet, there are lots of breezes and rarely, unless I'm weeding and messing around in the bushes, do I even see mosquitoes. Even by the beach, as long as there is a breeze the mosquitoes aren't a problem. The issue with mosquitoes is dengue fever so everyone works hard to keep the town clear of old tires and places mosquitoes can breed.

With a ceiling fan above running above the bed I never have problem with mosquitoes at night, even with no screens.

Moving – We got rid of tons of stuff before we moved. We had tons of stuff that belonged to the kids, everything from second grade papers to sorority keepsakes. We said to the kids, "It's your stuff and it's not going to Panama. Keep it or take it to Goodwill", and they did. But we had a lot of things that we'd accumulated over the years, things we just wanted to keep. So we shipped a forty foot container to Panama. We know folks who got rid of everything, and bought all new stuff in Panama. For us there were some things, like my wife's grand piano, that are difficult to come by in Panama.

We looked at a number of companies that specialized in overseas moves. We chose Marlog Cargo because we liked the people and because their rate was lower. Unfortunately at the last minute they added a number of extra charges that raised their rate to about what everyone else was quoting in the first place. They added a special extra charge because the "grand piano required special handling" by their local associates, Panama Storage and Packing. Fair enough, except when the container arrived in Boquete it arrived with four teenagers and two, spindly hand trucks – no "special handling" for the piano. Apparently everyone assumed a "baby grand" meant that it was a was a little, "baby" piano! Fortunately I was able to get the construction guys at Valle Escondido to jerry-rig a backhoe as a fork lift and help me get the piano out of the container and into the house! Despite repeated efforts I was unable to get Marlog Cargo to refund extra "piano handling charge" or cover my cost for the backhoe.

Nightlife – Panama City has loads of nightlife. Boquete, well . . . actually it's better than you'd imagine. There are bars and clubs appealing to Indians, Panamanians and expats. For a tiny community we have Mexican, French, Japanese, Italian, Chinese and American restaurants in addition to local Panamanian restaurants. But restaurants in Boquete come and go with breakneck speed. I leave on a cruise contract with one set of restaurants and come back in four months to a whole new set. Downtown is open weekend nights and very busy as all the Indians and Panamanians come to town to shop, play pool, and just wander around and see and be seen.

Old Panama – The ruins of the original city of Panama lie outside the current city and are visible driving in from the airport along Corredor Sur. The original city was plundered and burned by pirate Sir Henry Morgan in 1671 leaving the city in the ruined state you see today. Knowing Morgan was coming, the priests white-washed their solid gold altar praying that Morgan would think it was concrete. Although the church was burned, Morgan missed the gold!

Old Panama is a UNESCO World Heritage site and the restored tower from the original city has become the symbol of Panama City.

Orchids – Panama has 1,000 species of wild orchids in an amazing variety of colors and sizes. Wild orchids are fairly common in Chiriqui. Some orchids are large and showy and others are smaller than the fingernail on your little finger. Orchids aren't all by nature conspicuous, and you may have to search for them, but they are there if you look

You can buy them from road venders in bloom from $1 to $10 and stick them on tree trunks in your yard. Be cautious, however, since some varieties are endangered from over harvesting and others are protected.

Orchids tend to bloom in the dry season. Apparently the lack of water stresses the plant and the result of stress is a beautiful bloom. Something to remember in life! If I were still preaching I'd definitely work that into a sermon illustration.

There is an annual Orchid Fair in Boquete and on the other side of the volcano above Cerro Punta is the Dracula Orchid Farm, named after Panama's night-blooming orchid.

Panama City – Panama is not an island, but when you live in a primarily rural agricultural area like Chiriqui, you occasionally need a dose of big city life, and Panama City is it! By air it's an hour. By car it's a six hour drive each way on pretty good road with often beautiful scenery. You can get a great hotel room with a spectacular city view for about $100 or a cute bed and breakfast on Ancon Hill where the monkeys play outside your window for about $50. You get your fill of entertainment, casinos, shopping, and American standards like Hard Rock Cafe, giant malls, etc. The food courts in the huge malls are just like any mall in the US, so if you need a "fix" of US-style "civilization" I guess this can be it. There are traffic jams to be enjoyed, pollution, and even areas of the city to avoid – all the "comforts" of home that you left behind!

Panama Relocation Tour – There are a lot of real estate tours to Panama, some even free, where you are basically a captive audience to various developers who sponsor or co-sponsor these tours.

Jackie Lange is a friend I met through my blog, who purchased this book, and ended up retiring to Boquete! She is well-known for the seminars, training, and Web support she has provided to thousands of people in the US who have made lots of money following her advice buying and selling real estate properties. When she announced she was moving to Panama, suddenly she had scores of people who wanted her to show them Panama. Hence the Panama Relocation Tour. Basically the tour is a chance to get an overview of Panama, to visit some of the places North American expats have moved to including Panama City, the beaches, the mountains and, of course, Boquete. It is a chance to get an overview without anyone selling anything. The tour is designed so that participants have the opportunity to meet expats who are living here and ask questions, and find out about things like visas, setting up bank accounts and how real estate actually works in Panama.

Everyone participating in the Panama Relocation Tour gets a copy of this book and it is required reading. And whenever I am not on the ship and able, I join the tour.

If you are interested in the Panama Relocation Tour, and you should be if you are thinking about moving or retiring to Panama, check for links and details on my blog at www.RichardDetrich.com.

The Panamonte – The Panamonte Inn & Spa is one of the most charming places in Boquete. Opened in 1914 and operated by the same family throughout its history, the Panamonte offers around twenty cozy rooms, a spa, a wonderful traditional European dining room, and the most comfortable bar in town with two roaring fireplaces. Yes, at night in Boquete, especially during the rainy season, a roaring fireplace can feel wonderful!

Parrots – Parrots and big green parakeets are fairly common and most are green. They are noisy and travel in packs. They live mostly in lowland forests, feed on fruits and nuts and nest in tree hollows, although occasionally we see flocks in Boquete. You generally hear them first, and then see them. Although illegal, kids frequently raid the nests and you will see them selling individual birds along the Pan American highway. The colorful macaws have become rare, largely due to the practice of illegally capturing and selling the birds.

Pests – OK, no place is perfect. I've mentioned the coffee flies. Mosquitoes aren't a problem, but we're surrounded by tropical mountain forest teeming with insects and "interesting" creepy crawlies.

Like most places in the tropics, we have cockroaches that sometimes make their way inside. Normally the roaches live happily in the jungle under the leaves on the jungle floor. But when the heavy rains start they head indoors to get dry. And we have a cornucopia of spiders – one that's the size of your passport! – and scorpions. Most of our scorpions aren't the deadly poison type like the South West US, but, mindful of the neighbor in Valle Escondido who didn't shake out his pants before pulling them on and got stung in a most uncomfortable spot, I always shake first! You shake out your shoes and your clothes and the golf course manager gave me a spray for inside the house, made from chrysanthemums, that is lethal to insects but not to people or pets. We have an exterminator spray about every six weeks, just like in the States, and it's not much of a problem. We also encourage our "house geckos" who, in addition to being fun to watch, consume a lot of little bugs and spiders.

Yes, Panama has lots of snakes, something like 127 varieties, but only twenty are poisonous. Unfortunately a few are very poisonous. Generally snakes wisely avoid people. For the most part we don't see many snakes, even although we live on a farm. My workers did kill a seven-foot fer de lance, and we've seen some little ones, but . . . just like in a big city, you watch where you walk. And since I have three dogs, it really does pay to watch where you step! Most places in Panama, except deep in the jungle, you're within forty minutes of a state-run hospital that has antivenin. We found a small boa once in Boca Chica all curled up in a cinder block. I'd love to see a giant boa hanging from a tree, but you'd have to really go looking, in the right places, and be lucky to see one. My Embera friends, who live deep in the jungle, tell me, yes, you could find snakes if you went up on the mountain and went looking. There are snakes, you need to be aware, but you're not likely to be bothered. The mountains just behind my home in Ventura were home to loads of rattlesnakes and even mountain lions. Did I ever see any? No, But I was aware that they were there, and cautious when I was in their territory.

Norman W. Elton, M.D., Chief of Board of Health Laboratory, Gorgas Hospital for the Canal Zone back in the '40s wrote, "If one does not fear lightning one need have no fear of poisonous snakes, for it has repeatedly been demonstrated statistically that one's chances of dying from snakebite are not greater than those of being struck by a bolt of lightning. Furthermore, the mortality among people actually bitten by poisonous snakes in Central America . . . is less than 10 percent." With all the development since the '40s, one could argue that there are a whole lot fewer snakes in Panama.

Pets – Yes, you can bring in pets, but generally pets are subject to quarantine. With some animals a home quarantine can be arranged. There are different climate conditions and diseases and vets are not generally as available in the US, so sometimes it's better just to find a good home in the US for your pets, and adopt new animals in Panama, although people do bring in cats and dogs all the time.

We were never "dog people" until we retired to Panama. All our dogs are local, supposedly pure although without papers. And in answer to your question: two Dalmatians, a Rottweiler, and a "pure Palmira" street dog who looks just like 90% of the dogs in Palmira. We had an Indian worker who left to go back to the *comarca* and left his dog, Bobbie behind. Bobbie shows up faithfully at meal time.

We also we have four cats. These were feral kittens that my wife captured and took to the Spay Neuter Clinic. We kept them inside while they healed and then thought we'd never see them again. Now they and Bobbie sleep on the porch at my brother's house at the entrance to our farm.

When we first came to Panama Chiriqui vets traditionally had more experience with large animals (cows and horses) than small animals. There was one vet cat and dog owners even called "Dr. Death."

We have found a vet in Boquete who is wonderful with small animals and has helped us through several emergencies. She, along with a "snow bird" neighbor of ours, a Vet from Colorado have been instrumental in starting Boquete's spay/neuter clinics. At every spay neuter clinic they do 70-120 animals. At first it was 80% *gringo* pets, but now it's about 90% Panamanian pets and the Clinic is usually staffed by local vets and volunteers. The Spay Neuter Clinic has resulted in a noticeable reduction in malnourished street dogs. Animales, the organization that sponsors the Spay Neuter Clinic, is also a great place to adopt a pet.

Phone Home – The only problem we've encountered is the two to three hour time difference between Panama and the West coast, where our kids live. Actually it costs us a little less to call our daughter in San Francisco from Panama than it did calling her from Ventura, California. Calls to my daughter in Seattle are about the same as they were from California. But then we usually use Skype and talk for free!

Planning – Pretty much give up the idea! In Panama plans change constantly, if in fact there were plans in the first place. Yes, with building and construction, there is a plan and you'd better try to get people to follow it. But try and plan your day or your week – forget it. You'll be planning to go to town, or drive to David, and the workmen who you've been trying to corral for months will show up unexpectedly, tools in hand. Car repairs that might be expected to take a few days in the States can drag on for weeks. If you come to Panama used to maximizing your day with your Blackberry or phone in hand, give it up! You need to be flexible, to go with the flow, to expect the unexpected and not let it bother you. The upside is that this also makes for serendipitous adventures.

When we drive 40 minutes to David with a list of three or four things to get done, if we manage to get 50% accomplished we're ecstatic! Offices that are supposed to be open are closed, stuff that's been on order and was promised three weeks ago still will not have arrived, and half the things you needed at Price Smart won't be there. "Welcome to Panama!"

Promises – I am sometimes amazed that anything gets done in Panama! Really! Yet the country is booming. Towers, projects, new roads, and an expanded Canal attest to the fact that stuff does get done – eventually. Much of this is a cultural difference. It's like the hare and the tortoise. I doubt that Panamanians use many flow charts or PERT charts. "Just In Time" here can be assumed to mean when the client is holding a gun to your head. But it does eventually get done, and I guess that's the point. At times the slowness will drive your nuts, and it's not always steady, but it does get done. And to a Panamanian that's the point.

A cultural difference enters in as well. Panamanians are so polite they will tell you what you want to hear, as a matter of politeness. A builder friend told me, "If you ask, 'Can you get this roof on in one day?', and you know that even with no rain it is humanly impossible, as a matter of politeness the crew will say, 'Of course!', even when they too know it is humanly impossible."

The more I as a *gringo* extract promises – "OK, you'll have this done next Saturday, right?" – the more I exacerbate the problem . . . for me. It's not a matter of being impolite or rude or incompetent because they do not perform. In fact they were polite in telling me what I wanted to hear. It's a tough adjustment for a *gringo* MBA who has always wanted everything "Now!"

Quetzals – The Resplendent Quetzal is Central America's most famous bird, found high in the mountains of Costa Rica and Panama. Although rare, they are frequently seen high in the mountains around Boquete and Cerro Punta, near Volcan. The red, green and white birds are 14-15 inches high, but the male has brilliant green tail plumes that add another 15-30 inches. My wife Nikki has seen three. I've only seen one female, but it was right here in Palmira. This year we actually had a pair nesting on our coffee farm.

"Quetzal Trail" – The "Quetzal Trail" runs through Volcan Baru National Park between Cerro Punta, above Volcan on the West side of Volcan Baru, to Boquete, on the East side of the park. The trail is easier coming from Cerro Punta to Boquete, although it is still up and down all the way. The trail is fairly well-maintained, although bridges are frequently out and you will get wet. A $3 fee is charged to visitors ($1 to locals).

The trail is variously described from "easy" to "strenuous". My assessment is that if you are in good physical condition the trail is a good work out, but not overly difficult. For me, in rather dumpy physical condition, it was pushing the limit. The trail is 7.5 miles, but that is from trail head to trail head. If you're hiking from Cerro Punta to the town of Boquete, you can add another 7.5 miles. And you're not going to find taxis at the Boquete trail head! It is a spectacular hike through various kinds of forests! It took us 6.5 hours, with stops along the way for picnic lunch.

[Update: Unfortunately due to the death of a hiker on the trail the Quetzal Trail is now closed, The plan is to eventually upgrade the trail and reopen it.]

River Rafting – Chiriqui is one of the top areas for river rafting and there are several rafting outfits in Boquete. Trips run around eight hours, including transportation to the river. Many of the same rivers provide world-class white-water kayaking as well.
Chiriqui River Rafting is owned by our friend and neighbor in Palmira, Hector Sanchez. Hector has been doing this longer than anyone else in Panama and is committed not only to enjoying but also preserving the rivers of Chiriqui. We were impressed by the commitment to safety and the experienced and friendly guides. Unfortunately in Panama there is a trend to turn more and more rivers into hydroelectric resources which is destroying some of the great stretches for river rafting.

Safety – There are many areas of Latin America where you are not safe driving around in your car, particularly after dark and on remote rural roads. For the most part Panama is not one of them. The Darien area near the Colombian border is very dangerous but there are no roads, just impenetrable jungle. Much of Colon and in certain areas of Panama City you need to use caution and common sense. As anywhere in the world, if you're in a hotel, ask if the area is safe or for suggestions of safe places to walk or jog. Aside from minor opportunistic theft, in most of the rest of Panama you're fine. You wouldn't leave luggage and valuables in your car at home, so common sense says not to do it in Panama.

Boquete is far safer than Ventura County, which has some of the safest cities in which to live in the whole US! You are perfectly safe walking at night in town in Boquete. You never feel threatened. '50s-like values still prevail. People are courteous, friendly, and respectful. There are some cultural differences, but you won't encounter gangs of unruly and disrespectful kids. It's very refreshing! And of course you'll see very few cops.

Violent crime unfortunately has increased in Panama, mostly amongst people involved in the drug trade. Panama is a convenient destination for drugs as well as drug people meeting together and coming from Mexico and Colombia. The government is trying hard to crack down and receives US financial help, but until the US gets serious about the genesis of the problem, decriminalizes drug use and removes the profit incentive, the problem will continue. Rarely is this a problem in Boquete. Despite the "War on Drugs" more people use illegal drugs than ever before and as the US should know from history, prohibition does not work.

Clinton and Bush foolishly denied their own drug experimentation, while Obama admits that in his youth, like unfortunately many young people, he did use drugs. Yet Obama doesn't want to take the much needed step to end the drug prohibition, legalize drugs, and tax the hell out of them.

Unfortunately as Boquete has established a reputation for being home to a lot of "rich *gringos*" robbery in some areas has become a problem. We're only a $12 bus ride from Panama City, so if you're looking for spoils . . . and a weekend away from the big city . . . and if you are robbed, well, like I said, few cops. .Like anywhere in the US there are occasional home thefts, mostly folks looking for laptops, cell phones, and easy to dispose of electronics.

Some of the most problematic criminals have been a few unsavory expats who've come to Panama on the lam from the law in the US and preyed on other expats. We've had "Ozzie" who set himself up as the local computer expert for *gringos* and then proceeded to rob them blind, or "Wild Bill" who would become friends with other *gringos* and then kill them for their rights of possession land. And there has been the usual assortment of expats who want to run Ponzi schemes promising unrealistic returns.

Schools – I frequently receive emails from families anxious to escape the US and Canada who are asking about schools for their children. Local Panamanian schools do a heroic job despite a notorious lack of funds. There are a number of parochial and private schools in the Boquete/David area. A new Boquete International Academy has just opened. They opened with grades one through four have been adding a grade a year. It is a completely bilingual school with the object that "Kids whose native tongue is Spanish learn excellent Spanish and good English. Kids whose native tongue is English learn excellent English and good Spanish." Unlike most Panamanian schools, it has a very progressive philosophy. Interestingly over the past five years we have seen more and more young families with children moving to Boquete, particularly from Canada.

Social – You can be as active as you want, or just stay at home. People entertain, or eat out with friends. There are parties and events. Potlucks among expats and their Panamanian friends are fun and popular. There are email lists and local online bulletin boards, like BoqueteForums.org that keep everyone in the know regarding various activities.

Every Tuesday morning the expat community meets at the Boquete Event Center of Boquete Community Players to share information and have speakers on various topics of interest and concern. There is also a Tuesday Morning Market at the Event Center with dozens of vendors, both expats and locals, selling everything from art work to bread and pastries.

Some expats relate primarily to other expats, which seems a shame. We wave and great everyone – *"Hola!" "Buena!"* We were out driving a rutted mountain road and I spotted one of the workers on the house next door. We greeted each other and he introduced his family and showed me his garden. He'd watched me create my garden and knew I liked plants, so gave me start for a blackberry bush. That start has now expanded to four bushes and I enjoy fresh blackberries on my cereal thanks to that worker.

Sociedad Anónima – Or, S.A., stands for a corporation in which the owner's are anonymous, i.e. their names do not appear in the public record. The names that do appear in the public record are directors who by law must do the bidding of the holders of the bearer shares of the company. The nominee directors are Panamanian citizens who are "hired" by your attorney on your behalf to lend their names for a fee of $25 to $200 a year. This allows you to protect your assets from law suits and keep your investments and net worth private. Most people own property in the name of an S.A. corporation. S.A. corporations do have to pay Panamanian corporate taxes of 30% if they are in business, but generally S.A. corporations formed to hold property have no income. The new US-Panama treaties may eliminate some of the anonymity that has been traditional and Panama is seeking to reign in bearer bond corporations in order to collect more tax revenue.

Spanish – When we first said we were moving to Panama after the first question – "Why Panama?" – the second was always, "Do you speak Spanish?" The answer was no. Well, I had Spanish in high school and picked up some street Spanish in the South Bronx, but I knew very little. Of course I had gotten along well in Ventura County for eighteen years, and there are places in Oxnard where far fewer people speak English than in Boquete.

In school I've had to take Latin, Spanish, French, Greek and Hebrew, so naturally I hate languages. Needless to say, I'm not very good at it. But once you live here, and want to communicate, and it's all around you and seems so natural, it just comes. Really! It's not that bad! You can live in Boquete and get by with English 80% of the time if you want to, and if you want to limit yourself to *gringos*. But what a shame! Boquete has lots of classes for locals wanting to learn English and expats wanting to learn Spanish. The locals are very patient, gracious, and eager to help. They will struggle along with you until you both communicate.

There are two local Spanish schools in Boquete. People come to Boquete just to learn Spanish at these schools. They have special programs for locals as well: Habla Ya [HablaYaPanama.com] and Spanish By The River [Spanishatlocations.com]. I have found an affordable and very helpful Spanish course you can do on your computer, anywhere, anyplace. – check my blog for details. I know, since I work on it while I'm cruising.

Surf's Up – With two oceans, Panama has some of the best surfing in Central America. PANAMA: LONELY PLANET has some great detail on Panama's surfing spots, as well as a map showing surfing spots.

Sun – The sun generally always shines in Boquete, at least sometime during the day, with the exception being occasional days in October when it is like "June gloom" on the California coast. In the rainy season the mornings are generally sunny and spectacular. After noon the clouds build up over the mountains, and generally there are showers in the afternoons. In the dry season it can be sunny all day long. The sun is hot, even in Boquete, particularly at the middle of the day.

Television – Not to worry. Satellite TV is alive and well in Panama. Boquete also has cable TV and Internet. Basic service is about $60 a month. We don't have it, because we never had TV in Ventura. We were too busy and there wasn't that much on TV we cared to watch. We get our news from the Internet where we can dig as deep as we want and get an International perspective. We've got loads of videos and VCRs, and there are several sports bars in town.

Theater – You'd expect it in Panama City, but maybe not in Boquete. The Boquete Community Players "BCP" began producing plays several years ago and now has its own Boquete Event Center with a 115-seat theater and space for community meetings and events. Several other production groups have started as well shepherded along by individuals with Broadway and California acting experience.

Tipping – Outside of Panama City it is not automatically expected. 10% is pretty standard in nicer restaurants. In small cafes or family-run restaurants it's not expected, but I generally leave something. Bell hops are usually tipped, cab drivers are not.

Time –Because we're nine degrees north of the equator the sun usually sets at about 6:30 pm and rises around 6:30 am. No need to mess around with changing the time every six months! Panama time is the same as Eastern Standard Time.

Toilets – *Gringo* homes generally have US-style plumbing, but in many Panamanian homes and establishments because plumbing isn't necessarily of the same quality, used toilet paper is put in the "*basura*" containers next to the toilet. Just do it and get over it!

Public toilets are hard to find, especially ones that live up to US expectations. You tend to learn where they are located. (Driving from Boquete to Panama City, the McDonald's and Kentucky Fried Chicken in Santiago are favorite *gringo* stops, and not for so much for the food but the toilets.) Many public toilets don't always have toilet paper, so you are wise to take some along. Almost everyone keeps a roll of toilet paper in the glove compartment! Even public toilets are traditional American fixtures: don't expect squat toilets.

Tourist Requirements – Travelers from the US require passports. A tourist card, at the moment . . . and immigration requirements seem to change quarterly . . . is included in the price of your airfare and entitles you to a 30 day stay in Panama which can be extended for an additional two months, depending on the policy of the month.

Some would like to see a requirement for tourists to bring in $500 month cash for the longer visas. You need a return ticket, although officials rarely check. But all this can change overnight. When we came in we got a "*Pensionado*" visa and local residence indefinitely. One really great benefit of visiting as a tourist is that your tourist visa automatically gives you 30 days of medical insurance in Panama should you be in an accident or have a medical emergency. This is automatic and the date of entry on your passport qualifies you.

Tránsitos – the traffic police in Panama, responsible for all traffic-related issues. The Tránsitos fortunately all have identical, well-marked motorcycles and cars, and always park very visibly at the side of the road. Additionally, for safety, they wear bright orange, reflective vests. Unlike US cops they are not given to lurking in the bushes, ready to pounce and reach the ticket quota necessary to earn their salary. The idea seems to be that the laws are there for safety and to encourage good citizens to obey the law. Usually the Tránsito will be on his cell phone or chatting with locals. Sometimes there are check point stops, usually to check car registration, driver's licenses, or that people are carrying appropriate identification (Panama *cedula* which is an identity card or passport).

Often, rather than attempting English, Tránsitos will just wave *gringos* through. However, life is changing in Panama and Tránsitos now have working radar guns and computer links! There is also a national effort to get rid of the traditional bribery operations of individual cops. The current president raised the salaries of police officers just so they wouldn't have to rely on payoffs to feed their families.

Tuesday Morning Meetings – In Boquete every Tuesday morning an Information & Networking Meeting is held at the BCP Event Center along with a Tuesday Morning Market featuring home made goods and crafts. Meetings feature guest speakers of interest to the expat community and provide opportunity to share resources and information.

US Taxes – You'll want to check with your tax accountant. That being said, Uncle Sam in his largess wants not only you but your money no matter where you live. However, if you have a permanent residence outside of the US (meaning you are not in the US, or in US airspace – they are quite anal about this – more than thirty days in a calendar year), you may be able to exempt up to $92,900 per person of income earned outside the US. As a US citizen all income must be reported no matter where you live. Unfortunately you are probably still going to need your US tax accountant. I tried, but the IRS specializes in making things complicated to keep themselves and tax accountants gainfully employed and off of welfare.

Used Cars/Used Car Dealers – We've purchased used cars. The first we bought from a dealer, but it turns out the car had rear-ended someone and the dealer had just patched it up to sell. I guess used car dealers are the same the world over. The car and truck we have now we bought used from *gringos* who were leaving Panama.

UV Rays – We're nine degrees from the equator, and at 3,600 feet, so you need to be aware of the sun. Even at sea level, with the reflection of the water, you need to be sun-conscious. Neither of us generally burns, but when we're in the sun we use sun screen.

Valle Escondido – Valle Escondido is one of the first developments of its kind in Panama. A private, gated community of luxury homes, villas, and condominiums, Valle Escondido is set around a 9-hole executive golf course with restaurant, gym and spa. As Valle Escondido has evolved, after the developer sold most of the lots, the amenities were declared "private." Residents wishing to use the golf course and club pay up to $25,000 to become members. Of course there seem to be a wide range of membership deals including now a month-to-month rate so check for the deal of the moment.

One of the real advantages of living in a private community is that it is controlled. There is virtually no zoning in Panama, so for the most part outside a controlled community your neighbor can pretty much do what he wants. You may not want chickens and roosters crowing at 4 am in the lot next to you. Barking dogs are a problem in town or on lots where your neighbors may have a loud dog.

With round-the-clock security a gated community like Valle Escondido is ideal if perhaps you are only going to live in Panama part-time.

Valle Escondido is undeniably beautiful and it IS a reality. Unlike many developments which are just developer's dreams on paper, Valle Escondido IS . . . and in my mind that makes it head and shoulders above the rest. It is largely "built out" so you aren't going to have to live with construction noise six days a week.

Some big developments with grand plans and beautiful architectural renderings have either abruptly changed course mid stream, or the promoters have just up and left the country leaving homeowners and folks with homes under construction, high and dry. "So, sue me!" and god luck with that! There is a lot to be said for a project which IS a reality and not just a dream.

VCRs/DVDs – Even in Boquete, with a fair number of English speaking expats, we were concerned about finding movies in English. There is a Blockbuster in David, forty minutes away, and a lot of newer DVDs offer choice of language. And I saw an ad for Netflix - $60 a month so you'd have to watch a lot of movies. Before we left California, I watched eBay and Nikki got to know our local video store management and bought hundreds of videos and stuck them in our container, so we've got lots to watch in English. However, now that our VCR players are broken . . . finding a VCR player is about as easy as finding a player for 8-track tapes! Anyone want to buy boxes of useless VCR tapes?

Visas - Nothing having to do with government moves rapidly, anywhere in the world. It took months to get my Social Security approved in the US, and it took months to get my *Pensionado* Visa approved in Panama. I would suggest people start both processes early. There are papers required from the US which must be authenticated as genuine by the Panamanian Consul in the US before starting the actual visa process in Panama. I'd use an attorney who specializes in visas. The requirements aren't all that complicated, but they are always changing. As to all the *Pensionado* discount benefits, I'll ask for the ones from big companies, but many of the ones I could ask for from local businesses, I choose not to request.

Visiting – The Panamanian government is learning tourism and sometimes makes mistakes along the way. It used to be that when you came to Panama to visit you stood in line to pay $5 for a tourist visa that was good for 90 days. Because of problems, mostly with Colombians, Panama changed the Tourist Visa to 30 days. When someone pointed out this was equal to "shooting oneself in the foot" since it preempted gringo "snow birds" from the US and Canada, Panama promptly went back to the 90 day Tourist Visa for everyone, including Colombians, except the US and Canada. Now it's back to 30 days. Panamanian logic sometimes defies logic! This is still under discussion. It takes some hassle, and money, but after 30 days you can still get a 60-day extension.

Panama likes to think that all the prostitutes (legal here) come from Colombia, and that clamping down on Tourist Visas clamps down on an undesirable element. However, Immigration also issues "Prostitution Visas", some 500 of which were issued at the beginning of the year. Again, it defies logic!

Vino – Coming from California where there is an abundance of really good to great wine, we wondered. You don't see a lot of California wine in Panama. Some mass market brands. Beringer White Zinfandel, when you can find it, runs about $6 a bottle, about twice what we used to pay at Costco in California. But there is a lot of very good Chilean and Argentinean wines from $4 to $6 a bottle. Spanish sangria, which goes very nice in Panama, is about $3 a liter.

Volcan – Whereas Boquete and Volcancito are on the eastern slope of Volcan Baru, Volcan and the neighboring hamlets of Bambito and Cerro Punta are on the Western slope. This is another area that has been popular with expats. One little community is called Nuevo Suisse, and the area with its terraced vegetable farms going up the mountains is reminiscent of Switzerland. There's "Finca Dracula" that raises orchids, the "Dracula" being a rare, night-blooming orchid. There are beautiful farms where Arabs fly in to shop for horses.

Volcan Baru – Volcan Baru is the 11,407 foot [3,478 meter] high dominant mountain peak in the Chiriqui highlands. Some 5,000 years ago it erupted violently changing the culture of the highlands but leaving behind the rich volcanic soil which makes possible the abundance of flowers, vegetables, and coffee trees that grow today on its cool slopes. Its last eruption was around 500 years ago. It has not one, but seven craters and is the highest point in Panama. On a clear day you can see both oceans from the summit, although the summit is frequently in the clouds. A strenuous trail goes from Volcancito, above Boquete, to the summit.

The US Geological Survey has done a lot of study of Volcan Baru. Should the volcano blow the gas will go in the other direction, toward Volcan, and our home is not in an area projected to be impacted by lava flow. I will however have one of the best views of the "action" available.

Volcancito – Is a tiny coffee-growing hamlet on the slope of Volcan Baru high above Boquete Valley. It is a popular area for expats to build who want larger lots with spectacular vista views.

Voting – US citizens can continue to vote in US elections while living permanently abroad. You continue to vote wherever you had your last US residence. So I get my absentee ballot mailed from Ventura, California, my last residence. I choose not to vote in the local elections since I'm not living there, but I do choose to vote in Presidential and Congressional elections, not that my vote makes any difference in the dire directions the country is headed.

Water – Generally there is an abundance of water in Panama, but in some areas the infrastructure to get water to your home may not always be reliable. Generally water is safe to drink in Panama, although, since I have a "tender tummy" we usually boil water. Water bills in Boquete run $5 to $10 a month which compares quite favorably with the $90 a month we used to pay in California!

Too much water can occasionally be a problem. Panama can get downpours that you wouldn't believe. Flooding can occasionally be a problem in low lying areas, particularly if you build near to rivers and streams. Many people visit a place and assume it is always the same. Ideally you should visit an area in several different seasons of the year before you decide to move there.

Whales – We are on the 101 for whales migrating to warm waters to mate and give birth. I have watched a giant male leaping out of the water off Pedasi, just like in the Sea World shows, to attract the attention and interest of a nearby female. There are whale watching tours in season both from Panama City and Boca Chica.

What We Miss – I never thought I'd say this, but Home Depot! Price Smart in David is no Price Club/Costco/Sam's Club. The only time I feel really deprived living in Panama is when I visit my daughter in the States and she takes me to Sam's Club. I miss avocados from my yard. Panama has avocados, but as any Californian knows real avocados come only from California. The ones here are pretty tasteless by comparison. Most of all I miss every morning waking up and looking out over the Pacific Ocean. Well, I do see the Gulf of Chiriqui from my farm, but it's a long way off, and I can't see the waves breaking on the beach like I could from the hill in Ventura.

What We'd Do Differently – I would have made the move earlier, if I could have. A few months earlier and my Dad could have come down to visit, and maybe to stay. If I could have tempered my need to always get things done "on schedule" before I came to Panama, I might have had less frustration. Had I put my house in California on the market a few months earlier, I'd have made more. I'd also have brought more "stuff", like all of my tools including every power tool I could get my hands on. Hint: pack your power tools at the front of the container. Customs officials love to charge extra duty for power tools either not considering them as "household goods" covered by your *Pensionado* exemption, or just out of jealousy.

Winds – Some areas of Panama get strong northerly winds, particularly during the dry summer months of January, February and March. These winds can easily reach 60 mph and are reminiscent of the Santa Ana winds in California or the Chinook winds in Denver. There are times in Palmira when I think the house is going to blow away. Boquete has a lot of microclimates and amounts of wind and rain differ dramatically, so before you settle on a place to call your own, it's important to talk with locals and natives and find out about wind and rain patterns.

Work – Does not have the same "value" as it does in the US. In the States, you worked seventy hours a week, dutifully took your laptop home, didn't use all your sick days, or take your entire two week vacation, A Panamanian would think you were crazy! Come to think of it . . . maybe we in the US are crazy! No other country in the world works as long, as hard, or with as little vacation as the US. In Panama work for its own sake does not have the value it does in the US: it is merely a means to an end, and one works as little as possible without a sense of guilt.

Workers – The main principle of labor law in Panama is: the worker is always right. Whatever a worker says is taken as truth, unless the employer can prove otherwise.

You can hire a maid or gardener for around $10-15 a day. You're supposed to pay an additional almost 15 percent in social security taxes. If you are the only employer of that person and you've not enrolled them in social security and they are hurt you are responsible for their "lifetime care". Workers work a 5.5 day week, get 30 holidays a year, 30 days of vacation, 18 sick days, 14 weeks maternity leave and something called a "Thirteen Month Bonus." Even although there are only 12 months in the year, workers must be paid for 13. The "13th Month Bonus" is paid in three equal installments. This is a required "bonus" whether the worker performs acceptably or not. When someone ceases working for you the law requires you to pay them a severance. All of this has caused Panama to be less competitive on the world labor market and has contributed to a poor work ethic.

Working – Well, I can't work in Panama, because of my visa. We are both determined that no matter how much we enjoy our various projects, that we are not going to turn our lives in Boquete into another rat race where we don't have time to enjoy all the things that Panama has to offer. Plus I have the best of all worlds since a few times a year I can leave Boquete and do some real work on cruise ships!

X-Rated – Look, I needed an "X". Yes, for what it's worth prostitution is legal. However, outside of reputed areas of Panama City, we haven't seen evidence of it, but of course we haven't been looking. Should you be tempted, PANAMA: LONELY PLANET gives this sage advice: "Dudes: Keep your pants on. The risk just isn't worth the momentary thrill."

When we first came to Panama we'd see lots of establishments with names like Beverly Hills, Garden of Love, Paradise, etc., and suspected they were houses of prostitution.

Actually they are what are locally called a "push". Hotels are where you stay overnight; a "motel" is like a "push" or a place of "temporary hospitality". It is a place with long, hidden driveways where you literally "drive in" and rent a room by the hour. It's a place where you may steal away with your secretary or "prima" ("cousin") for an hour of illegitimate romance, but more likely it's a place to get away with your lover or wife and have some privacy. Panamanian homes are much smaller than US homes and often several generations live under the same roof, so privacy is not the given it is in the US.

Yellow Fever & Other Shots – Nikki worked for Public Health and so the first time we visited Panama they looked Panama up in the CDC (Centers for Disease Control) book and poked us with shots, loaded us with malaria pills, etc. Most of it was unnecessary.

There is some risk of malaria in rural farm areas of Chiriqui and Bocas. My understanding is that most malaria is cured by the same pills you take to prevent it. At the moment Panama does not require yellow fever shots for entry, but many countries do, so if you plan on traveling why not get it taken care of since protection lasts ten years. There is a small risk of yellow fever in the Darien, but if you're wandering around the Darien near the Colombian border I'd be more worried about Colombian rebels, drug runners, and poisonous snakes. To be on the safe side check on the current requirements in advance.

The bigger risk in Panama, as throughout Latin America, Florida and the entire Caribbean is dengue fever for which there is no preventative and no cure. For this reason Panama is very serious about combating mosquitoes and removing standing water, old tires, etc., and places where mosquitoes can breed.

"Yes" – "Yes" is a word like "Tomorrow" that is easily misunderstood if you assume you understand the true meaning of the word. Ask a worker to do something and the worker says, "Yes" – don't assume it will be done. "Yes" means "Yes, I understand", not necessarily "I will do it."

The Zone, Zonians – Refers to the old US Canal Zone, a fifty square mile area along the Canal that was home to many of US military and Canal employees.
After the 1979 Panama Canal Treaty this land was gradually turned over until the final turnover was completed in 1999. Over the long history of the US construction and operation of the Canal many people lived their entire lives, even for several generations, almost exclusively in the Canal Zone, which was kind of its own little country within the country. Those who lived or grew up in the Canal Zone are Zonians, and even have their own clubs and Internet sites.

Some Zonians, and those who worked for the US Army or the US Canal have an "attitude" toward Panama, Panamanians and those, like us, who have come to Panama since the US departure. Others love Panama and all things Panamanian and are very accepting and helpful to new expats.

Zona Libre – Duty free zones, in Colon and Panama Pacifico. The Colon Free Zone is the second largest in the world, second only to Hong Kong.

Unlike most of the Caribbean port duty free zones, the Zona Libre is mainly a commercial and wholesale zone where buyers come from all over Latin and South America to buy container loads of goods. Panama's central location makes it convenient for companies to keep stock in the free zone and reship throughout the world. Custom and duty regulations prohibit locals from taking advantage of the duty free zone and buying goods without paying duty. The Colon Free Zone is big business: $21.3 Billion a year big business!

12. Questions People Ask

On cruise ships, on my blog and via email I get lots of questions, some over and over again. Since you may just have some of the same questions, here goes . . .

What kind of government do they have?

Panama is a democracy that is in many ways far more participatory than in the US. To be in Panama and see everyone's involvement prior to an election is an amazing thing, particularly when contrasted to the election process in the US which mostly involves the citizenry just sitting back and watching TV ads!

The current President, Ricardo Martinelli, is a very successful businessman, owner of Panama's largest supermarket chain and educated in the US. He is a no nonsense, no crap guy who is running the country like a business and getting things done. He likes to point out that he has seven CEOs in his cabinet where Obama has none.

After Noriega, Panama abolished the military, and chose to invest instead in education. Like its neighbor Costa Rica Panama is officially neutral, and like Switzerland it holds everyone's money. There have been charges of corruption in Panamanian government centered on some former Presidents who has been accused of favoring friends and family. One former president is accused of spending $1,000 every day she was in office for personal clothing and jewelry, needing to "look the part." The difference between Panama & the US is that in the US we pretend there is no corruption, while knowing that there is, and in Panama and other countries it is acknowledged. In the recent elections there was a candidate who as a child had lost an arm in an accident. The joke was that he should be elected because he could only rob the voters with one hand.

Martinelli's administration is committed to transparency and has actually gone after government officials from previous administrations and that makes some of these folks nervous.

Is it like Costa Rica?

Yes, in the sense that it is Costa Rica's neighbor and has the same abundance of natural wonders and beautiful coastlines on two oceans. Like Costa Rica it is a neutral democracy without an army. Panama's current *Pensionado* program to attract retirees has similarities to ones Costa Rica used to offer. Many people took advantage of Costa Rica's retirement incentives, so they are well-known even although no longer offered. Most people know little about Panama other than the Canal and the Noriega episode. Panama now has one of the best retirement incentives in the world.

It is interesting that many US expats who moved to Costa Rica and have lived there for 5-15 years are now picking up and moving to Panama because of crime and the high cost of living in Costa Rica. Although the leading export of Costa Rica is not bananas, but computer chips, it still doesn't have the diverse and flourishing economy of Panama.

Costa Rica has its own currency, whereas the US dollar has been the legal currency of Panama since 1904. Panama has a strong economy based on the Canal, international banking, and business services for the many off-shore Panamanian corporations. Panama is leveraging its strategic position at the crossroads of the Americas as a free trade center, telecommunications center, and Internet hub. Although Panama enjoys the highest per capital income in Central America, it still offers an affordable and educated workforce that is familiar with US culture and customs. In Panama City many skilled workers are bi-lingual.

Panama is just now starting to develop eco-tourism. Tourism is now growing faster in Panama than any other Latin American country.

I've heard coffee is making a comeback in Panama. Is this true?

Yes and no.

Yes. European and American tastes in coffee are becoming more sophisticated. Boquete in particular is taking advantage of the many microclimates that exist in and around Boquete. It's similar to the Napa and Sonoma valleys only in our case the product is coffee. Different coffee farms produce different tasting coffees due to variations in climate and soil. Boquete coffee is becoming a unique, distinct, and increasingly recognized specialty or boutique coffee. This is helping prices to move up to levels where it may again be as profitable to raise coffee as sell off land for real estate development.

No. As land becomes more and more expensive, it becomes harder and harder to grow coffee and make a profit. You can't pay more than $4 a square meter for land on which to farm coffee, and farm land in Boquete is now going for $15 a square meter and up. The "*lata*" of coffee we sell for $8 costs us $2 to pick, $2 for fertilizer, and $2 for labor throughout the year. Do the math! That's making $2 per *lata*. That *lata* will end up in the US producing about 10 pounds of roasted coffee beans selling at $16 a pound, so we end up with about 20 cents on every pound. The money isn't in growing coffee.

And all of the certifications – "Fair Trade", "Rainforest", "Bird Friendly", etc. – all cost lots of money, which no truly small grower in Boquete can possibly afford. People are willing to pay $1 more per pound for these certifications which they think are helping the small grower and making life better for the Indigenous people who pick coffee. And while I admire people who are willing to pay $1 additional per pound to do what they believe is "the right thing", these are really clever marketing schemes which may help big growers and large cooperatives, but are of no benefit to the truly small farmer like us and our neighbors. In fact, assuming some of that money does get down to the person picking the coffee, it raises the rate paid to coffee pickers for everyone, actually making things more difficult and less profitable for the truly small farmer who isn't a member of the big cooperative or grower consortium that was able to afford to buy into the branding scheme.

Boquete is now fighting a new coffee disease which threatens the entire crop. The disease plus the soaring cost of fertilizer has caused little coffee farmers on both sides of us to give up. We are fighting but . . . I predict Panamanian coffee futures will soar, but the future of coffee is a big question. Culturally Boquete without coffee would be like Napa Valley without grapes.

Can foreigners own property?

Yes. Panama allows foreign ownership of property with a few exceptions like beaches (which belong to the people), properties within proximity to international borders, etc. Basically foreign owners/investors have the same rights as Panamanians. The tricky part is that some properties are "titled" similar to what we expect in the US, and other properties offer just rights of possession. Most often foreigners choose to own property not in their own names but in the name of a corporation, usually an anonymous "SA" corporation, as a means of enjoying some protection from liability.

Is it safe?

Safer than Oxnard, California! You don't listen to gun shots at night. Innocent people aren't being randomly shot by drive-by shooters. People don't talk about "respect", they live it! You don't have the gang culture. There is respect for the law. It's a given that you may have to resolve an issue by offering some direct assistance to a police officer who is struggling to make ends meet, but it is done without pretense. There's not the cop/gang banger mentality where it is a "we-cops" vs. "citizens-kids-criminals-anyone-who's-not-a-cop" mentality.

Do you know Spanish?

"Si, un poquito." About the same percentage of folks speak English and/or Spanish in Panama as in Oxnard or LA. Certainly more people in Panama speak English than in Miami!

I am a guest in Panama so I am trying to learn Spanish even if I do murder the language along the way. Actually I do know some Spanish, and when I'm in Panama I start thinking in Spanish, so I'm getting there . . . slowly! I'm not in Panama just to associate with English speaking expats! When we bought our coffee farm two years ago our Indian worker said, "Don't worry, in two years you will be speaking Spanish." Now he says, "Don't worry in five years you will be speaking Spanish." He will probably master English before we master Spanish.

Where is Panama?

OK, I thought it was kind of dumb too, but many Americans are amazingly ignorant of geography. I was walking out of the theater on a ship after giving a lecture about the Canal and there were two ladies up in front of me who didn't know I was behind them. One lady said to the other, "I didn't know the Panama Canal was man-made."

The Republic of Panama is the southernmost Central American country. It runs east-west bordering Colombia on the east and Costa Rica on the west. The Caribbean is to the north and the Pacific is to the south. And the Panama Canal actually runs north-south, not east-west.

Is that, like, a state?

Please don't laugh. I've been asked this several times! The Republic of Panama is an independent country, albeit one with a history linked to the US during the Canal Zone days. I like to think of US/Panamanian relations in terms of the US being a "big brother." You may not always want to live with or in the shadow of your big brother, but when in a jam it's nice to know you have a big brother for "backup."

Are the Indians who live in the jungles dangerous?

Of the several dozen Indigenous tribes who inhabited this tiny squiggle when the Spanish arrived, seven groups remain!

The Kuna are the largest and perhaps best known. The Guaymis or Ngobe–Bugle live in and around Boquete and work the coffee *fincas*. The Guaymis women wear brightly colored dresses and are often seen in town. The Embera are committed to maintaining their traditional lifestyle and if it weren't for my Embera friends and researching the Embera Puru I probably would not have "discovered" Panama. To stay overnight with my friends I drove one hour out of Panama City, then took a dug out canoe for an hour and a half into the jungle up the river to their village. The Wounaan are related to the Embera. There are three other tiny groups living mostly around Bocas del Toro.

The Indigenous in Panama are warm, friendly, interesting people who actually have considerable political clout.

Weren't you afraid visiting the Embera?

Of what? They were my friends. That we'd eat monkey brains? Well, the thought passed my mind! Actually we had the best tilapia I've ever tasted, right out of the river. The Embera are wonderful, contented, happy people who have made a choice to preserve their traditional lifestyle.

When I used my rental car to take my friend Erito into Panama City, Erito, who is like the village mayor or manager, whipped his cell phone (doesn't work in the village) out of his briefcase and started doing business. We visited three banks, one attorney, dropped someone off at a clinic, stopped at a sweatshop to pick up clothing, picked up videos (car batteries run two village televisions), and picked up supplies before leaving for the little town where we left our dug out canoe. At that time alcohol was not allowed in the village. Never-the-less, we left with me, four guys, and three cases of beer in the boat. Not to worry for by the time we got home, one and a half hours later, there was no beer!

The next morning Erito and one of the village elders gave me the same pharmaceutical tour of the jungle they give to representatives of drug companies looking to "discover" new cures.

How do you deal with the heat and humidity?

Being only nine degrees from the Equator with lots of rain, particularly in the rainy season, many places are hot and humid. The Caribbean side tends to be more humid than the Pacific side. During the dry season, on an endless beach with only two or three other people, it felt a lot like Cabo San Lucas in Mexico. Hot, dry with successive waves of cool breezes coming off the ocean, an 85 degree [29 Celsius] ocean!

Because Boquete is about 3,600 feet [1097 meter] up in the mountains the year round temperature ranges from a low of 65 degrees [18 Celsius] to an occasional high of 85 degrees [29 Celsius]. Frequently you want a light sweater or flannel shirt at night or a fire in the fireplace and you always pull up the blankets. It can be humid, but generally not hot and humid like in the lowlands. When it's 75 degrees [24 Celsius] in Boquete it can be 100 degrees [38 Celsius] in David which is forty minutes a way. Kind of like the difference between Ventura and Simi Valley back in California.

What will you do without the Internet?

Not to worry! Panama is very wired! There are Internet cafes everywhere - $1 an hour. Panama is actually a crossroads for much Internet traffic and the old US Army Fort Clayton has been turned into the "City of Knowledge" which will be a techno-park and high-tech incubator. Some believe that Panama's location at the intersection of five major undersea fiber optic cables may one day contribute almost as much economic revenue than the Panama Canal. Already many off-shore call centers are taking advantage of Panama's location and affordable workforce with a background in English and Americanized culture. We even have cable TV and Internet now in Boquete! However, now that Boquete has high speed cable Internet, we live outside Boquete and have only one incredibly slow and unreliable wireless Internet provider.

What does your family think?

They love the idea! They see it as a new, low-cost, all-inclusive destination vacation resort!

I've heard that cruise ships are now using Panama as a "home port"?

Because of security hassles in the US it has become difficult for Europeans wanting to cruise to use the Florida ports. Royal Caribbean has begun using Panama City as a "home port" for two of its ships and the response has been phenomenal. With the renovations at Tocumen and increased airlift into Panama from the US and Europe, and now using the old Howard AFB runway for charters, I think movement of ships from Florida to Panama will continue over the coming years.

Doesn't it rain all the time?

It rains a lot, but not all the time. And rainfall in Panama varies widely. The wettest areas are on the Caribbean side, and there are some dry areas on the Pacific side. The "dry" or summer season is from mid-December to mid-April. During the "green" or "wet" winter season Boquete gets 11 inches [279 millimeters] of rain a month (whereas Ventura, California gets 11 to 13 inches a year), but most of this comes in torrential tropical downpours, often thunderstorms, in the afternoon. Mornings are nice and sunny and usually in mid afternoon there will be a storm or a slow afternoon drizzle. Except perhaps during October, it's not Seattle rainy. And, even during the "rainy" season, we can go days without any rain.

What kind of diseases are there? Do you need shots?

Depends who you ask. Before we moved to Panama we went to the County Health Department, where my wife used to work. They pulled out the CDC Manual and gave us pills and injections for almost every disease known to mankind at a cost of almost $500! It turns out we didn't need any of this!! With the exception of a few areas in Bocas del Toro, where in all fairness we were headed, we didn't need ANY shots or pills, period. Live and learn. If you're coming to visit us, the only real hazard is consuming too much Panamanian rum ($8 a bottle)! Popular brands of US cigarettes at $15 a carton should be avoided if you are concerned about your health.

Can you visit Cuba from Panama?

There are direct flights from Panama City to Havana. The rest of the world enjoys the freedom to visit Cuba: US citizens do not enjoy the freedom of travel to Cuba. Despite the fact that we're all buddy-buddy with Viet Nam, China, the former Soviet Union, South Africa, and even talking with Libya, the US still can't get along with our nearest "enemy-neighbor" Cuba. Do we really think Castro can make the world a totalitarian Communist system when Russia and China couldn't make it work? So as a US citizen you can visit Cuba from Panama, but you may not. [Remember all the grade school teachers who used to play that silly can/may game?] But people go none-the-less. The Cuban government graciously insists you pay in US dollars and stamps a piece of paper rather than stamp incriminating evidence into your US passport. Just don't try to import a box of Cuban cigars into the US unless you are a member of Congress.

Can you drink the water in Panama?

One of the legacies of American involvement in the Panama Canal is that throughout Panama, with the possible exception of Bocas del Toro, municipal drinking water is usually safe to drink. I have a "tender tummy" so to be sure, we boil our drinking water. The water in Boquete is delicious: better than Evian! The water comes from springs that originate from deep within Volcan Baru. Pure, no chemicals added, and delicious!

What about shopping?

Panama City is rapidly becoming a shopper's paradise for South Americans who come to buy luxury goods and the latest fashions. Panama City has almost everything including loads of luxury brand shops.

In Boquete we have three small supermarkets and a farmer's market that is open daily with fresh, locally grown produce. The Boquete supermarkets (and we use the term "super" loosely!) will sometimes run out of common things like meat, bread and chicken and have seem to have difficulty keeping a reliable inventory. but forty minutes away is Panama's third largest city. There is a Price Smart store in David. It's not as big as the Costco stores we were used to in the States, but has the same "big box" feel and has some of the same things. Unlike the States, it is not always cheaper than the local stores and you often pay more, not less, for bulk sizes. The joke is that once *gringos* find something they like, Price Smart stops selling it because the *gringos* keep taking it off the shelves and buying it. If your tempted to ask, "But isn't that the point?", then you don't understand how business works or thinks in Panama.

What about "squatters"?

This is more of a problem in other Latin American countries and is not generally a problem in Panama. People are respectful of others property and property rights. Since there are "haves" and "have-nots" and as a *gringo* you are perceived to be fabulously wealthy, whether or not you actually are, it only makes sense to take care of your property and if you are an absentee owner to have someone locally looking after your property. Grates or "bars" on windows are a Latin American tradition. They do deter petty theft, but often have the more important function of conveying to your neighbors the message that you are so successful and have so much "stuff" inside your home that you need to protect it.

What about health care?

First, the life expectancy in Panama is about the same as in the US. And who knows, without drive-by shootings for some populations it might be higher. Second, because of the long Canal/US association Panama has a pretty good health care system without exorbitant prices, litigious culture and price gouging that characterizes so much US medicine. David has four large hospitals and many doctors have been trained in the US.

My wife has cardio concerns so we decided to visit the US-trained Boquete doctor who was highly recommended by local US expats. She went to his office without an appointment and waited twenty minutes because the doctor was making a house call. The doctor listed to her history and suggested since we'd been in Boquete a while that he do an EKG to see how she was doing at 3,600 feet [1,097 meter]. No problem. My wife asked, "Well, what happens if I have a heart attack here."

The doctor answered, "Well, you call me, and I'll call the ambulance and come over and ride with you down to the hospital in David. We'll get you stabilized and if necessary air-lift you to Panama City where the best cardiac specialists are located." He named the guy he considered to be the best, also US trained, picked up his cell phone and said, "Let me see if I can get him." He got him on the phone, described Nikki's condition and said, "Here, you talk to him", handing the phone to Nikki. After 45 minutes with the doctor (not sitting in an exam room waiting for the doctor), an EKG, a phone consult with a specialist, Nikki walked out with a bill for $60. Unfortunately, this particular doctor moved to Panama City.

Another example: my own experience. Ready to head off for four months on the ship, and not having had a checkup for a few years, I had gotten a bunch of tests including an EKG. The doctor who reviewed the EKG thought I should see a cardiologist. This is five days – FIVE days! – before I am to leave. I called my wife's cardiologist . . . and got an appointment for the NEXT day! That might ever happen in the US! He wanted to do a stress test and echcardiograph. So Saturday, two days before I leave, he and his staff stay late Saturday afternoon to do the tests. My cost for intial visit $40. Were I able to get my local hospital insurance to approve tests (this can take weeks!) they would have cost $300 of which the insurance would have paid half. Without the insurance, without the hassle, $175.

We're still working out health insurance issues. Expat international medical iInsurance is widely available and as long as you are having treatment outside the high-priced US it is not that expensive.

We finally settled on a local program a kind of modified HMO discount program. One of its selling points was that after two years it covered pre-existing conditions but apparently someone didn't run the numbers when it comes to selling to a largely senior group of expats. So they are merging with another larger company. We still have the "pre-existing" conditions and hopefully still have the "insurance". .

What are the people like?

Friendly. Delightfully diverse. Incredibly patient.
Panama has always been at the crossroads of the world. Columbus put in at Bocas del Toro to do ship repair. The pirates hung out here. Panama's heritage and people are a delightful blend of Indigenous, European (Spanish, Italian, Greek, Jewish), Caribbean (Jamaican), Oriental (Chinese) and American peoples. This is one of the few countries in the world that actually like the US! Because of the long cooperative history with the Canal, many Panamanians have US relatives.

There is a laid-back industriousness about Panamanians. They are neither driven nor lazy, but seem to have worked out an approach to life that works. Things get done . . . eventually . . . . although maybe not on an American time schedule.

Do they like Americans?

Panamanians still like and respect the US. The US supported and encouraged Panama's independence from Colombia in order to secure a canal route. Without US support and "gunboat diplomacy" the secession of Panama from Colombia would have taken longer and involved loss of life. There is a hundred year history of cooperation with the US.

Through the years there has been a lot of intermarriage between Panamanians and US nationals living and working in the Canal Zone.

The US invasion of Panama to remove Noriega was largely supported by Panamanians.

The national currency of Panama, although called the "Balboa" is in fact the US dollar. Panama has never printed its own currency. Coins have different imprints than US coins but are identical to US coins and work in US vending machines and are used interchangeably with US coins in Panama.

Isn't Panama a big drug center?

Depends on who you ask. According to the CIA it is a, "major cocaine transshipment point and primary money-laundering center for narcotics revenue; money laundering activity is especially heavy in the Colon Free Zone; offshore financial center; negligible signs of coca cultivation; monitoring of financial transactions is improving; official corruption remains a major problem."
Of course, according to the CIA every place BUT the US is a major drug center! But if drugs weren't demanded by the US population there would be no problem. If the US decriminalized and regulated drug use, all of those who suck at the teat of the drug industry (drug lords, law enforcement, prison industry, "justice" industry, etc.) would initially be out of work and on welfare, but eventually we'd save billions of tax dollars and be able to invest that money in education and treatment.

Because Panama's neighbor is Colombia, the drug lords are constantly trying to move drugs through sections of Panama to the US. Panama has a huge jungle coastline. There are major, major drug interceptions weekly, but the failed US policy of prohibition makes the drug trade so lucrative that the drug cartels don't mind losing tons of pure cocaine each week as a cost of doing business, and they just keep on trying.

In terms of drug use in Panama there is a lot less than in Ventura or Los Angeles.

How about moving?

You know those big shipping containers you see trucking up and down the freeway? They come in twenty foot and forty foot sizes. You can load your own or have a professional mover take care of everything. In LA they will bring the container to your home, it gets loaded, goes back to the Port of Los Angeles and takes about two weeks to arrive in Panama. The cost for a forty foot container is about $3,500 plus transport costs to/from the ports. The major cost is the moving the container to and from the ports. Moving is expensive anywhere, but it doesn't have to be any more expensive to move to Panama than Denver.

Were I doing this again, I might try and purchase the container outright so that when it arrived in Panama I had my own storage unit.

How is banking different?

Mostly it's point of view. The IRS used to call it "clandestine" and "secret." Others would call it "private." Now with the new US Panama Free Trade Agreements nothing is "secret" anymore for US citizens. Opening an account and dealing with the bank is worse than dealing with the Department of Motor Vehicles in the US.

We're used to working with banks in the US who generally seem to want your business. Here banks seem genuinely hostile, some more than others. And it's against the law to say anything critical about a bank you don't like. In a now famous one big international bank went after an expat customer who publicly his banking experience and tied up not only his access to accounts in their bank but also froze access to ALL of his assets in Panama until the case was eventually resolved. Like every other business in Panama, banking lacks a customer service orientation. The same giant international bank is now the target of a huge US investigation for money laundering. What goes around comes around.

With the new US trade agreement the US IRS is attempting to impose onerous reporting requirements on Panamanian banks with US customers so many Panamanian banks are already just saying if you are US go elsewhere to bank.

What kind of visas do you need?

US Citizens require visas to enter and remain in Panama. There are various options to meet various needs.

Type Visa	Duration	Notes
Tourist	30 days – can be extended additional 30 days while in Panama	Usually included in price of airline ticket – includes medical insurance
Pensionado	Usually permanent	Allows you to remain indefinitely in Panama and enjoy same discounts as Panamanian *Pensionados* – you cannot work for someone but you can have your own business – you must meet some minimum pension income requirements
Investor	Varies	To encourage foreign investment – some offer dual citizenship and Panamanian passport

[See Migracion.gob.pa **for** current information and details]

Don't you feel isolated from the rest of the world?

Not really. Unfortunately from Boquete you have to drive 7 hours to Panama City or fly 50 minutes to Panama City and frequently overnight before your flight due to flight times and schedules. But Seattle, where my daughter lives is 11.5 hours flying time from Panama City, Los Angeles 8 hours, Miami 3 hours. KLM and Iberia both offer direct flights to the Continent: Madrid 10 hours, and Amsterdam 10 hours.

Rumors persist that eventually there will be direct flights from our local airport in David to the US! That will make everything so much easier!

Aren't you worried about hurricanes?

I did not want to contend with hurricanes! One of the big plusses for me about Panama was that it is tropical but is below the hurricane belt. Sometimes the tropical depression vestiges of a hurricane will affect the Caribbean side around Bocas with heavy rainfalls, but the brunt of hurricane assault that you risk in most Caribbean islands is not a problem.

Aren't there lots of mosquitoes?

Everyone knows mosquitoes and yellow fever were problems in the building of the Panama Canal - over a hundred years ago! - the mosquito image has lingered in Panama. It doesn't help that ages ago folks who weren't into tourist and real estate marketing named things like "Mosquito Coast"! With the possible exception of the area around Bocas del Toro yellow fever is not an issue in Panama, and it's only a rare possibility in Bocas. You will find mosquitoes in some areas, but nothing like Alaska in the summer - where, incidentally they're called the state bird of Alaska.

Boquete has about as many mosquitoes as Ventura, and to the best of my knowledge does not have West Nile Virus like Southern California.

Frankly the bigger pests are flies. We have two kinds, coffee flies and regular flies and both are somewhat seasonal. The coffee flies are tiny, little flies that leave a bite like "no-see-ums", And a thin layer of skin lotion seems enough to discourage these guys. We didn't believe it at first, but after a while the insects seem to tire of you when you're no longer "fresh meat". The population of regular black flies seems to explode at the beginning of the rainy season. For about a month they are everywhere!

How is buying real estate different?

"You're not in Kansas any more!" Many of the things we're familiar with - REALTOR®, Code of Ethics, listing agreements, exclusive listings, offers to purchase, multiple listing services, etc. - are non-existent. Some things like licensing, title insurance, escrow companies are just beginning.

Pretty much anyone can and does sell real estate. Not all real estate offered for sale is even owned by the people who are selling it! In some places land is titled, in other places you are essentially just buying "the right to pick fruit" on the land. I saw folks selling building sites along the road overlooking the beach across the road - great view, great price - the only problem was the land they were selling is owned by the government was not for sale! But it IS possible to buy titled property and not get ripped off if you work with people you can trust, and proceed cautiously.

Often people utilize anonymous corporations "S.A." as a holding vehicle for property. So when you buy a property you don't actually purchase the property but ownership of the "S.A." company whose sole asset is the property you're acquiring. Purchasing property in this way is an anonymous way to own property that protects the property should you be named in a law suit and offers certain advantages.

You make it sound like paradise! What's the downside?

Nothing is perfect. Although from my farm I can see the Pacific and the islands in a distance, it's not the direct ocean view that I had in Ventura. And the ocean is an hour and a half away and not a 10 minute drive.

The business orientation is very different and there is no sense of customer service, and I miss specific businesses like Home Depot, and believe-it-or-not Costco.

If I want to fully communicate and become part of the culture of my new home I'll have to master Spanish. Not that I couldn't communicate without knowing Spanish, it's just that I want to communicate in the native language. It's a challenge at my age, but supposedly learning a new language is one of the things that keeps your mind working and slows dementia.

It does rain a lot. Actually during the rainy season I look forward to the rain at 3 or 4 pm. It's an excuse to kick back and read a book or take a nap! The only time it becomes somewhat oppressive (like Seattle in winter!) is in October, and I try to be away from Boquete in October.

Many of the things I've come to Panama for are, ironically, the things I'll have trouble with! Things like two-lane roads - of course I'm trying to get away from the 405 with its ten lanes! There are stores and supplies, just not as convenient as Ventura - of course I'm trying to get away from the commercial "strip"! Then there's the pace. I tell myself I want a slower pace, and I do, but sometimes I still want things NOW! Every governmental agency in Panama seems to operate like the DMV in California.

So, nothing's perfect, but for us, this is damn close!

Do foreigners and retirees have to pay Panamanian income taxes?

The Republic of Panama only taxes income that is generated within the territory of the Republic of Panama; therefore, foreign source income is not taxable in Panama.

What about American style schools in Boquete?

The Boquete International Academy is an excellent, progressive bilingual school right in Boquete. It started with grades one through four and has been adding a grade a year.

Panamanian schools are very different from US schools. Many of the very basic resources, like books and paper, that we would take for granted are lacking. Yet expats have sent their kids to Panamanian schools through the years and many of these kids have gone on to schools in the US and have become attorneys, doctors, engineers, etc. Some have returned to Panama and others have stayed in the US.

Some people use home schooling or online schooling or some combination. One young friend did most of his schooling on line, until he hit high school and then started a local school while continuing online. The local school offered one plus that the Internet didn't provide: girls.

What about security, self defense and gun laws?

Security - I feel more secure here than in Ventura and Ventura County has two of the consistently "safest" cities in the US. There are areas in Panama City and Colon where I'd rather not get lost, and even a few areas in David where I only go with Panamanians, but on the whole this place is MUCH safer than the US. Unlike much of Central America, you can drive anywhere in Panama safely. The only dangerous place in Panama is in the jungle along the Colombian border where only drug runners and Colombian rebels would be anyway.

Self-defense - a couple of the guards at Valle Escondido are black belts and teach karate, but it's more of a macho, young guy thing that they learned along the way. People really don't worry about that here. The more urgent worry is if you remembered to bring your umbrella in case there is a downpour!

Gun laws - There are LOTS of guns in Panama. There are gun laws; in fact there are lots of laws. But there isn't the budget to enforce a lot of laws. I don't want a "cop heavy" society so I guess I can't complain. I'm not into guns, but I understand it is fairly easy to get permits, so lots of people have guns.
On the whole Panamanians are generally very docile and non violent people. They would much rather discuss than have a confrontation: the discussion can go on forever, but what's the hurry? And by the way, it's much easier to get a gun license that a license for a chain saw.

Assuming you have no air conditioning how to you sleep at night? Is the breeze cool enough?

It depends where you are living. In Boquete you wouldn't need air conditioning. In David, Panama City or along the ocean, it is probably essential for expats, although locals might not need it. In Boquete, up in the mountains, it was probably a low of 61 degrees [16 Celsius] here last night; definitely need a blanket or two.

How is restaurant and bar life? Are there "Gentlemen's Clubs"?

Again, it depends. Panama City has fantastic restaurants, night clubs, and "Gentlemen's Clubs", as you put it. Boquete is a small town, but for a small town we have a Chinese restaurant, a Peruvian restaurant, two Mexican restaurants, a French restaurant, an Argentinean restaurant, a couple of Italian restaurants and a Middle Eastern restaurant. Some of these are tiny, and some may not be that great, at least for my taste, but there is increasing variety. The Panamonte Inn has a lovely formal dining room with candlelight, crystal, and china. There are lots of local restaurants as well.

We have a couple of sports bars, and bars for *gringos*, Panamanians, and Indians. Indians come in on paydays (two Saturdays a month); some like to get pretty drunk, they will sometimes fight each other over women, pull out their ever present machetes and someone ends up cut and can't work. But they stay to themselves. We're certainly not Panama City, which is very Latin and hip. In town during the "Fair of Coffee & Flowers", Carnival and holidays they bring in huge portable disco clubs with two story speakers and there is lots of partying to the early morning hours.

You and others talk about the super protective labor laws. So from what I gather, you can have for a bargain a maid and a gardener, but you have to pay them a thirteenth month, plus give them a month's vacation and sick days and holidays and pay their social security. So what's the workaround on that? Is there any?

The minimum wage is about $1.15 an hour. If you are "on the books" you pay an additional almost 15 percent in Social Security which allows worker coverage at Social Security hospitals. Sometimes workers aren't concerned or don't want social security and will work "under the table." However, if a worker gets pissed at you for any reason, or gets injured or hurt, they can take you to the labor department and if that worker is injured on your job you may end up supporting him and his family for life. As Panama moves ahead there are more people enforcing the law so you'd better know and follow Panama's labor laws, onerous as they may be.

Understand that the basic principle of Panamanian labor law is "the worker is always right." And you are the outsider. In my book you'd be a fool to try and avoid your responsibility. Labor law is about as big of a business here as lawsuits are in the US. My understanding is that if you employ someone for less than three days a week, or on an occasional basis, that you can avoid this, however, you have to have a clear contractual agreement or hire on a per diem basis for a short time. You can easily get trapped in Panama's labor laws, so it is important to consult with a Panamanian lawyer specializing in labor law.

I a retired Air Force, then trial lawyer, and now part-time REALTOR®. I'm 71 and ready to finally retire and move to Panama. Can we survive on $5,000 a month? We want a place where it is not too hot, but not too far from the beach. My wife is Russian and loves herbs, fresh vegetables and gardens, animals, birds, and is a nature lover. I am a lover of fresh coffee. Is there a nice furnished place we can rent until we can buy what we want?

Boquete just might be your place! The expats who have settled here are a diverse and international group. You will find much of what you like here in Boquete, except for the beach. We lived overlooking the ocean in Ventura, California, and the ocean is the one thing we miss. But we're less than two hours to the Pacific and four hours to the Caribbean, so we can get there when we need a "beach fix". My only caveat is that prices have gone up considerably, and continue to rise, so some price information people pull from old Internet pages is pretty out of date.

We live WELL on $4,000 a month, but I don't play golf and my wife limits her massage appointments! But you could live VERY WELL here on $5,000 a month. Food costs more than we expected, as does medicine. If you want to get a feel of rentals look at BoqueteForums.org - kind of our bulletin board here. I'd think twice about bringing down a car. Most folks have found it more expensive than purchasing here and lots of frustration. We brought down our furniture because it's "ours" and we're attached to it, but, you can pretty much find everything in Panama City. You might want to bring in overstuffed furniture, but anything rattan or wood, buy here.

I'm a single guy in my 40s living in Miami Beach and thinking of moving to Panama City. What is the night life like? The Bay looks beautiful: is it good for swimming? [Sorry, but I have to include his email handle: "Spoiledrichkid"]

Panama City is a vibrant Latin capital where the night life starts at 10 pm and goes until morning. You'll find lots to keep you busy! However, Panama City is not Miami Beach. And forget about swimming in the Bay! Due to an old sewage system when there are heavy rains raw sewage ends up being dumped into the Bay.

A new system is under construction and hopefully about the time the Canal Expansion program is finished (2015) the Bay of Panama will be on the road to recovery. The good news is that there are fantastic beaches within an hour drive from Panama City, or a puddle jump flight or ferry out to some of the Pearl Islands, one of the areas where the TV reality show "Survivor" was filmed.

My husband and I are looking into relocating to Panama. We are in our early 30s, so the retirement option is probably out. I have read a lot about reforestation but am not sure I buy it. I understand the only way to get residency, if you have some money to invest, is to use an attorney . . . there are so many on the internet. Is there someone you would recommend as reasonably priced and honest?

You're assuming many attorneys here are dishonest? Actually you'll find that Panamanian attorneys are just as honest as their American counterparts. For what it's worth there aren't as many lawyer "shark" jokes in Panama as there are in America. I think the key is to find a firm, as opposed to an individual attorney, who specializes in visas and immigration. The reforestation option is an interesting one that works for some people. As with everything in any foreign country, move cautiously, check out all the facts, and once you're sure, then move ahead.

I hear Panama City's high rise buildings referred to as "Cocaine Towers". Is Panama really a center for money laundering?

It depends who you ask. Some locals tell me that money laundering is a "secret everyone knows about", yet others say while there may be a few nefarious investors, most operations are legitimate investments. There are boutiques in high rent malls that continue in business year after year, yet nobody ever seems to buy anything. There are lodging operations which look perfect, yet never appear to have any quests. I'm told that the "secret everyone knows about" works like this. You build a building that you show as costing $12M, when in reality the actual cost was $4M. You sell it to another S.A. (anonymous) corporation for $12M and even if you pay some tax, you've cleaned and pressed about $7M. It helps if you have some key people with phantom jobs on your payroll. These are folks who may be paid $200K a year, who don't ever show up to work at your place, but do have real, albeit poor paying jobs, in key places in government. I don't know since I don't have the problem

Did you pay cash or finance your place and did you take out a loan? Is it more difficult to get a loan there?

We "cashed in our chips" and got out of the Southern California real estate casino and bought our home in Panama with cash. You can also get a loan. A loan requires all the US paperwork and more. And getting a loan approved can take forever in Panama! Also, Panamanian banks will not loan you money after a certain age, and the loan must be repaid before you are 70. The thought is that once you are retired you will no longer be able to service the loan.

With so much new building coming on line there do you have personal concerns as to Boquete loosing the feeling that brought you there?

Yes, it's a concern. Like most people we want to see our investment grow, but at the same time, once we're in, we'd like to "close the door" to prevent further growth. There are a lot of proposed projects for Boquete. Some of these will actually be completed, and others will die along the way. Local government is beginning to address growth and some of the challenges it brings.

Is it feasible to rent a car and see the country safely in two weeks time? I'm very interested in the non city experience in seeing rural Panama, both coast lines, the mountains etc.

Absolutely. Driving in Panama City is a hassle and not for the faint of heart. But once you are outside of the city, driving is fine. Main roads are generally in good condition. Except for one small section of the Pan American Highway, now being rebuilt, the Pan American Highway is a good road and the six hour trip from Panama City to Boquete is interesting and gives one a good view of life for most Panamanians. All the major rental car companies have offices in Panama City and in David should you choose to fly to David and rent a car locally. Here's my suggestion for two weeks.

Days 1-4 – Panama city area. You can hire a cab for around $15 to $25 an hour. I can give you suggestions or you can check with the front desk of your hotel. See Old Panama, the old French area of Casco Viejo including the Interoceanic Canal Museum, Opera House and Golden Altar. See the Canal itself including the Miraflores Locks visitor center. Your driver can call and check the schedule so you are actually at the visitor center when a ship is in the locks. There is a Hop On Hop Off bus that will take you to the main sights of Panama City providing a taped narrative in multiple languages and allowing you to get off, spend some time, and then get back on the next buss.

Arrange an all day tour to the Embera Puru maybe through Anne Gordon, a *gringa* who married an Embera guy.] They will pick you up at your hotel and it will be a memorable day.

[EmberaVillageTours.com]

Days 5-6 – Stay at the beach. Decameron and Sheraton Bijao are all-inclusive beach resorts about an hour from Panama City.

Days 7-10 – Fly to David, rent a car, and visit Boquete. We have hiking expeditions, river rafting, canopy zip line tours, coffee tours and more.

Days 11-12 – Fly to Bocas del Toro, a funky, laid back, somewhat noisy town in the Caribbean islands.

Days 13-14 – Fly to the San Blas Islands and visit the Kuna Indians.

Day 15 – Fly home.

That will give you a whirlwind tour of Panama and you'll be anxious to return for more.

What about the real estate tours? I understand these are sometimes free or at reduced prices.

Free? You get what you pay for. Have you been to a time share presentation? There are some outfits who offer travel seminars that provide a good overall introduction to expat living in Panama . . . for a whole lot more than the cost of this book.   Understand that many of these programs tend to be whirlwind tours so you end up being somewhat of a "captive" audience seeing only certain projects and there is not a lot of time to go off on your own.

Jackie Lange's Panama Relocation Tour is different. The tour is a chance to get an overview of Panama, to visit some of the places North American expats have moved to including Panama City, the beaches, the mountains and, of course, Boquete. It is a chance to get an overview *without anyone selling anything*. The tour is designed so that participants have the opportunity to meet expats who are living here and ask questions. Practical information, like visas and setting up bank accounts and how real estate works, are covered.

Everyone participating in the Panama Relocation Tour gets a copy of this book and it is required reading. And whenever I am not on the ship and able, I join the tour. If you are interested in the Panama Relocation Tour, and you should be if you are thinking about moving or retiring to Panama, check for links and details on my blog at www.RichardDetrich.com.

Do many foreigners live in the area as they get into their late seventies and eighties?

It remains to be seen. A lot of us have come here with the intention of spending the rest of our lives in Panama. We have seen some folks who have returned back to the States for medical reasons, mostly insurance and Medicare driven. There are some projects on the drawing board that will offer US-style assisted living for folks as they get older. A live-in care giver and companion is still relatively inexpensive. Our medical care is good and relatively inexpensive, although generally not covered by insurance and certainly not by Medicare unless we go back to the States for treatment.

Generally by the time people are already in their eighties, it is harder to make the transition to a society that is new and radically different. The argument can be made that people will live longer when they retire to Panama just because the quality of life and the quality and personalized aspect of medical care is better than in the US. Both my wife and I fought high blood pressure in the States. Since coming to Panama both of our blood pressures have dropped at least twenty points. The air is pure, the food is locally grown, fresh, relatively pesticide free, and better. At least in Chiriqui we don't have much violent crime.

People do come here and stay and that number is increasing. So a group has started a Hospice program in Boquete to assist people in their final days. Dying here is different, and in some ways maybe more "complicated" than in the States. One of the goals of Hospice is to provide expats with the information they need to know about planning for the inevitable.

Do roads ever get washed out due to the heavy rains?

Sometimes. Usually when this happens they are repaired within a few days, or an alternate temporary route is devised. A bigger problem is trees that fall over the road due to heavy rain or wind or just the inside of the tree being infested with termites. These are usually cleared rather quickly by enterprising individuals who then sell the wood to coffee *beneficios* who use it to fire up the coffee bean dryers.

Are you still enjoying it there?

Absolutely! We love it! Is it perfect? No. Are there frustrations? You bet! But on the whole we love it and only wish we had made the move sooner.

I've read about heavy winds. How bad and how often?

If you've lived in California with Santa Ana winds or Colorado with Chinook winds, you know what they are like. We get strong winds blowing down from the North generally off the volcano during January, February and March. They are not continuous, but come and go. Some valleys and canyons feel them more than others. There is no place in the world that is perfect 100% of the time. I'd rather put up with a few windy days three months out of the year than deal with snow for five months of the year! We get strong winds in Palmira where we built our house, but we designed the house to accommodate the wind and it is oriented away from the winds.

Do you feel it is best to buy an existing home or to have home built? There seem to be good reviews on a company called "PAC" that builds in the new housing developments. Any knowledge of that company or opinions?

This was an old email question, but I've included it because the company in question went out of business a few years ago leaving a number of folks high and dry.

Whatever you do in Panama, as anywhere else, you need to do your due diligence and make a thorough investigation. Take your time and talk to many people, not just the reference names that are suggested contacts. If it sounds too good to be true, it probably is.

The company referred to in the email was asking for 80% of the cost of construction up front. That wouldn't make sense in the States, so why would it make sense in Panama? Being "American" or a US builder is no more guarantee of success than using a local, Panamanian builder. It is tough to build in Panama, but it can be done, if you are on site to supervise. The chances of building long distance and being happy with the result are minimal. If you intend to rent in Panama and live here during construction, go ahead and build. Otherwise, buy an existing home where you can see what you are getting and someone else has endured the hassles of building. Be sure and read the next chapter!

What do you actually DO?

Before we moved to Panama, this was the question we emailed to everyone we'd met in Boquete. Our greatest fear was retiring to Panama with nothing to do! Our friends would laugh and say, "We're as busy as ever!" And it's true! But the busyness you have here is busyness of your own choosing. You make the schedule. You do what you enjoy and you find new things to enjoy. We have a lot more friends here because in California we were both so busy we really didn't have time for friends. We socialize more, largely because we have time. You can be as busy as you choose to be!

How often do you do cruises?

The easy answer: as often as possible! The real answer: it depends. Depends on the opportunities available and how interesting the itinerary is, and the arrangements.
I've been to most of the Caribbean, and many of the islands have just become one Diamonds International and Colombian Emeralds store after another. I love the Canal trips because I get to talk a lot about living in Panama, but you can only do so many trips through the Canal and keep it interesting. I like doing world cruises especially if they have interesting itineraries. Generally I'm at sea six months a year, and the rest of the time in Panama.

Have you heard about "Canoe Man"?

"Canoe Man" and his wife may be the British saints of con. John Darwin apparently faked his death in a kayak accident as a scam to escape debts in Britain. His wife collected his life insurance policy and the couple moved to Panama where they purchased an apartment in Panama City. Two things undid the scheme: John's longing to see his adult sons, who thought their father dead, and an Internet photo of the couple on the Web site of a Panamanian real estate agent. As the escape and scam unraveled it was the top story in Britain for weeks . . . and generated a lot of interest in Panama. Apparently record numbers of Brits are leaving merry old England, tired of crime, dreary weather, taxes and the high cost of living. Many go to Australia and New Zeeland, and a lot go to Spain, Gibraltar and even Turkey. The lower cost of living and warm weather make Panama particularly appealing.

Peter, a blog reader from Hampshire, England wrote,

"Richard that dude John Darwin is the one who alerted us to Panama! Shame he is in prison now for collecting squillions [this must be a British word] in death Insurance and pensions claimed by his wife who not surprisingly is also in custody since arrival back in England this morning.

"To me Panama was the quintessential Central American hellhole drug store run by a manic Fascist named Noriega.

"There are millions of GI bred 'victory babes' (I could never understand why they called me Hank as a baby) in the UK, you call them boomers, retiring over the next five years who, like me, are 61and looking to retirement where it is warm and affordable.

"I live in the South of England, Hampshire, Winchester is the capital (the original one) which is by far the richest region in all of Europe with a house worth a million US $, huge gardens etc. Along with that comes 52% government tax, $4000 local community tax, gas (petrol to us) at $10 a gallon, a loaf of bread $4, a pint of beer $5. Now see the potential for Panama if it remains stable?

"The only negative is no direct flights from London. We will have to use the hubs of Atlanta or Miami which makes it somewhat torrid journey, but after living in Africa, Zimbabwe and South Africa I am sure Panama would be a superb environment. I have considered Spain but so has everyone else and house prices for a 3 bedroom villa in a good spot now costs $500,000 to $750,000US for English to live there. It is now completely overpriced and the bubble is ready to burst.

"That's why this golden nugget called Panama is worth investigating for we wish to retire in style and in the quality of environment you have."

So, Sir Peter, come on over . . . Sell your house, cash in your chips, get out of the casino, and come and enjoy life. Just forget the "canoe" route! Actually we have a lot of "Brits" in Panama and in Boquete. The town of Boquete was started over a hundred years ago and developed largely by Europeans because of its wonderful soil and agricultural climate. One of our first settlers was a retired English sea captain who fell in love with a Panamanian. His descendants, the Watsons, are pillars of the community! It's not unusual to find long-term Boquetanians with very English names.

Condor flies to Panama City from several cities including Manchester, and KLM and Iberia offer direct flights from the Continent. Emirates has just signed an open skies agreement with Panama.

Have you heard about "Wild Bill", the mass murderer?

Another infamous con artist, this one from the US, who tried to reinvent himself in Panama.

Some of the folks come down to Panama from the US trying to get away from the long arm of the law. Thanks to the Internet and the "Coconut Grapevine" most eventually end up getting caught and deported.

It took a while to catch up with "Wild Bill Cortez" whose real name was William Dathan Holbert. Holbert and his wife were wanted in the US and decided to hide out in Latin America. Holbert reinvented himself as William Cortez, and moved to Bocas del Toro where he established himself as a larger-than-life, local character (of which there are many in Bocas) who went by the moniker "Wild Bill".

Holbert was a real estate scam artist who would befriend people who held property in bearer bond SA corporations. With a bearer bond company whoever physically holds the bond owns the property. Once he established the friendship and knew where the bonds were, "Wild Bill" simply took the people out and put bullets through their heads, buried them in shallow graves and took over everything they owned. People simply disappeared!

In expat communities people come and go so their sudden absence did not seem unusual until their friends and family back home started making inquiries. Unable to find their friends or family members, people began making deeper inquiry. Their concerns came to the attention of a somewhat muckraker blog journalist named Don Winner whose Panama-Guide.com is a popular source of local information in English. Winner is a former US Air Force intelligence agent who came to Panama during the Noriega years, liked Panama, and stayed. Winner[20] went after the story like a hungry bulldog and eventually uncovered a gruesome trail of bodies.

Holbert and his wife escaped to Costa Rica where they ran the same scam until they were recognized then ran on to Nicaragua where they were captured at a routine check point. Both are now sitting in jail in Panama.

Can you really live in Panama on $600 a month?

---

[20] Winner is a former US Air Force cryptologic linguist and strategic intelligence analyst with Special Forces experience throughout Latin America.

I get this question a lot. People get this $600 a month number because in order to get a retirement or *Pensionado* visa you used to have to prove you have outside pension income of at least $600 a month for a couple. That number is now $1,000 a month "for life" or you have to have purchased property in your own name for at least $100,000 in which case the pension amount need only be $750.

Can you live on that? Sure. It may be a struggle, but Panamanian retires do manage to live on much less than that. But most folks from the US and Canada do not want to live that way. For most retirees from the US $1000 a month is going to be nowhere near what they need! One of the problems with the Internet is that information is not dated and is often outdated, particularly when it comes to "cost of living" information from Panama. Food seems to cost almost as much as it does in the States, unless you are going to shop like a Panamanian in a local market at Panamanian not *gingo* prices, and steer away from prepared and imported products. Most Americans aren't going to shop that way! Price Smart looks comfortably like Price Club/Costco but has nowhere near the selection and really doesn't offer much, if any, savings, unlike Costco in the US.

Don Winner, the expat blogger who really was instrumental in uncovering and capturing "Wild Bill", has a very helpful blog called Panama-Guide.com which expats and folks considering moving to Panama should read. Realizing that one of the most frequent questions people by people considering moving to Panama is "what is the cost of living" and recognizing that there is a lot of outdated and misinformation on line, Winner asked his readers to share what their "real" cost of living was in Panama. He gave specific parameters of what to include and how to respond. He received a myriad of responses for expats living all over Panama, everyone from self-acknowledged spendthrifts to folks struggling to get by. Singles, couples, families responded from several dozen communities across Panama.

Presented on his blog, it gave a snapshot of the cost of living for various expat families with various lifestyles. Winner went on to analyze the responses which were across the board form $1,995 to $295 per person per month. In a way kind of what you expect: people's expectations and life styles are different, even in Panama. You can get the snapshot on Panama-Guide.com and it makes interesting reading.

Depending on you expectations, your needs and wants, it doesn't have to cost a fortune to retire in Panama!

I am a state-certified building contractor in Orlando, Florida land figure it is time for a change. I have always done what I set out to do and feel I can do the same outside the country. Is there a demand for a reputable builder to come down, immerse themselves in the community, develop crews and could he be successful? I have read all the pitfalls and issues, but I also had similar pitfalls here, and if anyone thinks building in Florida is a piece of cake, they obviously haven't tried it. Let me know your thoughts!

I think you might do well. You have the right attitude. You have the experience. If you live in South Florida you must speak Spanish because nobody speaks English in South Florida. I think there is demand. Some guys like you have come and succeeded; others have turned out to be crooks or just didn't have the stamina to make it work. My question is do you have the resources, i.e. deep enough pockets, to be able to put out for a while before you start making money? Locals seem to understand and do well with cement, block, steel and wood. With the exception of tile work, finishing is another story. Electric isn't bad, but plumbing, drywall and roofing are disasters.

While you can't work as an employee for someone else, you can be a consultant or own your own business. Be sure to read the next chapter about "Building In Paradise" before you give up your business in the US!

It seems from all I've read, I still can't retire to Panama unless I'm very well off because of the lack of availability of medical insurance for those over 62. I'm not there yet, but close and certainly could never afford an intensive care unit or other prolonged hospitalization out of my own pocket with only Social Security and a small pension. So why is everyone promoting retirement to Panama? It seems like so many other places that are only for the wealthy. Mind you I'm, not poor, but have only so much money for retirement. Am I missing something?

Not everyone who retires in Panama is wealthy! Most people choose to retire here because it is cheaper than most places in the US. Just like in the States there is a wide variety of housing options. You can rent a fairly nice place for $750 a month, or a more luxurious place for $2000 a month. There are houses for sale in Boquete for several million dollars, and ones for under $50,000. I built my brother's very cute and comfortable 1,100 square foot casita for under $50,000 including the cost of land.

There are insurance schemes available some last, some don't. Because medical care is so much cheaper in Panama than in the US, some people choose to self-insure knowing that once they are 65 they can always go back to the US and use their Medicare, but sometimes the full cost of the treatment in Panama is less than what they would have to pay out of pocket in the US with Medicare.

It's nice to be retired, live anywhere in the world you wish and have no business deals with locals. But there are several problems with this perfect picture. First, you can't increase your income. Second, you can't stop using your brain. You need something not only to keep you occupied, but also happy. Third, you have to wait until retirement age to live the dream.

Is there a secret and what is it?

Secret: the guts to get out of the rut and do it!

Nothing is easy! If it was easy everyone would do it. There will always be problems. My way may not necessarily be your way. "Business deals with locals" ARE a problem, no question, but in my opinion, the reward outweighs the hassle, which is why I stay in Panama.

I've found a way that works for me to "increase" my income by working on ships half the year - granted for a whole lot less than I made before I retired, but with lots of bennies like seeing the world – which at the same time really stretches my brain, having to put together all these lectures. People can and do retire early. I did. But you have to really understand the numbers and see if it will work for you. Most people don't understand their own money: how much they have, how they spend it, what retirement will cost, etc. Run your numbers and see what is possible. Don't just assume you can't do it!

Is Boquete suitable for a single woman in her late fifties?

Absolutely! There are a lot of single gals here that are active in lots of activities and have no problems. Compared to most places in the world, Boquete is very safe.

Why did you move out of Valle Escondido?

Easy answer: I bought a piece of property in Palmira as an investment. It was an old coffee farm and my wife decided to have a go at restoring it. We liked going up to the farm and letting the dogs run, and decided to build our dream home on the farm.

More difficult answer: Our home in Valle Escondido was one of the first built. When we went the Valley was pretty much a jungle with few buildings. Over the years we watched it build out and a resort develop. Although beautiful, even spectacular, and secure, it slowly began to feel less like the Panama we came to experience and more like a very nice, very upscale development which could have been almost anywhere in Southern California. I'm not a golfer, so for me, aside from the beauty of the golf course, it wasn't an incentive.

In Palmira I hear the neighbors, their dogs, and sometimes their music. At 4 am the roosters start to crow. When we're away we need someone to housesit. It's a long way . . . not that long, but it seems long at 10pm at night . . . to drive home from a party. In Valle Escondido you could drink too much and walk home! So there are a lot of advantages of Valle Escondido that we miss. It's just that we came here to experience Panama which is exactly what life on a coffee farm is like.

Are your books available in Spanish?

Not yet, but several students at the University in David, studying to be English translators are working on translating this book at CRUISING THE PANAMA CANAL for their final senior project.

I understand Panama is building a new airport?

Actually two new, or renewed airports. David [DAV] airport has had a major makeover with improvements to the runway, new radar, and a beautiful new and expanded terminal. It is an "international" airport because it has several flights a week to Costa Rica. What it needs now is a major airline flying to the US! Hopefully Copa will step up and start providing direct service to Tocumen International in Panama City, Copa's hub for the Americas, as well as direct service to the US [most likely Miami or Houston].

Prior to the US Invasion the main military airport in Panama was at Rio Halto in the middle of the country. During the US Invasion this was the major airport used by giant US planes. Although closed since Panama abandoned the military after the Invasion, the basic runway remained. Now Panama is building a major international airport at Rio Halto which is scheduled to open next year. The Pan American Highway will run underneath the main runway.

Rio Halto will serve the expanding beach resorts on the Pacific coast as well as being more accessible to the Azuero Peninsula , Chiriqui and Boquete.

Interacting

1. So, what additional questions do you have?

Start making a list. If you have questions you'd like me to answer just send them to me on my blog - RichardDetrich.com -and I will respond. Just know that if I am on a ship there is sometimes a delay in responding.

13. Building In Paradise

Here's a question similar to ones I get all the time: "My husband and I recently bought property in Boca Chica with a beautiful view of Playa Hermosa Bay. We are still in the States but thinking of building. Do you have any recommendations, suggestions or tips?"

My best advice if you are considering building in Panama – don't!

I don't think that I am a novice to building. In my career as a pastor I built three churches, working with architects, builders, and city planning departments in New York City, Milwaukee, and Jefferson County, Colorado. We built a second home in Door County, Wisconsin. And I partially remodeled two brownstones in New York, and remodeled our home in Ventura, moving bearing walls, building sheer walls, doing electric, plumbing and rough and finish carpentry. I've installed three kitchens. I'm not an expert, but I'm not a novice either.

All-in-all I am pleased with the home we built in Palmira in spite of the worst efforts of some of the folks who should have been on my "team" and weren't. What was promised in one year took almost two years and never was finished by the builder whose ass I fired after he took all my money and only did 70% of the work. I put together a crew and finished it myself.

I would never do this again in Panama nor would I recommend it to you. Panama is a great place to live and a wonderful place in which to retire. But building here is nuts!

I know when you come down and see a beautiful lots or beautiful graphics for a development, it looks tempting, but my advice is to look around and find something already built. Even if an existing place isn't perfect, with a little money, and a lot less frustration, you can do some upgrades, some redecorating and landscaping and make it into your dream home. Trust me, the house you build, even if you are on site 100% of the time, will not be perfect either!

I had planned to build some other stuff in Panama, but after this experience I've decided to abandon those plans. There! My wife wanted it "in writing" so here it is. "I may be stupid [to do this in the first place], but I'm not crazy [to do it again]!"

I love and admire good architecture. I like Frank Lloyd Wright and Frank Gehry, even although their style isn't "my style." As far as I'm concerned the art deco Chrysler Building in New York is near perfection. I admired Richard Neutra who did the original buildings for the Crystal Cathedral when it was Garden Grove Community Church and Phillip Johnson's Garden Grove Church when it was the Crystal Cathedral[21]. And The Getty by Richard Meier is close to my definition of architectural perfection. I also love the old gothic architecture of cathedrals in Europe, and some modern church architecture, like the tiny chapel at Seattle University.

I've hired architects and worked with them to design and construct three church buildings. So I'm not a novice working with architects. I have had very good architects and we have worked well together. I know what an architect should do and what to expect . . . but not in Panama!

To my regret I have discovered that architects in Panama generally draw a pretty picture, farm out the engineering, and then let the builder figure out the details . . . if it will work, and how it should work. "Specs", which were generally a one to three inch thick book in the States, are sketchy at best and are limited to notes on the plans.

---

[21] Due to the unfortunate demise of the Crystal Cathedral and Robert Schuller Ministries, the church has been purchased by the Roman Catholic Archdiocese of Orange and has been renamed, perhaps more appropriately, Christ's Cathedral.

The architect doesn't specify much of anything and the details are left to the builder.

So why do you need an architect in Panama? In my opinion, you don't! If I were doing it again, I would have a US architect draw up the plans and specs, then get a responsible, reputable Panamanian engineer with great references and impeccable attention to detail to draw up plans for Panama and get them approved.

Panama City is a sea of architectural extravagance some designed by local architects and some by firms from outside the country. I am sure there are good architects in Panama City.

We started out on this project working with a friend and neighbor, Brad Abajian. Brad retired early as a successful Poker player. His dad has a construction company that did high end custom homes in the Los Angeles area and Brad grew up in a contractor's world and knows a lot about construction. He worked with us over months as we defined what we wanted and drew up plan after plan. I spent hours and hours with Nikki working out what we wanted on an inexpensive computer design program. Brad went over it with us and made excellent suggestions, but it is our house.

I wanted something with a Tuscan country feel that would somehow fit in a tropical mountain coffee farm setting. We wanted a home that was light and airy and open. We wanted a home with an inside/outside feel since after all you come to Panama to enjoy life outside. I wanted our bedroom to be as close to sleeping outside as possible. And we wanted a patio that was an integral part of our home. Since it rains a lot in Palmira during the rainy season, we needed outside living areas that were protected from wind and rain.

So we take full credit for the design of our house! If you like it, credit us. And, despite the architect's best . . . or worst . . . efforts, it came out looking almost like we designed.

The "hot" architects for *gringos* in Boquete were mostly young men whose fathers had construction companies. We talked around and it came down to two guys we should talk with. I liked them both. I had seen a lot of the work of both and it wasn't bad, but we already knew pretty much what we wanted. One guy told us it would be at least two months before he could start on our project, and the other guy told us he would start right away. We chose the guy who could start right away . . . only the reality was that he put us off for two months!

He charged us a design fee. I figured since he was an architect, and going to charge us a design fee no matter what, rather than show him what I had designed, I would describe what we wanted, and see what he came up with. He speaks English fluently and so I described what we wanted in a house, how we wanted it to flow and feel, our life style, how we wanted to use the house, and our budget.

A few months later he came back with a plan. It was immediately obvious that he hadn't listened to a word we said. Parts of the unimaginative plan looked vaguely familiar from houses he'd designed that I had seen under construction. At first I thought it was someone else's house. It appeared as if he had cut and pasted together – not very well, I might add – parts of other houses he had designed. So much for design and although he had done nothing we paid him for the design phase. I pulled out the computer and showed him the detailed plans we had designed with Brad that were VERY detailed including light circuits, cabinetry . . . the works. I said, "Here this is exactly what we want. We need you to take it and work on the roof lines and prepare working drawings. We're going ahead and ordering Burmese cherry cabinets from China, so we need to have you keep the exact dimensions."

So he prepared plans. And we spent lots of time going over and over the plans, pointing out things he had omitted or changed, discussing the plans. Eventually we had listed all the changes we needed and he came up with the final set of plans. We reviewed those and pointed out a few glaring errors . . . like dropping a skylight out of the kitchen that had been included previously . . . changing our fireplace (US style proportions) to a Panamanian style fireplace (totally out-of-proportion by US expectations) . . . that he promised to change . . . and waited for our final, approved, stamped plans.

The architect spoke fluent English. The plans were in meters, a language we didn't speak and although the builders work in inches and feet, he refused to do the plans in feet since it wasn't what he usually did. And I'll admit that he was busy making plans for a wedding so that may have distracted him, but . . . as the construction progressed we discovered:

• A window in the laundry room that was in the final plan had been dropped;

• The plate line which I had specified as 10 feet [3 meter] had been reduced to 9 feet [2.7 meter] which caused a lot of scrambling and builder adjustments so our furniture would fit;

• Large bathroom windows had been reduced to typical Panamanian size bathroom windows, reflecting some sense of modesty I guess even when it was impossible for anyone to look in the windows, not only did this limit the light we wanted, but eliminated my wife's view of the mountains from the her tub, but increased the cost of decorative tile borders;

• The large hopper-style windows in my shower – for view of the volcano and ventilation – had been changed to small, fixed windows totally defeating the purpose;

• 8 foot [2.4 meter] doors had been reduced to standard doors;

• Two walls didn't meet;

• The corner of the tower – a wall which supported one quarter of the weight of the tower, ended midway in mid air with no support [Fortunately my builder was smarter than my architect and pointed out that there was no structural support for 25% of the weight of the tower roof. To correct this we had to angle the corner which meant the side clear story windows had to be different sizes than the front and rear clearstory windows];

• The electrical plan required a humongous steel box, larger than most developments and commercial buildings in Boquete, and this wasn't discovered by the contractor (how I will never know, since he bid the job) until 16 months into the job when he was hooking up the electric and if we wanted to make a change we would have to have new electrical plans drawn up and approved;

• The kitchen plans which had to be exact since we had pre-ordered cabinets were changed;

• The architect stuck in a 36" [.9 meter] dishwasher, when every household dishwasher in the world is 24" [.6 meter] or 18" wide [about .5 meter];

• Electrical circuits and outlets were seemingly randomly placed, or placed by computer, with no regard to our requests;

• He drew in things, like doors to the patio, which were supposed to open all the way and stack, without specifying how they were to be constructed – in general details were absent and left up to the builder;

• The architect changed the fireplace back to Panamanian proportions from our US design which I had to rework and redesign on the spot;

Along the way the skylight/cupola that was supposed to flood the kitchen and dining room with light was carelessly shifted on the plans to the back porch, which didn't need any more light!

I suspect, because his dad builds a lot of his designs that pops "catches" and fixes his errors. The guy didn't listen. He didn't pay attention to the client or to detail and isn't detail what an architect should be all about. He didn't adequately check and recheck plans and didn't make corrections as promised . . . all-in-all our experience was for me an architectural disaster.

In spite of the architect, we have been able to create a home which still has 90% of what we had specified.

It is a lovely home to live in and admired by all. The fact that it is in spite of the architect and not because of the architect is a shame. I know this is not the US. In the US we are accustomed to building in a seemingly hectic, but actually very organized and efficient process:

- Building permit is pulled
- Surveyors arrive and stake out site
- Heavy equipment arrives and cleans site
- Cement crew, plumber and electrician arrive, construct forms, lay
- pipes and conduit, pour footings, foundations, and slab
- Rough carpentry crew arrives to frame house and as they
- progress the electrician and plumber are doing their stuff
- Roofers show up
- Windows, doors, and cabinets show up
- Finish carpentry crew shows up
- Painters and tile people show up
- Carpet arrives
- Certificate of occupancy is secured
- "Check list" corrections are made
- New owners move in

It's a neat, organized, carefully choreographed process. When one house is finished the crew moves to the next pad and starts another. Labor is expensive so adequate materials show up "just in time". It's so well choreographed that TV shows can build a house (granted with fifty workers!) in a week, start to finish!

Well, Virginia, this ain't the US of A!

And from our US cultural background building in Panama seems all backwards! We had spent two years watching contractors build in Valle Escondido. When we came here we were the second house in Valle Escondido, so we've watched most of them being built. The favorite Sunday afternoon activity in Valle Escondido used to be traipsing through homes under construction and critiquing everything! So based on our observations and feedback from lots of folks, we submitted our plans for bids to five different contractors.

Contractor A was an expat *gringo*. Young guy, asked a lot of the right questions that I would have expected in the States (soil studies, topographical studies, etc.) and had built a home outside Valle Escondido that I liked.

Contractor B spoke English and was one of the largest Panamanian contractors in Boquete and does residential as well as commercial work. We'd seen a lot of his work, and he built a friend's house in Valle Escondido. It was a big outfit with lots of jobs running simultaneously. But in my humble opinion the onsite management for my friend's project was poor and some of the quality of work left something to be desired. They did however have resources in terms of money and access to workers and subs.

Contractor C also spoke English, certainly better than my Spanish, and had also done the house of a friend. We liked his quality, and we liked him. He'd built in other Latin American countries but had been building in Panama for about ten years, mostly low-end Panamanian housing projects. He had his own ironwork and window shops and seemed to have a pretty efficient operation. He had resources in terms of money and access to workers and subs. But he had established a cooperative relationship with an expat promoter that gave us some reservation.

Contractor D spoke only Spanish and was definitely a small operator. He built a few homes a year, but was a local and had been building in Boquete for something like fifteen years. Frankly, we were skeptical until we saw a few of the houses he had built. We were impressed by the quality of his workmanship and frankly, by him. He had a small crew with whom he had worked for years, and since he was a small player had limited financial resources. We knew from friends that he had difficulty wrapping up projects but that is pretty much a universal problem with Panamanian builders. [This is where the sirens and red lights should have gone off!]

Contractor E was a couple just starting out. Both were graduates of Texas A&M with impressive credentials. They had just completed a friend's house right on schedule and their work was as good as any we had seen in Boquete. The father of one was an established builder of larger projects in Panama giving them entre to workers and subs, but they lived in Panama City so would not be on the job on a daily basis.

We gave all five a complete set of plans (well, as "complete" as plans are in Panama), along with five pages of introductory explanation about us, and our expectations, and specific concerns and, if you will, demands.

Contractor A – Disappeared with our plans. Fortunately all I lost was a set of plans!

Contractor B – Came in with the high bid. He had a couple of other big projects getting underway. He had built our friend's house and knew our friend was not totally happy, and I think was a little concerned that our friend would be helping us as an advisor, and I'm not sure he really wanted the job.

Contractor C – Came in with a bid right in the middle. He was definitely a major contender. He had the resources, his quality was good, but we were concerned about the business relationship he had with this expat promoter. He assured us that he was severing the relationship, but it didn't appear that way.

Contractor D - was the low bidder, but the quality of his work made him a definite contender. He only spoke Spanish and we really only spoke English, so that was a concern. The fact that he was a small operator we viewed as both a blessing (more attention to our project with only one or two a year) and a curse (limited crew and resources).

Contractor E - Also came in with a bid right in the middle. Their background, fluency in our language, the quality of their work, and the enthusiastic recommendation of a friend made them definite contenders. We were concerned that they were new with only one, albeit very good, *gringo* house under their belt, and that they were in Panama City.

So, which did we choose?

You know that if this were on Home & Garden TV that there would be a commercial break at this point. Since I can't do that, I will hold you in suspense while I share some general observations about much of the building in Boquete.

1) It looks disorganized . . . and it is!

"Choreographed" is not a word that you would use to describe building in Panama.

It's a little like traffic flow in Panama City or David . . . somehow, in the end, amazingly, everyone eventually gets where they are going without major loss of life . . . but the process of getting there is a zoo! With the exception of the Panama Canal expansion project, I doubt if these folks ever heard of a PERT chart or know how to use MS Project.

Panamanians in general seem to think lineally, certainly do in construction. The idea that you have multiple trades working simultaneously to reach a goal without stepping on each other or destroying each other's work seems totally foreign.

2) Labor is relatively cheap . . . supplies aren't.

"Just in time" can be a very good concept, except in Panama stuff is never "in time."

God forbid that anyone should order enough of anything, let alone some extra.

They always run short! So you have guys sitting around waiting for things like cement, sand, wire . . . No matter how big the operation, Panamanians are used to living and thinking "on a shoe string." The concept that you might buy and store major chunks of the materials you need so the materials are on hand when needed, is totally foreign. Buying what you need up front would make sense especially as construction supply costs are going through the roof. But generally that's not the way things are done. But I now know that often money is being siphoned off each job to finish the job that precedes it. Would that it were just as simple as continually running to the construction supply store! Of course the store doesn't keep items in stock. They have to order . . . and wait . . . while you wait and wait. It could be simple . . . and planned . . . but it isn't.

You are not, repeat NOT, going to change that basic way of doing things in Panama!

3) OSHA would go bonkers!

Some of the larger builders issue hard hats to workers, but chances are the hard hats won't be worn but will be used as mixing buckets for tiny batches of cement with which to patch up. Crude, improvised ladders are made on the job . . . and not a single one would get OSHA approval. Where in the US we would call in a crane to lift I beams into position, here they are lifted by hand with workers often standing on the top rung of rickety hand made ladders holding the I beam above their heads while someone welds it into place. We routinely run eight different saws, drills, etc., off one jerry-rigged electrical line which sometimes gets changed to 220 and heaven help you if you plug in your drill and don't know that for the moment its 220. Worse yet we get one of the frequent afternoon downpours and you are standing on a wet surface using an electrical tool which is plugged into a jerry-rigged extension cord that isn't grounded.

My daily prayer while we were building was, "Lord, first, let us get through this day; second, may we get through this day without anyone getting hurt or killed; and, third, assuming we are allowed several requests, may I get through this day without killing the builder!"

4) Estimates are guestimates.

I suspect that jobs are estimated with guestimates and that quotes are put together on a guestimate of square foot costs and not actually costed out down to each nail and cinder block. Sometimes this works, but sometimes, especially when material costs are soaring, it doesn't work.

Construction times mean nothing. Absolutely, positively, nothing. Safe bet: take whatever a contractor says and at least double it.

Panamanians like to please and they tend to tell you what they think you want to hear whether it is true or makes any sense or not.

5) Tools of the trade.

There are none.

Want to work construction in the US? You'd better come equipped, not only with skills, but also with tools. In Panama a really equipped worker MAY have his own tape measure, but that's it. All you need is two hands and a strong back. And the contractor isn't much better. All a contractor seems to need to be a contractor is a cement mixer . . . generally one he is borrowing. If that doesn't work, a hoe will do. Panamanians are inventive and they are good at recycling and making tools as needed.

6) Promises, promises, promises.

OK, that's not unique to Panama! When we built a cottage in Door County, Wisconsin, some neighbors who had used the same builder, gave us some advice. Our builder was a great guy who had built and paid for the local church. He was a great Christian guy and we enjoyed working with him, but before we started our neighbors warned us, "He may be a Christian, but remember, he's a contractor first."

7) Prayer, booze and money . . .

Prayer, booze and money are the essential tools for anyone who is foolish enough to build in Panama.

The prayer is to pray for the safety of your workers and that the contractor actually delivers and finishes in this millennium.

The booze . . . it's the key to patience and accepting that things aren't as they are in the US, and that's why you moved to Panama in the first place.

The money . . . well, particularly if you are building, Panamanians see all *gringo*s as multimillionaires with nothing but money and more money, so you'd better have an endless flow because you will need it!

* * * *

Oh yes, we choose the builder behind Door D: wrong choice as you will see!

After I first published some of these thoughts on my blog, I received this well-written and thoughtful response comment on my blog from Charles Metz which anyone who even thinks about building in Panama should read.

"My name is Charles Metz. We have met at Valle Escondido. You may recall that I am a custom home builder and developer living in Naples Florida. I have designed and supervised the construction of one house in Valle Escondido long distance which was also a bit of a disaster.

"No matter what quality of American plans you have, your plans must be submitted by and in the name of a Panamanian architect in order to get a permit. This is largely taken advantage in Panama with the typical asking price being in the neighborhood of $15,000 to $20,000 by local architects who do nothing. Custom plans for a house in Boquete end up costing more than for a house in Naples, Florida one of the most expensive markets in the US.

"In addition once you turn your plans over to a Panamanian architect they are owned by him. If you ever decide to change anything or remodel you will need that architect's permission. I have heard of architects charging $10,000 just for their permission. So it is good to get something in the contract about this. If the architect is also the builder you will not be able to fire the builder halfway through the project since he controls the plans. You also will not be able to fire the contractor half way through the project and finish the job yourself since your original contractor must sign the paperwork for your occupancy permit, meaning you will have difficulty holding out the final 10% of the contract price as a penalty for shoddy or incorrect work. And forget taking anyone to court. The courts are not very dependable and you are a stranger in a strange and.

"It is important to remember that few of the local architects have had experience with the budgets that are used in the States to build custom homes. The few who are experienced have generally only designed for wealthy Panamanians with lifestyles and design expectations totally different than those expected by North Americans. Because of limited availability of trained craftsmen, local architects have learned to keep it simple. A large Panamanian house is generally a smaller Panamanian house with enlarged rooms.

"There is very little supervision on a Panamanian construction site. I don't care who the builder is. And if you want your house to look like your plan, you had better be on the site every day. The workers will do what they are used to doing unless told otherwise. And unless you are there they will not be told otherwise. There will likely be no plan at the jobsite and if there were the electrical engineer is probably the only one at the job who could read them anyway.

"For those thinking they can buy and American architect plan on the Web and build it in Panama think again. In Panama you are building a concrete block house for earthquakes not hurricanes, so your generic tropical plans will not work. The steel reinforcement bar designs are very different and specific. A house plan developed using California earthquake code won't work since the Panamanian system is very different.

"A Panamanian house is built more like a high-rise condo than like a single family house that North Americans have experienced. All floor systems are poured concrete. We are talking welded red steel here. And although the first house that I designed in Panama was of M2 and not block construction, I would not do that again.

"I have seen many 'experienced' Americans try to go to Panama and 'tell them how we do it back home'. Frankly, nobody cares how you do it back home and being the 'Ugly American' will likely cost you more money. It is amazing to me how easily the Panamanian people get insulted if they think you are being disrespectful. It is the Latin macho thing. So you need to have your contract very specific and then treat everyone with kid gloves. And unless you write your own contract it will be full holes and opportunities for extra charges. It does not take long to learn that there are Panamanian prices and there are *gringo* prices.

"To those American builders who think you are going to go to Panama and take the business from the local builders to build for the *gringos* please don't be so foolish. It is a closed and protected system. Not only do you not know what you are doing, you do not have the labor nor understand how to manage the labor. You do not know the true costs, the construction systems, or the local laws. The locals will blackball you in a minute. They are related and you are not. They know who to pay off and you do not. Heck, if you are like me you probably do not even know the language very well.

"So what is a person to do if you want to build a home in Panama? I have a few thoughts.

"1 - Find those Web site plans that you like and buy them. Make sure they are designed for block construction and not wood frame. Buy the plans on disk in auto cad so they can be easily modified and if you have any changes to make have 'the original architect in the States' makes them. Keep in mind there are few flat lots in Panama and foundations are expensive as is site work for the grade. Make sure your plans work for your grade and will fit on your lot before you buy them.

"2 - Go find a Panamanian architect who is willing to redraw your plans in metric and in Spanish and for the local seismic construction code. All Panamanian architects are licensed over the entire country. So look in the larger cities rather than in the hot spots for development in the boonies.

"3 - Negotiate with the architect that you will 'own' the plans. Negotiate what he will charge for future revisions and what, if any, supervision of construction you expect from him. Keep in mind that your architect will have to visit your construction site and you will likely have to pay his expenses, so try to select someone within your region.

"4 – Find a bilingual Panamanian attorney to work for you in the creation of your requirements for a contract. Your contract will have to be both in English and in Spanish. English so you understand it and Spanish so that it will be a legal contract in Panama. Make sure your attorney has the power to legally 'authenticate' the translation: this is typically a specialty service from an authorized agency.

"5 - Establish an agreement with a local bank to make disbursements to your contractor based upon pre-agreed to phases of completion. They are not used to this but will do it for a fee. You will have to likely pay for each inspection by a bank person once your contractor requests a payment, but it will be worth it. The contractor will be less likely to try to jerk you around if the bank is involved. And at least you will have somebody speaking your contractor's language and who is paid to be on your side.

"6 - Now put your plans out for bid. Make sure your architect has detailed the specifications to your satisfaction. What you will find is that most of the contractors will no longer be interested in your project because you have taken away from them most of the tools to take advantage of you. But the ones remaining are the ones you want to talk to anyway.

"7 - If you are still inclined to 'do it yourself and save money', I suggest you at least contract with a local to build the shell of the house, what is locally referred to as 'in the gray' and then finish it yourself. Anyone can contract for laying of tile or painting, but keep in mind your 'in the gray contractor' will still have to submit the paperwork to get your occupancy permit, so get that agreed to upfront in writing.

"If you want to go to the next step, contract for construction management only. Go to your Panamanian bank and deposit enough funds to establish credit and then go to the building supply houses and establish your own builder account. You place the order for materials and you make the payments. This is a good strategy for several reasons. First, if you don't do this your builder will be getting a 10 to 15% discount and still will be marking up the materials to you at 20 to 30% over retail. And what did he do but make a phone call? Secondly, it is the only way you will know that all subs and materials have been paid for at the end of the job so you won't be stuck with the same kind of mechanic leans you are used to in the States.

"9 - Keep in mind that building only the shell is like building a log cabin. The log shell is a long way from the final cost of a house, so budget appropriately.

"10 – Finally, don't even think about doing it long distance: you have got to be on site. Period.

"Sound daunting? Sort of, but this is my recommendation after building one house in Panama and a few hundred over a thirty year period in the States.

"So let's see. We need a qualified architect willing to work under the terms outlined, we need a qualified attorney charging fair market fees, we need a banker willing to perform the service outlined, and we need a contractor willing to bid on the project under the terms outlined. And, it would not hurt to find some fresh out of university student willing to work by the hour as your translator.

"Wishing you continued success! Charles Metz"

There, Charles Metz just saved you hundreds of thousands of dollars, saved you from being ripped off, and, perhaps more importantly saved your marriage and saved you from a nervous breakdown.

I WISH, how I wish, I had his advice before we started building! Our experience wasn't as bad as some, but just to give you an idea.

The "nice guy" builder we contracted with turned out to be not so nice after he took 97% of my money and only completed 70% of the job, after taking twice the amount of time he promised. Unfortunately he's pulled this same scam with other *gringos*. The lesson here: you can't talk to too many people!

Even more unfortunately, Panamanian contractors typically intentionally underbid the job! And this guy is still doing it! "Sue him!" Yeah, but he knows the scam so all of his assets are in his wife's name and even if they weren't it would take ten or fifteen years, and we, being outsiders to the system would probably lose anyway.

Like all these guys he takes his profit at the beginning of the job, knowing in advance that there won't be anything left at the end. So I still see him driving around town in the new green Toyota truck with the little loop rings on the back to tie stuff down with . . . the truck that I bought!

But he was such a nice guy and played it so sincere and like most dumb *gringos* I bought it. I knew the cost of supplies was going up and he hadn't built any cost increases into the contract so frankly I expected to cough up some additional money at the end.

I wanted to help the guy out, which is why he ended up with 97% of the contract money and I only ended up with 70% of the job being done . . . a year late.

It all came to a head when he asked for an advance to purchase a septic tank, and then after I gave him the money kept telling me it was on order, and there were no septic tanks in David. It was two months before I was to leave on a five-month cruise contract and the house was already a year late. I sent my wife to David to check out septic tanks and she came home with this huge septic tank strapped on our truck.

The next day, September 1st, I fired his ass on the spot and told him and my caretaker that he was not allowed back on the property for any reason whatsoever. I then hired two of his workers who were now out of work. Of course they weren't his legal workers, just day workers, so now they were mine for two months. We moved into the partially completed house and roughed it while I worked with a team of three guys to complete the job. Two months later, the day I was leaving for the airport to work on the ship for five months, I was finishing up putting doors on the kitchen cabinets.

We were sitting in a restaurant just last week with some folks on the Panama Relocation Tour when another expat, who'd been here about two years, started talking about this contractor who did such nice work. I asked his name . . . and just about choked spitting out my wine when he said the name. The guy is still at it! Good first impression, not bad quality at least on the gray building (that's before any finishing), I guess still living off *gringo* suckers. So . . . ask around! And then ask some more! Obviously the guy making the recommendation had just "heard" but had never tried to build anything with . . . well, I can't tell you his name, but if you ask around, and ask expats who've been here a while and built, you'll find out!

Everything Charles says above, about firing your contractor and needing approvals is technically true, as is the fact that we shouldn't have been living in the house without a certificate of occupancy. I left the responsibility for getting a certificate of occupancy in my wife's hands. It took her four months of trying to track down the contractor, the architect who had signed the plans, etc., etc.

One of the big hassles was that the building department couldn't find the records or plans for our house. Not particularly unusual since back then nothing was really computerized and the building department was overwhelmed with plans and paperwork.

Finally, it turned out that the builder had never bothered to pull a building permit!! In spite of the fact that the fire department, of which the building department is a part, and the health department, and the electric company had all visited the house many times during construction and approved and signed off on everything . . . there never was a building permit!

It took some doing on Nikki's part, but when it all came out that there never was a building permit, meaning that both the licenses of the builder and the architect who signed for him were on the line, somehow the builder did come up with the permit fee and fine and the permit was issued retroactively and we got our occupancy permit.

Despite the architect, the builder and the "FUBAR" process, we ended up with a beautiful house.

Maybe because I was able to escape to five months on the ship, I never actually did have the nervous breakdown, although my wife came close.

So my best advice if you're considering building in Panama . . . don't! Find something already built and if necessary put some money into it to remodel it to your specifications. It will still be a hassle, but you will hang onto your sanity and a lot of money.

Interacting

1. The "big question" about building . . . why?

2. The "follow up question" . . . are you sure?

3. The "rubber meets the road question" . . . are you willing to physically be on site if you decide to build?

14. People Come . . . People Go

Why do people leave Boquete?

Great question! It has always interested me to know not only what brings folks to Boquete, but why they leave. I wish someone would do a study on this, but here are some of my own observations and those of others.

Perpetual Adventurers

Let's face it, picking up and moving to a foreign country requires a certain sense of adventure! Some folks we know have left Boquete and moved elsewhere because that's just the kind of people they are. They are always looking for another place . . . maybe another spot of the world that hasn't yet been "discovered" and where property is still ridiculously low-priced.

There are some folks who the moment they move to Boquete are already scouring International Living and the Internet, looking for the next "hot" place to move.

Relationships on the rocks

Moving is always a high stress event, and moving to a new country with a new language, new customs, and new mores make it an even higher stress event. Folks who thought that making a new start in a new country might "fix" things in their relationship soon find out it doesn't work that way. The stress is greater so, like a tiny crack in the windshield, the cracks in the relationship are soon going in multiple directions.

For a lot of folks, moving to Panama is breaking out of the mold or rut if you will, of the traditional commute, nine to five job, social obligations, and family expectations – whatever. Suddenly feeling free, and frequently knowing that this is the last big adventure of life . . . folks break loose . . . one stays, one heads back to the States, or they both move on elsewhere in different directions.

Folks who didn't do their homework

If you came to Panama looking to shop every other day at the Galleria, or expect museums, openings, Broadway, and symphonies in Boquete, or want a tennis club, US-style country club, shopping at Pavilions or Bristol Farms, or a 30-screen Cineplex . . . you ain't going to find it in Boquete! So why are folks surprised when they move here and don't find those things? Didn't they do their homework?

The novelty wears off

You chuck off everything in the States and move to Panama! It has a certain excitement and novelty to live in a new country where everything seems different. All the folks back home want to hear about your new adventure. But after two, or three, or four years the novelty wears off, and you begin to miss the familiar and the comfortable feel of wherever "home" used to be. You get homesick for Home Depot, Bed, Bath & Beyond, Wal-Mart and even the bureaucracy of the DMV where at least they – usually – speak English.

Looking for a fast buck

There are those who came to make a killing . . . and didn't, or maybe did. For some Panama was seen as an opportunity to get rich quick as the world's attention focused here and real estate and condo speculation was manic. Everyone saw the opportunity for instant cash: just buy a farm cheap, throw in a road and sell lots to unsuspecting foreigners. Well things rarely work out that way.

There is still great opportunity in Panama, but the day of the "fast buck" is disappearing quickly. Scam artists are gradually being sent back home, either by being rooted out by Panamanian authorities or being extradited back to authorities in their own countries. The question, "How can you become a millionaire in Panama?" The answer, "Come to Panama with two million!"

"Rain, rain go away!"

There are those who don't like the weather. Some folks never bothered to check the weather. Living in a rain forest is incredibly beautiful, but, guess what? It rains! And it rains a lot, particularly at certain times of the year and that isn't for everyone. There have been a lot of friends for whom Boquete is too cool and too wet and so they have left, not to go back to the States, but for beach areas where it's a lot hotter and there is a lot less rain.

Been there, done that.

Yes, we get a lot of expat retirees, "baby boomers" looking for a better lifestyle in their retirement years and come intending to stay. But interestingly we are getting a lot of young people, sometimes families with kids, or people who did well, retired early and are looking for a new and different experiences. These folks come, enjoy Boquete for a few years, and then move on to another adventure.

OK, we built the dream house, now what?

Most people have this dream of the house they'd like to have someday. So they retire, maybe cash out of the US and are in a new country where the cost of building is a lot less than it was back home and, for the moment at least, they are flush with cash . . . and so they build the dream house.

"Mea culpa!" When we moved to Panama we "downsized" from a 1,680 square foot house on the hill in Ventura - which by the way was very adequate for two people! - to a 3,000 square foot house in Valle Escondido, to a 4,500 square foot house on a 4.5 acre farm in Palmira. What's wrong with this picture?

We have some neighbors who sold the big estate-sized house in the States and bought a 3,000 square foot house while they built their 11,000 square foot Boquete mansion. Over drinks the wife said to us, "I love our little 3,000 square foot house and I have no idea why we are building this mansion for the two of us!"

Other friends built this incredibly well-designed and well-built French country chateau with a killer view and every amenity in the book. It's on the market. They bought a condo back home in Phoenix for a song in a depressed market, and are looking for a condo in Boquete. I bumped into the guy in the restaurant the other night and he said, "Richard, I'm tired of the upkeep and all the work! I just want a place where we can lock up and walk away for a few months."

I understand. Don't get me wrong: I love the farm and I love our house, but it is a lot of work and responsibility, especially when I'm on the ship half of the time.

Another couple moved down and bought a very nice home, and then proceeded to add anything and everything that could be added spending money like water. When the rest of us were paying gardeners $8 a day they paid their gardener $20 a day and naturally upset the order of things since he had to brag to all the other gardeners and then they wanted the same thing. The guy bought the big Harley and every other toy and the wife lavishly decorated the house. After a few years the house is on the market and they are back in the States.

What ever happened to "free and easy"?

Panama isn't the "tax haven" some people thought it was. Panama, like every place in the world, has taxes! The taxes may come in different forms, like fees, etc., but they are there none-the-less. If you're a US citizen and thought you were going to escape the IRS, no matter how many seminars you've attended or books you've purchased, think again. Short of renouncing your citizenship there is no way out.

As Panama moves from being a second world country to a first world country the government is becoming more computerized making it harder for those who would seek to avoid taxes illegally. But, as anywhere, there are ways to legally minimize your taxes, but there are taxes. Panama does not tax on income earned outside Panama. If you are a US citizen and your permanent residence is outside the US you do get to deduct up to $92,900 of earned income provided you are not physically in the US or US waters more than 30 calendar days a year.

"I'm not ready to retire . . . what I really needed was a Sabbatical".

My wife helped me define this after talking with a friend who was returning to Atlanta saying, "I still have ten years that I could be working!" Nikki has sometimes said, "I feel guilty . . . like I should be doing something . . . like I should be contributing." I found myself scouring potential cruise jobs, not that I want to leave Boquete, but I sometimes want to be back in "the action" for a few months of the year . . . and here I am. This isn't anything unique to living in Boquete; it's just a challenge of retirement. Perhaps more of a challenge to boomers than it was to past generations.

It's about the grandkids.

I grant you grandkids are a life-changer. When we moved here we didn't have any. Now our grandson is four and yes we miss him dearly! Thankfully with a combination of Skype and iPhone we can follow him around the house and visit with him regularly. Both my wife and I are preacher's kids, so neither of us lived near our grandparents. And since I was a minister much of my career, my kids never lived near their grandparents. And we didn't have Skype back then! Did we and our kids miss out on something? Absolutely! Did we in a way cheat our parents out of watching our kids grow up? Yes. But even if we did live nearer to our kids, we are not the kind of parents who would want to be intruding into their lives. Our kids love to visit us in Panama and we love to see them. Hopefully as our grandson gets older he will want to spend some time exploring Panama. Everyone's different, but before you make the move you need to figure out how the rest of the family fit into your plans.

Life changes.

Some people's lives change dramatically. Aging parents back in the States suddenly require more direct attention and involvement. Properties back home don't sell as expected. Businesses you thought you left in good hands suddenly need direct involvement. Spouses die and what was once your dream of a life together in Panama now rings hollow. One or another partner develops a medical condition best faced in the company of family and familiar medical resources and/or Medicare assistance.

Our new house in Palmira is on the road to the tiny cemetery in Palmira. My wife has informed me that she is "not moving again!" She has made it clear that her next move will be in a pine box, where she doesn't have to pack anything, to the cemetery down the road. Well, that's our plan . . . now. But, as Heraclitus pointed out, "We are living in a world of constant change." Things do change. People change. Plans change. And because of that, not everybody will stay in Boquete.

I posed this question on my blog and received a number of interesting responses.

From Scott and Belinda . . .

"Richard - The North Americans that I know personally who left Panama came here with little or no money and little to no continuing retirement income. They typically had exaggerated expectations of earning a living in Panama (bad idea, in my opinion). When that didn't work out, they had no choice, but to go back to their former jobs in the U.S. If someone wants to have a business to keep them occupied or for fun or to employ locals, fine . . . But don't count on making a living or getting rich. Come to Panama with sufficient income or assets to pay your bills, which may be higher than you expect."

From Diana . . .

"From my observation, it is not until you have made the move and experienced the lifestyle, experienced the differences for more than a few months, and endured the real challenges that anyone can judge and accept or reject the way of life here in Panama.

"Boquete (if considered as a separate entity, which I think it should be) seems on the surface to be the paradise that so many retirees are looking for. The climate is cooler and the views of Volcan Baru and surrounding landscape are stunning. Boquete is marketed as 'the place to be.' It is where so many have invested a lot of money, time and patience! It is where so many have made it their home, or invested for the future. It is the place that boasts many housing developments, hotels, sporting and leisure activities and is one of the biggest tourist destinations here in Latin America.

"It is a place where people have chosen to live in the safety of numbers, behind bars and security gates, in gated communities and advertised that they had something the local people could only dream of. As a result many fall victim to 'Gringo Bingo' where they end up being charged greater sums of money for products or services than locals. Many local people see us as an opportunity and feel there is much money to be made or just a little to supplement a pitiful income, as rich Americans and Europeans flaunt their previous lifestyle expectations in their faces. [Of course forgetting the Panama City Panamanian weekenders who really do have money and tend to be the ones with the really big houses.] Many come here with the thought that they can have their cake and eat it but will not change or adjust to a new way of living. We share responsibility for how things progress and should realize that before we try to change this country into the one from which we escaped . . . There is the need for patience here and many are so used to the fast pace they left behind, that the exceedingly slow pace here is intolerable. I think in reality, for many of us, is that we find ourselves way out from our comfort zone where the old rules no longer apply."

From Roger . . .

"I've observed that many come here with little or no knowledge of what to expect, assuming it'll be like it was from whence they came. Sometimes they try to recreate their 'comfort zone' here, but eventually give up. Many make little or no effort to learn Spanish, understand the people, customs and how things work here, or involve themselves into (not onto) the Panamanian community. Sometimes they retreat into their homes, like a turtle into its shell and, after they get bored doing nothing, despite everything there is to do, they leave. A foreigner here has to be proactive and friendly to be accepted and make a new life in a new land. Sometimes it's a matter of culture shock and sometimes just a lack of commitment."

One size does not fit all.

"Different strokes for different folks." Panama is not for everyone. Nor is Boquete, Coronado, Bocas, Ventura, Panama City or wherever. For us Panama has been wonderful! We only wished we would have made the move sooner. But . . . like anything in life it can become routine. We moved here to retire and to escape the rat race. And yet, as my wife noted the other day when we drove over to Volcan to buy plants, we may be as busy now as ever.

Granted, for the most part we have chosen the busyness we have now. We're working because we want to. As I tell the cruise line, "When this isn't fun anymore I'm out of here!"

A number of folks we know are moving back to the states, some who've been in Boquete as long as we have, or longer.

So Nikki and I had this big discussion as we drove the winding road up to Volcan. What did these couples have in common? Well, with these three, the men all seemed to love Panama, but the gals had gotten bored with the "adventure" of it all and missed the familiar accoutrement of home. Face it, going out for lunch with your friends at Tammy's isn't quite the same as lunch at the Cheesecake Factory. And shopping at La Reina isn't Nordstrom. Have these folks had a good time in Panama and great adventures? Of course! But for them it was an experience and after a while it was time to move on.

What I've tried to do in ESCAPE TO PANAMA is provide you with information and raise some of the questions you need to consider if you've ever thought about moving to Panama or anyplace else that is radically different from that to which you are accustomed.

If there are two factors which you must take into consideration if you are considering adopting an expat lifestyle they are these:

Your attitude toward CHANGE . . .

And your attitude toward RISK.

When you move from one country to another, one culture to another, there is going to be change – a lot of change.

Interacting

1. How well do you cope with change? Is it something you avoid or something you embrace? Do you find change threatening or stimulating.

2. Moving to another country and culture and adopting a lifestyle involves a lot of risk. What is your risk tolerance?

I welcome your thoughts, comments and questions. The easiest and quickest way to get in touch with me is via my blog RichardDetrich.com. Generally I try to blog every other day and I check out your comments almost daily.

15. Fifteen Things Not To Like About Living In Panama

If you are looking for paradise you probably won't find it.

Thanks to the screw up by our first parents, Adam & Eve, you're not going to find perfection or paradise this side of heaven. Accept it. Nothing is perfect. No one is perfect. But, as far as we're concerned, life in Panama is damn close, at least for us.

Folks decided to move to Panama for a lot of reasons. Escape. Adventure. Discovery. Whatever! And for many folks it is an excellent choice, as it has been for us. So there is a whole lot to like . . . make that LOVE! . . . about living in Panama. But, given as nothing is perfect . . . sometimes folks ask, "Richard, what's not to like about living in Panama?"

So here is my list of the top 15 things not to like about living in Panama.

15. Re-frozen Häagen-Dazs

OK, I admit it. There are times when things are so frustrating that only a pint of Häagen-Dazs will do. At around $5 a pint, naturally more than in the US, it's not something you do every day. So you root through the freezer at Deli Baru, or almost anywhere in Panama, for the most decadent-sounding flavor. Well, don't expect much. If you're lucky there will be two choices, three maybe if you dig all the way to the bottom. And then when you take it home and you sit down to forget all of your troubles, inevitably the Häagen-Dazs will have thawed somewhere along the supply chain, probably sitting out in the sun because someone was taking their break, and instead of being creamy and delicious will be nothing but a mass of frozen ice crystal.

Welcome to Panama! Take it back? This is Panama! You bought it, you got it: end of story.

14. Dirty Propane

Panama runs on propane. You can be convenient, like we do and buy big tanks for $80. We use gas for cooking, drying clothes, and on-demand water heaters and a tank lasts us around a month and a half. If you don't mind running to the corner store frequently you can buy the small tanks (about the size of the ones you use for your barbecue) for about $5.50, cheaper because they are subsidized by the government. But don't assume you can use these for your barbecue, since they have totally different connections and so it's a hassle to get your barbecue gas tank filled. There are two different companies providing propane and they use two different connection systems just to keep things difficult. Now, the big problem: it's not really propane. As I understand it, what we get is a "dirty propane" more like butane, so things are always burning out. Some *gringos*, like us, come down and since we're used to it, have hot water tanks. We had two burn up, yes burn up, until we switched to on demand gas hot water heaters. They cost about $200 each. Most are made in China and yes, will stop working after about two years.

13. No Bagels

OK, this is about Boquete. There is a Jewish community in Panama City so they have bagels, but we don't . . . not real bagels like Western Bagel or Noah's. We had great hopes when we heard that a bakery called "Shalom" was opening but the owner turned out to be the Chinese pastor of a Baptist church. Restaurants come and go and change names and owners in Boquete with breakneck speed. Shalom bakery has new owners and a new name and I haven't had time to check out the bagels.

12. No Decent Pizza

This is about Boquete as well, since I know, and always make a point to get what I consider good pizza from Pizza Italia when I am in Panama City. Unfortunately they don't have a place in Boquete. Yes, we do have some pizza parlors and there are folks who even like some of them, so this really is, "No pizza that I happen to like."

Granted, I end up in Italy frequently on cruises and sometimes in Naples where pizza was born. Many ships have fantastic pizzerias. But my standard for pizza generally comes from New York. My first church was in the South Bronx and we had a wonderful family owned and operated (and take that "family" both ways because the Italian social club was just across the street) called Yolanda's. Yolanda's on East 149th Street had, and still has I am told, the best Italian food. Neal, the son of the owner and now the owner himself, kept feeding us for six years. The cops liked it too. They'd come in to get out of the cold, spend the afternoon eating and drinking "grape soda" as they called wine, hoping not to get a call, and sometimes, after too much "grape soda", showing off how they could fast draw and twirl their guns like cowboys.

11. No Home Depot

Don't laugh: it's one of the things I miss the most. When I go to visit my kids in the States I always get them to take me to Home Depot and they keep telling me I'm embarrassing them by fondling the power tools in public. When we came here eight years ago it was hopeless. Now we have Do It Center and Novey in David but they are nothing like Home Depot. Locally we have the two Chinese hardware stores, Ivan's and El Dorado, both of which are almost like old hardware stores and have almost everything. Unfortunately it's all made in China. At least at Home Depot there was the possibility of finding something not made in China and therefore providing a reasonable expectation that it would work.

I'm told Home Depot isn't what it once was. What you're looking for probably is in some other bin somewhere and you may not find it even although it's there. I'm told that the days when I'd go in and buy whatever I thought I might need, and then return what I didn't need only to have my money cheerfully refunded without a receipt, are long gone. But even still, I'm told that if something just doesn't work that you can bring it back: it's no skin off Home Depot's back; in fact they make money on returns. Believe me, it's not that way in Panama.

Maybe worse yet, no Costco, Sam's Club or Wal-Mar!

We do have something called Price Smart run by the same family that used to run Price Club in California before it merged with Costco. There is a look and feel about Price Smart and a layout that is y familiar, but don't be mistaken this is not the old Price Club or Costco.

Let me count the ways:
- A hot dog and soda costs $2.50, not $1.50.
- Buying in bulk is not cheaper: believe it or not, the idea here is that you often pay more for the convenience of buying a larger size – incredible, but true!
- The employees lack the enthusiasm and ownership that they've always demonstrated, at least to me, in club stores.
- If something sells it is frequently discontinued. Why? Now, I know this will be tricky but try to follow. If it is a popular item people remove it from the shelves and buy it making it difficult to keep the shelves neatly organized and full, therefore it has no place in the store. [If you mind is spinning don't even think about moving to Panama!]
- Customer service – say what? If a popular item, say dog food, is sold out, you'll have to chase down someone to find someone who will get a forklift and bring another pallet of dog food down for the masses.

Never-the-less we use Price Smart faithfully because it comes closest to what we are used to. Hopefully with the new Free Trade Agreement with the US we will see more of the familiar Kirkland brand products on the shelves. Price Smart doesn't have it all down yet, but it is getting there and encouragingly there are more and more Panamanians who are shopping Price Smart in David.

10. Microclimates

OK, microclimates can be wonderful when it comes to fine wine and great coffee. But a place like Boquete has so many microclimates it boggles the mind.

During the dry season where we live in Palmira can be as dry as the desert with dusty winds howling (think Santa Anas and Chinooks) while just few miles away, in some of the areas around Boquete, it is pouring rain, and other areas, like downtown Boquete are getting their late afternoon mist called "*bajareque*".

This is a good reason to spend six months, and preferably a year, in Boquete before you jump and buy or build. Or at least spend a few months and talk to as many people as you can. True, we are in the tropics and don't have the traditional four seasons, but we do have definite seasons and they are different. Add to that all the microclimates in an area around Boquete and you understand why you need to ask a lot of questions and do a lot of research.

9. Forced Overnights in Panama City

This relates specifically to Boquete. If you want to fly to or from the US or Europe almost inevitably you end up with a forced overnight in Panama City coming and going because of flight schedules. All this will change if and when some airline with a vision for the future begins direct service to the US from David Airport which is now less than 40 minutes from Boquete. The runway, radar and terminal at DAV have all been upgraded and all that remains is for an airline to introduce direct service to the US and a new international airport is under construction in the middle of Panama at Rio Halto, scheduled to open 2014..

8. The Way of Doing Business

Here's the stuff they failed to teach me in my MBA course at Cal State Northridge. It took retiring in Panama to understand the way retail business is supposed to work, at least in Panama.

The customer is the enemy. The customer comes only to steal and wanting to walk out of your store with whatever your employees have not already stolen. There are a myriad ways to keep the customer from buying goods and emptying your shelves or from returning to interrupt your employees' day.

The customer is always wrong. Period. No ands, ifs, or buts. Heaven forbid that the customer should return to shop with you again.

Always promise way more than you can deliver. Your advertising must always create expectations that you cannot possibly deliver.

Never actually have advertised items for sale. Use loads of brand logos and pictures in your advertising for stuff you don't actually have.

Unload whatever you can on the unsuspecting customer. If you know it doesn't work, by all means sell it! Even if it's last year's model or a floor sample, sell it at the new, higher price for the new model. Hopefully the customer won't know the difference. And if they find out feign ignorance. Everything is, after all, the customer's fault.

Have a "no returns" policy. Whatever you do, do not take anything back, defective or not! In small print on the fifteen copies of your *factura* state someplace in the smallest type font available, "Absolutely no returns after 36 minutes."

If something sells out, do NOT reorder! If an item sells out then there will be an empty spot on your shelves! Only order stuff that people are not going to buy. If an item sells out it means the customer's like it, and if you restock it they might start coming back, which is not the goal of retail business in Panama.

Spend a lot on a logo. A logo is THE single most important thing for your business. Don't waste money on things like training employees, customer service . . . just get a sexy-looking logo.

Have a Website. It doesn't matter that nobody in your organization ever looks at or updates the Web site, nor that it has nothing of value to customers. Like a logo, just having a Web URL is essential to your business.

Have uniforms! Everyone loves uniforms, especially employees who don't have to start the day by thinking what they are going to wear and who, if you are really successful in the retail business in Panama, won't have to think all day.

Have a cast of thousands! The more employees you have standing around, talking on their personal cell phones, and chatting with one another, the better you can ignore your customers.

Eliminate competition. Either through your family members in government, or by establishing uniform pricing in your sector of the retail business, do not compete. Competition is bad and divides the essential control of business by the few.

Paper is the essential element of business. Even if you have a computer system, in addition to the computer write everything out on paper longhand, and also have a notebook in which you also write everything in longhand. The reason for this should be obvious: you can't rubber stamp a computer! If you have 15 *facturas* to stamp you will give your employees something to occupy their time.

Do not train your employees. A trained employee is dangerous and can turn against you.

Do not empower your employees. An employee should never, repeat never, be permitted to make any decision, no matter how small. The key to success in retail business is for every employee to have to check with his supervisor before making any decision. Thus it is important that all managers carry their cell phones at all times, leaving them turned on at all times even when they are having coffee, at lunch or visiting a push. [A "push" is a place offering "temporary accommodation" by the hour for various recreational activities.]

Do not incentivize your employees. If you reward your employees for service they will start taking care of your business and treating customers knowledgeably with enthusiasm and respect which is the last thing that you want!

Never have inventory! Whatever the customer wants, must always be in Panama City or need to be imported from abroad, thus discouraging the customer from purchasing or coming back.

Never have adequate parking. If you do have a parking lot, assume that nobody drives a SUV or pickup in Chiriqui and that everyone arrives on horseback. Therefore a 3 foot wide parking space is more than adequate.

Never trust a computer. Computerization looks good and improves corporate image, but it should never replace traditional hand written inventory and invoices, all of which must continue to be in triplicate and rubber stamped and signed by at least four other employees. [See #13 above.]

Above all, encourage inefficiency! Efficiency is the bane of retail business in Panama. The more steps you can create to prevent your customers from emptying your shelves by buying your goods, the fewer goods they will buy and the less likelihood they will return.

And Panama is becoming the "Singapore of Latin America"?

I feel sorry for Panamanians who have always had to deal with such a hostile customer environment. David is booming with lots of new stores under construction. I hope that retailers in Panama will learn that their customers are the most valuable asset of their business and invest in their employees, most of whom want to do an awesome job and would happily contribute more if they knew they were valued and were trained, empowered and rewarded. My gripe is not with the employees, but with management that needs to move into the 21st Century. Panama is no longer a backwater country but is emerging as a powerhouse of world commerce and retail businesses need to start operating as such.

7. *Mold*

Come the rainy season it is everywhere! It is a constant battle. Mold gets inside dressers on the backs of the inside of the dressers, so you need to pull out the drawers and clean the inside of the dresser. It gets on books. It gets on the inside and outside of kitchen cabinets. Leave an extra leather wallet or purse, or the leather dress shoes you only take with you for formal nights on a cruise . . . mold! Yes, it wipes off. And vinegar seems to the best mold-buster. We've even had it on seriographs and lithographs. I pull the pictures apart and generally, although not always, it will wipe off. I've actually used a very light application of Pledge and even wiped the print itself lightly with vinegar. I've discovered that all the layers framers in the States put on the back as part of their framing process, just breeds mold, so after cleaning I put as little on the back as possible. We've started putting little blocks of wood on the corners to keep the artwork from touching the wall and allowing air to circulate.

Panamanians have discovered ways to prevent mold and the best way is with lots and lots of airflow. A good Panamanian closet or cupboard doesn't have doors and has shelves that are actually slats instead of solid wood, thus allowing airflow. You can keep the lights on in closets, or in the rainy season we use de-humidifiers in our walk in closets to deal with the humidity. Ceiling fans and windows aren't a bad idea in walk in closets. *Gringos* like nice windows that we can shut tightly to keep out bugs. Traditional Panamanian houses have windows that are made from open cinderblock so the breezes can blow right through.

6. Creepy Crawlies

It's the rain forest. There are bugs and creepy crawlies everywhere. It is a fact of life. You either accept it and get used to it, or YOU go bugs! We have an exterminator come in every other month, as you do in most warm areas in the US, but you still have Fly Season, Ant Season, Roach Season (when it starts to rain and the little critters who are usually at home under leaves in the jungle decide to come in out of the rain), "June Bug" season (although not necessarily in June, those heavy shelled little buggers who sound like pebbles bouncing off the walls), and Gnat Season (those tiny flies that love to take a swim in a good glass of Merlot adding a degree of protein to the mix).

There is even a "Scorpion Season". Our scorpions are mostly harmless aside from stinging and, if you have a ultra-violet flashlight you have the added joy of going "scorpion hunting"!

The good thing about the bugs is that you are always finding a new bug you've never seen before and many of them are unbelievably beautiful!

5. Poor Work Ethic

Most Americans are driven! It is all about work. If you're with a company, almost forever (Although who in the US is with a company for more than a few years, let alone "forever"?) you're lucky if you get two weeks vacation a year. And even at that, you may be reluctant to take the full two weeks lest your job disappear while you are on vacation. You're expected to take work home and to be online evenings and weekends . . . it never stops. It is what drives. Given this, it can take Americans a while to adjust in Panama.

Europeans have a better perspective on work and life. At 12 noon Europeans walk away from whatever they are doing, whether it needs completed or not. It's time for lunch. At the end of the day, they drop what they are doing regardless and go home. They have lives outside their work. They get reasonable vacations. So the Panamanian way may make a little more sense to Europeans . . . not much, but a little.

Panamanians generally work to eat. They are not driven and they enjoy an abundance of worker benefits. The upfront wage may not compare with the US or Europe, but they get about 21 days a year of paid holidays (Take that you poor US corporate slaves! Even government workers in the US don't enjoy that kind of largess!) Add to that 16 paid sick days. And, oh yes, be you a gardener or executive, 30 days a year paid vacation after you've worked a single year. And, you won't believe this, IN ADDITION you get paid for a phantom "13th month"! Yes, the Panamanian calendar is the same, 12 months in a year, but the Panamanian worker, whatever his job, is gratuitously and by law paid for an additional month. This is not a "bonus" but just a free-be required by law!

Add to that a Labor Board which assumes the worker is right and the employer is wrong, so the employer bears the burden of proof. All this adds up to a poor work ethic which, unfortunately in the world scheme of things, limits the attractiveness of Panama for international corporations. Once a robust Panamanian economy increases the average wage, the benefit of a "low-cost" work force, when you factor in all of the extra gravy, disappears.

This doesn't mean that Panamanians are lazy. Some are and some aren't like anyplace else. The Indigenous guys who work on our farm and those who pick coffee work their butts off. Panamanian workers can be very ingenious, making something work, improvising, not giving up when most Americans would have called a service department somewhere and just gone off on a coffee break. Individuals can be very industrious, but the government and the laws encourage workers to do the minimum.

4. *Communication Infrastructure or Lack Thereof*

OK, it's MY list.

Some folks may find the communications infrastructure in Panama great or passable or to their liking. I don't! Which may be because I live in what I think of as the real Panama, the countryside. But I think two tin cans on a string would function better than either the available cell phone service or Internet, at least where I live and with the companies I've dealt with.

When we moved to Panama almost eight years ago, Valle Escondido promised high-speed Internet. We fought for four years trying to get any decent Internet service and then we moved out to the country to our coffee farm. No sooner did we move than Cableonda came to Boquete and Valle Escondido now has cable Internet and .5 M only runs around $20 a month. Six months later I'm still fighting with the mobile Internet company for the 1 Mg service for which I've been paying all along.

So where I'm at now I've been paying $60 a month supposedly for .5 M but never really getting it and unbeknownst to me everyone else has been paying $40 a month for the same service. When I went to these guys and said as nicely as possible, "You're screwing me even although I've been your customer for 3 years" . . . I talked them into giving me the full 1 M for $65 a month. It took 3 MONTHS before I finally tracked them down in David to get them to commit to the upgrade . . . for more money. They promised, "Oh yeah, you'll have it the first of the month." First of the month came around and I was lucky to get .5 M which is what I'd been paying for and not getting. No news here: you already know customer service sucks in Panama.

Panamanian President Ricardo Martinelli wants the whole country wired with free Internet access and wants to give students, even in rural schools like ours, laptops since Panama doesn't have schoolbooks, skipping ahead a whole generation. I wish him luck! If anyone can create a paradigm shift, Martinelli can and probably will.

So there are areas with good Internet access, I just don't happen to live in one.

Telephone service: scratch "service". Scratch: "telephone."

I'm sorry but the best phones ever created were the heavy black ones that sat on the corner of your desk. You never had to yell, "Do you hear me now?" There were no buttons to push designed for the hands of 1-year-olds. If you wanted to talk with me you simply used the rotary dial to dial MOtt Haven 6-5643. You knew you were calling the Bronx, and Mott Haven area. When people talked seemingly to themselves you just walked on the other side of the street.

First off the major telephone company with the government's blessing is Cable & Wireless. They don't "do" land lines any more in our area, since every Panamanian comes out of the womb with a cell phone in hand and talks on it constantly for the rest of his or her life despite the threats of the traffic police, who are likely busy talking on their own cell phones . It is either struggle with a cell phone, use smoke signals or remain incommunicado.

So what's wrong with cell phones aside from the fact that they aren't waterproof? I get the cheapest phone I can buy since I know whether it's a $39 phone or an expensive iPhone that plays games with me and meets all my personal and interpersonal needs, eventually it's either going in the river, the spa, or as in the case of my last phone, the washing machine.

Never mind that every phone likes to pretend it is a miniature super computer designed to foil attempts to use it as a damn telephone. Never mind that even if you do choose "English" the phone company only speaks "Spanish" and all of the messages are in . . . guess what, Spanish. Never mind that the cell phone provider sends you commercial messages which beep and grunt and ring 24 hours a day promising that if you buy another $5 cell phone card you will get 50 zillion free minutes . . . which expire 30 minutes after you get them.

Every cell phone company promises the best signal and they do this by painting everything in sight across the country with their logos and often horrible signature colors. If they just invested a fraction of the advertising budget in actually improving their signals, it wouldn't be bad.

Where we live you really need three cell phones, one from each of the competing companies, in the hope that when you need to make a call one of the three might actually work.

I'm retired. I don't need a cell phone and I don't want one. You want to contact me, send me an email . . . and we'll both hope my Internet service works. Besides I spend half of my life cruising around the world. Show me a connectivity service that works world-wide at a reasonable cost, and I'm in. It's coming, I know and who knows, I might live to see the day.

3. Spanish

 "Dude! It's a Spanish-speaking country, what do you expect? You're a guest, so don't start dissing the local's language!"

Reminds me of the lady who came down from the States, thinking of retiring to Boquete, and said to the real estate agent, "Just don't show me anywhere where the people next door are speaking Mexican."   To say nothing of the fact that this is Panama, not Mexico, but, yes, the language is Spanish. A romance language which can be very beautiful unless it is slurred rapid-fire like a machine gun.

I live in a Spanish-speaking country so I should speak Spanish, although it would be nice if all those Panamanian companies who love to take *gringo* money would be considerate enough to add, "Press 2 for English".

The problem isn't that Panama speaks Spanish, but that I don't speak Spanish, at least not fluently.

Here's my hang up with languages. I went to a private junior high school where we had one required language choice: Latin. A "dead, dead language that killed the ancient Romans" and came close to killing me. Two years. Get through. Get the grade.

Then high school. Guess what! Spanish! EL CAMINO REAL was the text book. I never knew that in California I would actually live on EL CAMINO REAL, the trail or the Spanish missions, or live in Panama, home to the richest city in the world at the time of the Spanish conquest of the Americas. We had a Spanish teacher who was forever sexually propositioning half of the girls in the class and generally was a world-class asshole, but I did learn some Spanish. Not much, but enough to get the grade and get out.

College. French. Mainly because I thought . . . still think . . . a woman singing in French is about as sexy as language can get. I worked my way through college. Worked all night as a watchman so I could study on the job and after working all night would head into the language lab and do my French. So I struggled and never did find the sexy women singing in French, but I learned enough to get the grade and get out.

Language was always a requirement to be fulfilled without any really "live" purpose.

On to seminary. More languages. Really useful ones: ancient Hebrew and Greek. Two years of each. Passed. [Hebrew only by memorizing vocabulary words using the most pornographic images imaginable.] Requirement fulfilled. I guess the idea was that in the church everyone was going to inundate you with questions about the meaning of the text in the original Greek and Hebrew. Thirty years in the ministry: nobody ever asked or seemed to care!

Something did happen in seminary. I spent three months one summer in Europe and encountered people actually speaking different languages. Too late I got it! Yes, the French laughed at me but I frequently did get the room, the road, the train, the entre I wanted, never the French girls, but . . . hey, my French wasn't perfect.

Out of seminary and six years as pastor of an all-black church in a Puerto Rican area of the South Bronx. This should have perfected my Spanish, and in a sense it did. If I ended up in prison on Riker's Island I could communicate fairly well in street Spanish. Lots of useful stuff about your mother and her various romantic liaisons and I could do pretty well putting down your particular sexual habits. Once I left the Bronx for a staid, old, emphasis old, very traditional, emphasis very, church in Milwaukee, Wisconsin the only time I really got to use my Bronx street Spanish was when the Xerox machine wouldn't work.

So I have this long history with languages . . . and I can't communicate.

In the almost eight years we've been in Boquete, thanks many Panamanian friends with unbelievable patience and the ability to "dummy down" their language for my benefit, I can get by with some basic Spanish communication. My tenses are wrong. Feminine words are masculine and vice versa. [We have unisex toilets, what's wrong with unisex words?] Lots of the locals are trying to learn English and the *gringos* are trying to learn Spanish and when we relax and are willing to make fools of ourselves in the other person's language, amazingly communication takes place.

But . . . when you want to get beyond the basics of "How are you?" and "How is your family?" and "It's very windy, rainy, whatever" and you want to share feelings with friends, and ideas and talk about life, and meaning in life and all the stuff that friendships are made of . . . then you need to be able to really communicate. And that's my frustration.

So I have decided to bite the bullet and learn Spanish. I've been researching a lot of Spanish programs. I don't have the time to go to a Spanish school. Immersion? I'm already immersed living in Boquete. I need to move on. Like a lot of folks I looked at the most expensive Spanish program assuming that because it was the most expensive it must be the best. Then I discovered how much they spend on advertising to reinforce that image. And I talked to folks who'd used the most expensive program available . . . and unhappily sent it back to get something else, or let it just sit . . . like most of us do with exercise machines. Finally I discovered a less expensive program, went to their Web site and tried the program, liked the approach, and decided to try it.

The first thing I had to do is unlearn a lot of things I have been doing wrong. The pronunciation module has helped me realize why people don't understand my attempts at Spanish! People learn in different ways. I have never been a rote learner which is why I enjoy this program. I get to hear the correct pronunciation at normal speed or slowed down, so I can work at my own speed on my pronunciation. There are little pictures to go with the vocabulary, which may help some folks, but doesn't particularly help me. What helps me is to visually see the words, and then see visually how sentences are put together, not in the old "diagram" a sentence way, but how you take different pieces and put them together.

So I'm plugging along . . . slow and steady . . . and I like the basic materials enough that I've ordered some of the more advanced modules as well.

2. Locals, i.e. Panamanians, may be quite different culturally

Yes, the food preferences are different, more rice, less potatoes, more fish and chicken, less beef. The music may be different (and louder and go all night). And as a whole Panamanians, as most Latinos, seem to know how to enjoy life and seem less uptight and "driven" than many of their North American and European cousins.

Panamanians are beautiful, gracious and polite people. (Where else would folks entering a crowded waiting room or a restaurant feel compelled to greet the room before entering?) But as a whole Panamanians have some traits which many *gringos* find irritating. You either accept the good with the different from what you may be used to, or you go nuts.

Lots of people are not dependable. It's almost a national trait. Part of the politeness is to tell people what they want to hear, which may or may not be what they need to hear, and may or may not be an accurate representation. If someone says they will take care of it, or do it, or be someplace at a given time, they may actually mean it (it does happen) or they more likely are just telling you what you want to hear.

Like card players, people keep information close to their chest and don't volunteer information. What do you need most as an expat moving into a new culture and community? Information! Americans love to share their knowledge, insights and know-how, whether the world wants it or not. Getting the information from Panamanians can be like pulling teeth. You have to ask, over and over and over again. People don't volunteer what you need to know.

North Americans are a pretty trusting lot. Generally we like to trust people and tend to trust them until they prove that they cannot be trusted. Panamanians aren't very trusting of each other, which I guess tells you something.
Example: We owed a guy who had helped us initially as a consultant on our coffee farm and we said we would drop it off at his house, with his mother. But he didn't trust his mother! [Our relationship with this guy grew and we let him use a car and eventually "sold" him the car. *Gringos* who've lived in Panama a while are now on the floor laughing because they know how the story ends up: that he screwed us out of $8,000.] "Not to trust anyone" has been a tough lesson for us to learn. We've learned it . . . at a cost of almost $50,000 overall if you count my conniving contractor. Know that if you move to Panama, rightly or wrongly, you are perceived to be fabulously wealthy and of course there are folks who will assume that the reason why you came to Panama is to spread that wealth around.

Even within Panama there are different cultural idiosyncrasies between Latinos and the Indigenous. The Indigenous always assume that you will pay, for everything. And what you are already offering is never enough: they always want more. But then you are the rich *extranjero* ("foreigner").

1. There Is No Escape

I know that the title of this book is ESCAPE TO PARADISE . . . we "escaped" to Panama and we love it! But . . . there is no perfect place in the world, because, unfortunately, we aren't perfect. However, Panama comes damn close!

There are folks who think that if they change jobs, change partners, change locations that all of the problems will go away and life will be good. Unfortunately it doesn't just work that way. Sometimes you need to change you. Don't get me wrong: I am a big proponent of change. But change just for the sake of change . . . or thinking that moving to Panama is going to make everything right is a big mistake. *Por ejempl*o: if you have problems in your relationship deal with them before moving to Panama. The stress of a new culture will only make things worse. It seems nary a week goes by but the latest "Coconut Telegraph" gossip is who is breaking up this week.

If you're going through some midlife, late-life, retirement, "senior citizen" crisis, deal with it. Picking up and moving to Panama and buying a Harley and trying to become a senior-citizen-Hell's Angeles-want-a-be is not going to solve your crisis!

Now this is directed mainly at my fellow US citizens. Much of the world is dreaming and scheming to get a US Passport. Yes, we all hate the Federal Reserve and the IRS. We, as well as the rest of the world, know that the US has a totally dysfunctional government. We know things are screwed up beyond recognition. We inherited something precious and we are leaving something tainted and tarnished to our grandchildren. As a US citizen Uncle Sam is going to chase you everywhere to claim his pound of flesh.

There is no escape from the IRS. Just accept it. It's a cost of business, the price of citizenship in the US. You're not going to find a sandy island anywhere where you are off the radar due to the chip in your passport (and within 15 years I predict a chip embedded in your right arm, or better yet, on your shoulder). So what are you going to do? Are you going to give up your US passport for Dominica? Good heavens! Or St Kitts and Nevis, with Nevis already looking to break away? Get real. There is no escape.

Try travelling the world on a passport from Dominica or St Kitts. I travel around the world on a ship with a crew from some 35 different nationalities. You would not believe the confusion folks with other passports endure which you don't have to put up with if you have a US Passport.

I tell people I didn't drop out in the 60s, but now that I am in my 60s I'm dropping out. Panama is as good a place as any to live in exile. And, should you need it, Uncle Sam is here to help you! The IRS has just added 10 agents in Panama, not, mind you to help you with your taxes, but to put your in handcuffs. But it's helpful to know our spendthrift Uncle is not far away. In the second Carter-Torrijos Panama Canal Treaty the US agreed to protect the neutrality of the Canal in perpetuity and ipso facto the neutrality of Panama. There are times when it's nice to have a big brother.

OK, so Panama isn't perfect and it isn't for everyone, but it's worth taking a good, long look at Panama. It's been great for us, hassles and all. My only regret is that we weren't able to make this move sooner.

Interacting

1. That's my list, what's yours? What are your "Top 15 Things Not To Like" about the place where you live now? About your life? How will moving to Panama, or someplace else, change those things?

16. What People Won't Tell You . . . And Can't Tell You

There are a lot of things you should know that nobody will tell you . . . at least in print.

"If you can't say something nice, don't say anything at all."

I can hear my mother saying this. And it can be very good advice. But what if there are things that you really need to know . . . stuff that could hurt you if you are not in the know?

Turns out that in Panama my mother's advice is not only good advice for being nice and polite, but good legal advice as well. Panama does not have "free speech" in the same sense as the US does. Libel laws are much more onerous so you have to be careful what you say. In the US generally if something is true, then it's not defamatory or libelous to say it or repeat it. Not so in Panama! While Panama may not be as litigious as the US, it is actually quite easy to sue someone for saying something about you that you don't like, true or not. It will all eventually – meaning eventually in the sense of *"mañana"*, i.e. sometime in the future, which may be years - get sorted out in court but in the meantime the person who is suing you can have all of your assets in Panama tied up and sequestered.

So people are very careful, particularly saying things against individuals and companies in public.

There is however the "Coconut Telegraph" . . . which is a very effective and "uncensored" source of communication.

If you are looking for a builder, a maid, a hospital, a doctor, a supplier, an insurance company, a bank, whatever . . . ask around and you will get positive and unfiltered negative opinions. Panama is a small country. Understand that people are all related, by blood, marriage and friendships. Panamanians are often too polite to say negative things even if they need to be said. Sometimes Panamanians will say one thing and while they are saying it roll their eyes: read the eyes. *Gringos* are by nature more direct, one might even say "blunt" and will generally in person tell you exactly what sucks and what they think: the good, the bad and the ugly.

Had we talked to more people and maybe listened more carefully and read the eyes of locals as well as listening to what they had to say, we might have picked another builder.

If you want to come to Panama and avoid other *gringos* and go native, fine but you need t keep in contact with other expats to be in the loop on the "Coconut Telegraph." Don't count on just what you read online in chat forums, etc. That is public and saying the wrong things or something that could be interpreted as libelous in public can get you in trouble.

"Welcome to Panama!"

* * * *

Lest I paint too rosy a picture of life in Panama, I thought I really should include a blog I wrote. It's about yesterday, as I was struggling to go over the final proof for this book. It wasn't a good day. You have those days, even in Paradise. Here 'tis . . .

When All Else Fails Drink!

Of course since I just came from the dentist and am taking pain pills, etc., I can't drink! But hold on pilgrim, it gets worse! Less I paint too rosy of a picture of expat life in Panama . . . there are days! If Princess offered me an unexpected contract today, I'd be out of here!

It's all the little crap that gets you.

Every time I come back from David I'm pissed at the rotten customer service that's everywhere in Panama. I admit that I come off a cruise ship where everyone is striving to achieve "service excellence" and hitting Panama is like running into a cement wall. Except for the Panama Canal, I can't think of a single business in Panama where the customer isn't treated as the enemy and an inconvenience. Sorry.

The checkers at the grocery store sit there like they are doing you an enormous favor to check out your items. They don't smile. They don't say anything. They just look like you've terribly inconvenienced their day dreaming or visiting with one another.

I went to a big paint store in David. Nicely designed. Nice waiting area with decorator books to read while you wait. Ordered and paid for a gallon of paint. Nobody else in the store. 20 minutes and no paint. So I asked the guy mixing the paint. Oh, I had to take my receipt to him and ask for my paint to be prepared. The kids who took the order, who were ten feet from the preparation counter, couldn't be bothered to either take the receipt to the preparation counter or tell me that I had to take it, or, worse yet, just trigger the computer to send the order!

The energy-saving "USA *Productos de Calidad*" "Quality Energy Saving Lamps" with a "7 year or 8,000 hour lifetime guarantee" that I bought at the home improvement store . . . two out of the six burned out in one week! So much for quality! Oh, and those "USA Products" are made in China.

I bought curtains for the guest bedrooms – the kids are coming for Christmas – at the big new department store in David. I managed to ignore all the security guys with their earphones and scowling looks – "The customer is the enemy!" – and buy my curtains. Same identical model and skew numbers, same labels, everything identical . . . only one curtain panel is 8" longer than the other!

You can't assume anything!

And the dentist, who I really like, has a staff of assistants who either have never sat in a dental chair for treatment, or else attended the Dick Cheney School of Water Boarding! Their job is to stick the aspirator thingy in your mouth periodically without any concern if it is actually sucking up the blood and water, any pain or discomfort you may be feeling, or if you happen to be drowning.

And I'm just beginning . . .

We have two cars, neither of which works. The Nissan X-trail, which only came with a manual in Spanish – hell, the cheapest toy has assembly directions in 27 languages! – won't run. Those clever Japanese decided that someone may want to steal the car – Steal a Nissan, you've got to be kidding! – so they have an antitheft thing that sometimes randomly kicks in, maybe because of the rain and humidity, who knows. Anyhow, the manual as near as I can translate it, says is this happens you should take the car to the Nissan dealer – who happens to be in David forty minutes away! And, by the way clever Nissan folks, how the hell are you going to get the car there if you can't start your own frickin' car? Have it towed? Sure, what's $150 among friends or $160 to have someone come out and look at it and maybe, just maybe fix it?

And the truck, which because it wouldn't start got taken to a local "shade tree mechanic" who installed $400 worth of "genuine Mazda parts" . . . of course we never saw the boxes, the old parts, or his receipt . . . isn't working either!

And the roofer! The only one around who seems to know anything about roofing . . . and "guarantees" his work, but who never can be found, and for whom you have to truck in a ladder because, although he is a roofer, he rides a motor bike and doesn't have a ladder, and after a half dozen attempts the roof is still leaking . . .

If all that were not bad enough, a colony of tiny ants has set up housekeeping inside my laptop!

And me, unable to drink!

Yes, I know this shit happens everywhere, but it's compounded when you live out in the country and when you don't speak the language.

So folks, it ain't all perfect.

Now you know.

For Further Reading

Detrich, Richard. CRUISING THE PANAMA CANAL. Boquete, Panama, Richard Detrich, 2012.

Dinges, John. OUR MAN IN PANAMA: HOW GENERAL NORIEGA USED THE US AND MADE MILLIONS IN DRUGS AND ARMS. New York, Random House, 1990.

Doggert, Scott. PANAMA: LONELY PLANET. Melbourne, Lonely Planet Publications.

Frair, William. ADVENTURES IN NATURE: PANAMA. Emeryville, CA, Avalon Travel Publishing.

Galbraith, Douglas. THE RISING SUN. New York, Atlantic Monthly, 2001.

Green, Julie. THE CANAL BUILDERS. New York, Penguin Press, 2009.

Heidke, Dianne. THE BOQUETE HANDBOOK. Boquete, Heidke, 2010.

Independent Commission of Inquiry on the US Invasion of Panama, THE US INVASION OF PANAMA: THE TRUTH BEHIND OPERATION JUST CAUSE. Boston, South End Press, 1991.

Kempe, Frederick. DIVORCING THE DICTATOR: AMERICA'S BUNGLE AFFAIR WITH NORIEGA. New York, G. P. Putnam's Sons, 1990.

Koster, R.M. & Sanchez, Guillermo. IN THE TIME OF TYRANTS: PANAMA 1968-1990. New York, W. W. Norton & Co., 1990.

Lindsay-Poland, John. EMPERORS IN THE JUNGLE: THE HIDDEN HISTORY OF THE US IN PANAMA. Durham, Duke University Press, 2003.

Mc McCullough, David. THE PATH BETWEEN THE SEAS: THE CREATION OF THE PANAMA CANAL 1870-1914. New York, Simon & Schuster, 1977.

Noriega, Manuel and Eisner, Peter. THE MEMOIRS OF MANUEL NORIEGA: AMERICA'S PRISONER. New York, Random House, 1997.

Parker, David. PANAMA FEVER. New York, Doubleday, 2007.

Perkins, John. CONFESSIONS OF AN ECONOMIC HIT MAN. San Francisco, Berrett-Koehler Publishers.

Ridgely, Robert S and Gwynne, John A. Jr. A GUIDE TO THE BIRDS OF PANAMA. Princeton, NJ, Princeton University Press.

Snyder, Sandra T. LIVING IN PANAMA. Panama City, TanToes, 2007.

Key Dates in Panama History

- January 9, 1503 – Christopher Columbus built a garrison at Rio Belen

- 1509 - Spanish colonization began in what is today Colombia, Ecuador, Venezuela and Panama

- September 25, 1513 – Balboa claimed the "Southern Ocean" (later renamed the Pacific) for Spain

- 1519 – Panama City was founded

- January 27, 1671 – British privateer Sir Henry Morgan captured Panama City

- December 26, 1848 – First American Invasion as California-bound gold seekers arrived en Panama

- 1850 – Colon founded as the terminus of the Panama Railroad

- 1855 – Panama Railroad opened

- 1880 - Ferdinand de Lesseps began the French effort to build the canal

- May 3, 1881 - Compagnie Universelle du Canal Interoceanique incorporated under French law

- February 4, 1889 – The French effort was abandoned and Compagnie Universelle du Canal Interoceanique declared bankrupt and dissolved

- 1894 - Philippe Bunau-Varilla became stockholder and spokesman in the New Panama Canal Company, offering to sell the company's assets to the US for $109 million, asking price later reduced to $40 million

- June 19, 1902 - US Senate voted in favor of Panama as the canal site

- June 28, 1902 - The Spooner Bill authorized US to construct canal and purchased concession from France for $40 million

- September 17, 1902 - US troops sent to Panama to keep railroad open as local Panamanians struggled for independence from Colombia

- January 22, 1903 – Hay-Harran Treaty with Colombia giving US right to build a canal was passed by Senate, but not ratified by Colombia

- October 10, 1903 - Philippe Bunau-Varilla met with US President Theodore Roosevelt warning him of imminent rebellion in Panama

- November 3, 1903 – With US NASHVILLE standing by in Panama and Bunau-Varilla standing by in Washington, Panama proclaimed independence from Colombia with the only casualties being a shopkeeper and a donkey

- November 6, 1903 – Panama officially declared independence

- November 7, 1903 – The US officially recognized the Republic of Panama

- November 18, 1903 – Claiming to represent the newly created Republic of Panama, the Frenchman Bunau-Varilla granted the US a strip of land across Panama and the rights to build a canal and in return the US agreed to protect the new country

- February 3, 1904 – US Marines clashed with Colombian troops attempting to re-establish Colombian sovereignty in Panama

- February 23, 1904 – The US paid Panama $10 million for the Canal Zone

- May 4, 1904 – The Second US Invasion began as the US took over construction of the Panama Canal

- 1904 - Panama adopted US dollar as its currency calling it the "Balboa"

- 1904- Dr. William Gorgas took over as chief sanitary officer

- November 8, 1906 – US President Theodore Roosevelt visited Panama becoming the first US president in history to leave the country while in office

- 1907 - George Washington Goethals took control of the Canal Zone and construction

- August 24, 1909 – The first concrete was poured in the locks

- 1912 – The Chagres River was damned

- October 10, 1913 – US President Woodrow Wilson pushed a button in Washington triggering an explosion in Panama, exploding the temporary Gamboa Dike and allowing water to fill Gatun Lake

- August 15, 1914 – With the world occupied by a World War, the Panama Canal quietly opened with the ANCON making the first official crossing Southbound from the Atlantic to the Pacific

- April 20, 1921 -Thomson-Urrutia Treaty signed – US paid Colombia $25 million in return for Colombia's recognition of Panama's independence

- January 9, 1964 - Anti-U.S. rioting broke out and 21 Panamanian civilians and 4 US soldiers were killed including 6 Panamanian teenagers; now celebrated as a national holiday called "The Day of the Martyrs"

- January 10, 1964 - Panama broke off relations with the US and demanded a revision of the original Canal treaty

- October 11, 1968 - Panamanian President Arnulfo Arias was ousted in a coup by General Omar Torrijos

- August 10, 1977 – US and Panama began negotiation for Panama Canal turnover

- September 7, 1977 – US President Jimmy Carter and General Torrijos signed the Torrijos-Carter Treaties abrogating the Hay-Bunau Varilla Treaty and setting 1999 for the turnover of the Canal

- April 18, 1978 - US Senate ratified the Torrijos-Carter Treaties by a vote of 68 to 32

- October 1, 1979 – Under terms of the 1977 Panama Canal Treaties the US returned the Canal Zone to Panama, excluding the Canal itself

- July 31, 1981 – General Torrijos died in a plane crash

- August 12, 1983 - General Manuel Noriega assumed command of the National Guard

- 1985 – Dissident leader Hugo Spadafora was decapitated – Noriega later sentenced in Panama to 20 years in prison for the murder

- February 25, 1988 – Panamanian President Eric Arturo Delvalle removed Noriega as commander and was subsequently ousted as President and Noriega took control

- March 18, 1988 – Noriega declared a "state of urgency"

- April 8, 1988 – US President Ronald Regan issued an Executive Order blocking of all property and interests in property of the Government of Panama

- May 7, 1989 – Voters rejected Noriega but Noriega refused to recognize election results

- May 9, 1989 – US President George Bush in the light of "massive irregularities" in Panamanian elections called for Noriega to step down

- May 10, 1989 - Noriega nullified elections won by his opposition

- May 11, 1989 – US President Bush recalled US ambassador and beefed up US troops stationed in Panama

- October 3, 1989 – Noriega foiled attempted coup and had coup leaders executed

- December 20, 1989 – US invaded Panama with "Operation Just Cause" – the "Third US Invasion"

- December 24, 1989 – Noriega took refuge at residence of Papal Nuncio in Panama City

- January 3, 1990 – Noriega surrendered to US forces, was flown to Miami and arraigned in Federal District Court in Miami on drug-trafficking charges

- January 18, 1991 - US acknowledged that the CIA and US Army paid Noriega $322,226 from 1955-1986 and that Noriega began receiving money from the CIA in 1976 giving credulence to the claim of Noriega's lawyers that he was the "CIA's man in Panama"

- April 9, 1992 –Noriega convicted of drug and racketeering charges, sentenced to serve 40 years as a POW, entitling him to maintain his rank as a General . . . of an army of one since Panama had abolished the military

- 1995 - Noriega was convicted in Panama in absentia for the 1989 murder of officers involved in a failed coup

- October 1, 1996 – Fort Amador was transferred to Panama

- November 1, 1999 – US turned over Howard Air Force Base, Fort Kobbe and other territories to Panama

- December 14, 1999 – Former US President Carter symbolically turned over Panama Canal to Panamanian President Mireya Moscoso

- December 31, 1999 – US officially turned over Panama Canal to Panama

- 2000 – "Fourth US Invasion" began as North American and European retirees relocated to Panama

- September 1, 2004 – Panamanian President Martin Torrijos proposed an $8 billion expansion of the Panama Canal

- October 22, 2006 – Voters approved $5.25 billion Panama Canal Expansion proposal by 78%

- September 3, 2007 - Construction began on the Panama Canal Expansion adding a "third lane" of new locks

- April 26, 2010 - Noriega completed US prison sentence and after lengthy legal fight was extradited to France where he began serving sentence for money laundering, not as POW treated as a General, but as a common criminal

- September 4, 2010 – The one millionth ship transited the Panama Canal, a Chinese vessel named FORTUNE PLUM, carrying steel and crossing from the Pacific to the Atlantic

- December 2011 - US and France agreed to let Noriega be extradited home to Panama where he faces a 67-year prison term. Noriega was incarcerated in El Renacer Prison in Gamboa, next to the Panama Canal

- February 2012 – Panama introduces a one Balboa coin equal in value to $1 US because of the short lifespan and high expense of US paper $1 bills

Cruising The Panama Canal

Lecturing on ships transiting the Canal I realized there was a need for a simpler, more readable book written for cruise passengers that included information about the Canal as well as information about Panama. I wanted to write a book that would be helpful to folks planning a Panama Canal trip as well as serve as a guide during the voyage.

CRUISING THE PANAMA CANAL combines on board guide for both Northbound and Southbound transits.

* * * *

"CRUISING THE PANAMA CANAL is the essential companion for your cruise: what to expect, the past, present and future of the Canal and insider information on shore excursions."

"Richard's commentary, history and background made our Canal trip come alive!"

"The ultimate authority on cruising the Canal . . . Easy-going writing style makes this a cinch for anyone to read."

"This is the book you will want to buy for planning your cruise and to use as a guide during the Canal transit."

"This is the best Panama Canal book for cruise ship passengers."

CRUISING THE PANAMA CANAL is available online in print or on Kindle and in bookstores.

Coming from Richard Detrich

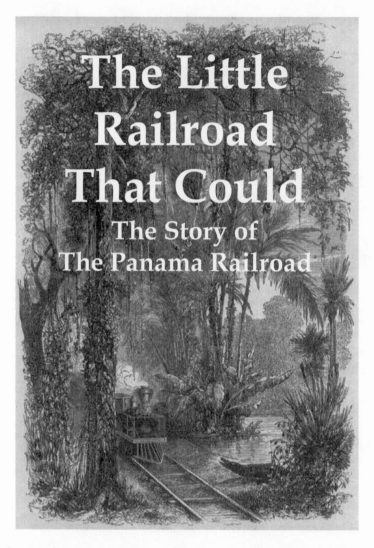

The fascinating story of the world's first "trans-oceanic" railroad . . .
the railroad that made the Panama Canal possible . . . and is still
rolling along over 155 years later!